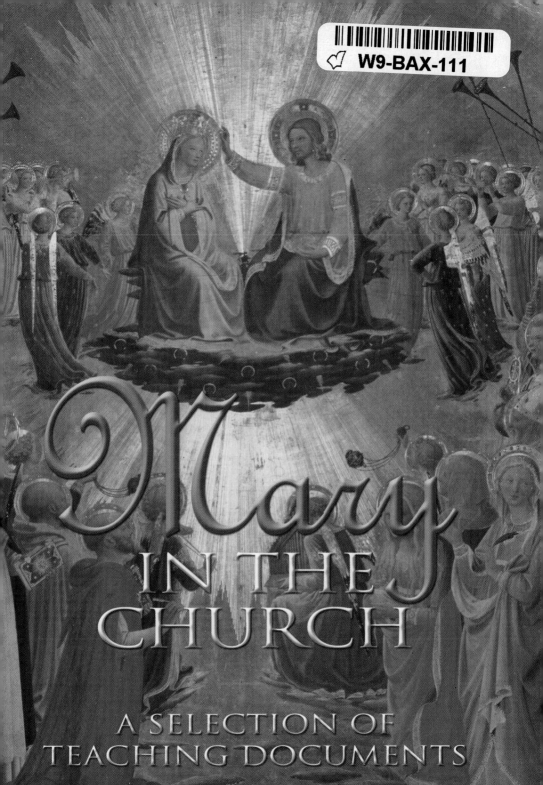

Mary
IN THE
CHURCH

A SELECTION OF
TEACHING DOCUMENTS

United States Conference of Catholic Bishops
Washington, D.C.

This resource of official church teachings, *Mary in the Church: A Selection of Teaching Documents*, was produced in collaboration with the Secretariat for Doctrine and Pastoral Practices of the United States Conference of Catholic Bishops (USCCB) and is authorized for publication by the undersigned.

Monsignor William P. Fay
General Secretary, USCCB

Images used with permission. Cover: copyright © Scala/Art Resource, NY, *Coronation of the Virgin* by Fra Angelico (1387-1455); page iv: © Charles and Josette Lenars/Corbis, *Our Lady of Guadalupe*; page 4: © Erich Lessing/Art Resource, NY, Cella 25: *Crucifixion, Virgin Mary, Saint Mary Magdalen, Saint Dominic*, 1438 by Fra Angelico; page 52: © Scala/Art Resource, NY, *The Immaculate Conception of the Escorial*, ca. 1565-1660 by Bartolomeo Esteban Murillo (1618-1682); page 92: © Scala/Art Resource, NY, *The Nativity* (The Creche) by Fra Angelico; page 148: © Alinari /Art Resource, NY, *Madonna and Child* by Fra Angelico.

Text of the bishops' 1973 pastoral letter *Behold Your Mother: Woman of Faith* is reprinted from *Pastoral Letters of the U.S. Catholic Bishops, Volume III, 1962-1974*, copyright © 1983 United States Conference of Catholic Bishops. All rights reserved.

English translation of Pope Paul VI's 1974 apostolic exhortation *Marialis Cultus: For the Right Ordering and Development of Devotion to the Blessed Virgin Mary* courtesy of Eternal Word Television Network at *http://www.ewtn.com*, 5817 Old Leeds Road, Irondale, Alabama 35210. Copyright © Libreria Editrice Vaticana, Vatican City. Published in the United States by the United States Conference of Catholic Bishops in 1974.

English translation of Pope John Paul II's 1987 encyclical letter *Redemptoris Mater: On the Blessed Virgin Mary in the Life of the Pilgrim Church* (*The Mother of the Redeemer*) is from the Vatican website, *http://www.vatican.va*. Copyright © Libreria Editrice Vaticana, Vatican City. Published in the United States by the United States Conference of Catholic Bishops in March 1987.

English translation of Pope John Paul II's 2002 apostolic letter *Rosarium Virginis Mariae: On the Most Holy Rosary* is from Libreria Editrice Vaticana, Vatican City. Published in the United States by the United States Conference of Catholic Bishops in November 2002.

First printing, November 2003

ISBN 1-57455-601-0

CONTENTS

FOREWORD

On November 21, 1973, the Catholic bishops of the United States issued the pastoral letter *Behold Your Mother: Woman of Faith*. In the letter they expressed the Catholic tradition regarding the Blessed Virgin Mary. Summarizing this tradition, they wrote, "We honor Mary as the Mother of Jesus Christ, the Incarnate Word of God. We recognize her unique and exalted role in the redemption her Son brought to men. We love Mary. We try to imitate her virtues of faith, purity, humility, and conformity to the Will of God, which are part of the very texture of the Gospel message" (no. 8).

In recent years *Behold Your Mother* has been available only in Volume III of *Pastoral Letters of the United States Catholic Bishops*. Nevertheless, there have been repeated calls for the bishops to re-issue the letter, especially as its thirtieth anniversary drew near. In the meantime, however, the Church's teaching about the Blessed Virgin Mary and devotion to her has been considerably enriched by documents from Popes Paul VI and John Paul II.

On February 2, 1974, Pope Paul VI issued his apostolic exhortation *Marialis Cultus: For the Right Ordering and Development of Devotion to the Blessed Virgin Mary*, in which he stated an intention "to help the development of that devotion to the Blessed Virgin which in the Church is motivated by the Word of God and practiced in the Spirit of Christ" (Introduction).

On March 25, 1987, Pope John Paul II, who dedicated his pontificate from its beginning to the Blessed Virgin Mary and has sought her intercession throughout it, issued his encyclical *Redemptoris Mater* (*The Mother of the Redeemer*). In it he conveyed how the Blessed Virgin Mary's "exceptional pilgrimage of faith represents a constant point of reference for the Church, for individuals and for communities, for peoples and nations and, in a sense, for all humanity" (no. 6).

More recently, on October 16, 2002, Pope John Paul II issued an apostolic letter *Rosarium Virginis Mariae* (*On the Most Holy Rosary*), in which he proclaimed the period from October 2002 to October 2003 as the Year of the Rosary. Also, to the previous fifteen mysteries of the rosary he added the mysteries of light—"a meditation on certain particularly significant mysteries in his [Christ's] public ministry" (no. 19).

In seeking to respond to the many requests for the re-issuance of *Behold Your Mother*, the bishops decided to enrich the reading and study of this important letter by creating a compendium that would include these significant Marian documents of the papal magisterium in order to provide a valuable source of recent church teaching on the Blessed Virgin Mary. These documents consistently demonstrate an ecumenical sensitivity as they present the authentic teaching of the Church on the Blessed Virgin Mary, and reading them can prevent misunderstandings on the part of other Christians.

It is gratifying to note that ecumenical discussions have led to deeper understandings of the role of the Blessed Virgin Mary in salvation history. In particular, there has been fuller study of Mary in the New Testament and of her role in different historical traditions of the Orthodox Churches as well as with some of the Churches of the Reformation. Particularly important have been studies undertaken in the Lutheran-Catholic and the Anglican–Roman Catholic dialogues. As so often happens in ecumenical discussions, these studies have brought new light to the meaning of Mary's place and role in the Church, and they have led to conclusions that the differences about Mary's place in the mystery of Christ's salvation can no longer be considered "Church-dividing."

The eighth Lutheran-Catholic dialogue in the United States, published in 1993 and entitled *The One Mediator, the Saints, and Mary*, is particularly helpful for Roman Catholics and other Christians to read together. Another work of value is *Mary in the Plan of God and in the Communion of Saints*, published in 1999, which presents the insights of a diverse group of Christian theologians known as the *Groupe des Dombes*. Another document on Mary is being prepared for publication in 2004 by the Anglican–Roman Catholic International Commission. These documents make clear how a number of other Christian communities share with Roman Catholics a recognition of the profound significance of the Blessed Virgin Mary for God's people.

It is to be hoped that this compendium of important Catholic documents on the Mother of God will enrich the faith and love of all who seek to imitate her on their way to Christ.

+ Most Rev. Wilton D. Gregory
Bishop of Belleville
President, United States Conference of
Catholic Bishops

BEHOLD YOUR MOTHER: WOMAN OF FAITH

A Pastoral Letter Issued by the
National Conference of Catholic Bishops
NOVEMBER 21, 1973

INTRODUCTION

Dearly Beloved:

1. We your bishops and your brothers in the faith are addressing to you a pastoral letter on the Blessed Virgin Mary. We wish to share with you our faith in the truths concerning her and together with you to express publicly our filial love for her. The Gospels summon us all to recognize the special place the Mother of Jesus has in God's plan for the salvation of mankind. The teachings of popes and Councils lead us to an ever-clearer understanding of Mary's privileged position in the Church. Singular honor has been given her in piety, art, music, and literature. Surely this Catholic tradition is a fulfillment of her prophecy: "All ages to come shall call me blessed" (Lk 1:48).

2. In order to serve better the current needs of men, the Church seeks to adapt herself to the widespread social and cultural changes of our time. Nevertheless, under the guidance of the Holy Spirit, she must preserve intact the divine message that she has received from Christ. This includes the special role of Mary in the mystery of the salvation of the human race. Through this letter, we hope to reaffirm our heritage of faith in Mary, the Mother of God, and to encourage authentic devotion to her.

3. First of all, we should clearly understand that the Second Vatican Council in no way downgraded faith in or devotion to Mary. On the contrary, the eighth chapter of the *Constitution on the Church* is a clear and penetrating account of Catholic

teaching on the Blessed Mother of God. Other ages have erected shrines and temples in her honor. This chapter, fashioned from the inspired texts of Sacred Scripture, the teachings of early Christian writers, and the practice and prayer life of the Church, is in reality a beautiful spiritual shrine in which the Mother of Jesus is honored and from which she continues to speak to us with a mother's loving concern. Our Holy Father, Pope Paul VI, has repeatedly affirmed the position of the Council. He called the chapter on Our Lady "a vast synthesis of Catholic doctrine" concerning her place in the mystery of Christ and his Church. He also recalled that she was the heavenly patroness to whom Pope John entrusted the Council.[1]

4.   These words of ours are the preamble to our full pastoral petter on Our Lady. We have called upon dedicated theologians to aid us in restating the teachings of the Church about her. Here again, the Council documents have guided our approach. We hope and pray that our presentation will be a subject for serious study and loving reflection. We desire with all our hearts that it be received into homes and rectories and seminaries, into schools and institutes of higher learning, into adult education groups, confraternity centers, campus ministries, and religious communities.

5.   The intercession of Mary extends not only to individuals but to the whole community of believers. She has a place in the ongoing work of redemption, which has as its goal, "to bring all things in the heavens and on earth into one under Christ's headship" (Eph 1:10). The full sense of Mary's role is summed up in the title Pope Paul gave her, "Mother of the Church."[2] Because of her divine maternity, Mary stands in a unique relationship with her Savior and her Son. "Believing and obeying, she brought forth on earth the Father's Son . . . whom God placed as the first-born among many brethren, namely, the faithful. In their birth and development she cooperates with a maternal love."[3]

6.   Sometimes anxiety is expressed that devotion to Mary may detract from the position of Jesus, our one Lord and Mediator. Such fear is unfounded. The more we know and love Mary, the more surely will we know and love Jesus and understand his mission in the world. It is also true that the more we know Jesus and love him, the better we will appreciate his Mother's place in God's plan for man's redemption. This is the teaching of the Second Vatican Council. Her motherly intercession, the Council made clear, in no way diminishes the unique mediation of Christ, but rather shows its power. God's free choice is the reason for Mary's place in the plan for our redemption. She is totally dependent on her son. Commenting on the words of the Council, Pope Paul VI declared: "Devotion to the Virgin Mother of God does not stop with her, but has to be regarded as a help which of its very nature leads men to Christ."[4]

7.   Dearly beloved brothers and sisters, this is the faith we share with you:

8.   We honor Mary as the Mother of Jesus Christ, the Incarnate Word of God. We recognize her unique and exalted role in the redemption her Son brought to men. We love Mary. We try to imitate her virtues of faith, purity, humility, and conformity to the Will of God, which are part of the very texture of the Gospel message.

9.   We acknowledge that devotion to Mary, the joyful duty of all of us, has a special function in exalting the dignity of woman and fostering respect for her person. We believe in the power of Mary's intercession to bring us, as individuals and as a community, under the influence of Christ's redeeming mercy.

10.   With all the affection of our hearts and the full submission of our minds to the truths of our holy Faith, we repeat the Church's familiar words in praise of the Mother of Jesus:

> Blessed be the great Mother of God, Mary most holy.
> Blessed be her holy and Immaculate Conception.
> Blessed be her glorious Assumption.
> Blessed be the name of Mary, Virgin and Mother.

11.   United with our Holy Father we proclaim once more the preeminent position of Mary in the mystery of Christ and the Church. We urge the restoration and renewal of the ancient love of Christendom for the Mother of the Lord as a tribute to lay tenderly at her feet. In this Holy Year, we pray that she may fill the hearts of all men with peace and lead them to know and love Jesus Christ, her Son, and to share in the abundant fruits of his redemption.

Chapter One
OUR LADY IN THE BIBLE

12.   The Holy Spirit led the Second Vatican Council to describe Our Lady's life on earth as a pilgrimage of faith.[1] This approach to the Virgin Mary based on the Bible is especially suited to the needs of our day. Remembering the coming of the Son of God among us as the Son of Mary, in one of the earliest New Testament passages, St. Paul wrote: "When the designated time had come, God sent forth his Son born of a woman, born under the law." According to the plan of the Father of mercies this took place "that we might receive the adoption of sons" (Gal 4:4-5). Following St. Paul, the Evangelists portrayed the special significance of the Virgin Mary.

St. Luke's Annunciation narrative stands in the tradition of Old Testament announcements delivered by angels, in which God chose men to play a special part in the messianic preparations.

13.   In the history of Israel, women as well as men had privileged roles in the accomplishment of God's saving plan. The Old Testament shows a line of great men of the Bible as "standard-bearers" of redemption—Adam, Abraham, Moses, and others—and a parallel line of believers in the saving action of the Lord, the great women—Eve, Sarah, Miriam, and even the whole people of Israel under a feminine image, "Bride of Yahweh," "Daughter of Zion."

14.   The future Eve, to whose offspring victory over Satan is promised, is realized in the great Old Testament women, but preeminently in Mary of Nazareth, whose obedient expression of faith, "Let it be done to me as you say" (Lk 1:38), heals the disobedience of the first Eve. The comparison between the first Eve, primitive mother of the living, and Mary, the new Eve, is the oldest Christian reflection on the Blessed Virgin outside the Bible, and accords well with the New Testament teaching that Christ is the new Adam (Rom 5:19).

15.   The Eve-Mary comparison is rooted in the covenant theology of the Old Testament, in which God's free initiative stirs up man's response of faith. Faith, God's gift, becoming then truly man's possession, marks the moment when mankind receives salvation. In Mary's response, "Let it be done to me as you say," the expectation of the old covenant achieves perfect expression. God bestows his grace freely. He chose Mary, prepared her, guided her to a fully human consent. Mary, then, has a central function in the fulfillment of redemption. Her faith opened the way for Jesus to perform his salvific mission. God's free election made Mary the representative of the believing remnant. In the Council's words, "She stands out among the poor and humble of the Lord who confidently await and receive salvation from Him" (no. 55). Mary is the "exalted Daughter of Zion" in whom, after the long waiting for the promise, the times are fulfilled and the new dispensation is established. "All this occurred when the Son of God took a human nature from her, that He might in the mysteries of His flesh free man from sin."[2]

16.   The designation "Daughter of Zion," evocative of Mt. Zion and the temple, is used in the Old Testament for the messianic community, especially that remnant of the Chosen People who returned to Jerusalem after the Exile. "Daughter of Zion" includes "the poor and lowly," the humble of spirit, the devout believers who counted on God for salvation.

17.   Luke begins his Gospel by taking us into the company of poor and holy people: Elizabeth and Zachary, Anna and Simeon, Joseph and Mary. Jesus himself and the Good News came from this circle, cradle of the Christian Church. For St. Luke, Mary is the perfect example of awaiting the Messiah with a pure and humble spirit. Luke sees in Mary the Daughter of Zion who rejoices because God is with her and who praises his greatness for pulling down the mighty and exalting the humble.

18.   God's guidance of his people of Israel culminated in the exemplary role of the Daughter of Zion who was to give the world the universal Redeemer. God's favor was expressed in the initial gift of grace to Mary that we call the Immaculate Conception. Mary was the person who acted on behalf of "the total remnant"; she stood out among the Lord's poor and lowly who looked for salvation. Kept free from Original Sin, she was able to give herself wholeheartedly to the saving work of her Son. By accepting the Annunciation, she became intimately associated with all the saving mysteries of Jesus' life, death, and Resurrection. "Just as a woman contributed to death, so also a woman should contribute to life."[3]

19.   Even the books of the Old Testament, as they are understood by the Church in the light of Christian Revelation, "bring the figure of the woman, Mother of the Redeemer, into a gradually sharper focus" (no. 55). In the fulfillment, we find the vague "figure of a woman" realized in *the* woman who is Mary of Nazareth, the "predestined mother" who would not merely "contribute to life" but bring into the world the One who is Life itself and who renews all things.[4] The light of completion shows that the Redeemer's Mother was "already prophetically foreshadowed in that victory over the serpent which was promised to our first parents after their fall into sin (cf. Gen 3:15)."[5] With St. Matthew, the Church holds that the Mother of Jesus is likewise the Virgin who will conceive a Son called Emmanuel (Mt 1:22-23; cf. Is 7:14; Mi 5:2-3).

20.   The bridge role of Mary between the Old Testament and New, between expectation and fulfillment, appears not only in individual texts, such as St. Matthew's use of Isaiah, but is an integral element of the Gospel view of Mary. For St. Luke and St. John, the Mother of Jesus is the typical, the perfect believer. The "handmaid of the Lord" in St. Luke's infancy chapters, and the "woman" in St. John's Cana and Calvary narratives is at once the individual "Daughter of Zion," in whom Old Testament hopes are achieved, and the type of the Church, Bride of Christ, new mother of all men. The primitive Church saw in Mary the fulfillment and personification of the Church, Mother of the messianic people.

21.   Thanks to the recent researches of scholars, we have become aware of new depths in the Gospel portrait of Mary. In the past, as in the image of the "Daughter of Zion," the liturgy, both for Advent and the Immaculate Conception, has, in fact, incorporated such texts long before their scientific exposition. The Holy Spirit leads the Christian people in many ways. The celebration of the mystery of Mary in the liturgy and other prayer is a school of the faith and a profession of doctrine.

22.   Under the inspiration of the Holy Spirit, the early Church had long reflected on Jesus, who he was and why he had come, before any book of the New Testament was written. A rich "allusive theology" is characteristic of the first two chapters, the most mature section, of St. Luke's Gospel. The author went back to the Old Testament for words and phrases to describe New Testament events. By multiple allusions to the Old Testament, St. Luke shows Jesus as the promised Messiah. These allusions can be illustrated here by a summary of the Annunciation story. The opening words of Gabriel, best known as the beginning of the Hail Mary, repeat the promise of hope that the prophet Zephaniah addressed to his people ("Daughter of Zion") as they faced the threat of invasion 625 years before Christ:

> Shout for joy O daughter Zion!
>   sing joyfully, O Israel!
> Be glad and exult with all your heart,
>   O daughter Jerusalem!
> The LORD has removed the judgment against you,
>   he has turned away your enemies;
> The King of Israel, the LORD, is in your midst,
>   you have no further misfortune to fear.
> On that day, it shall be said to Jerusalem:
>   Fear not, O Zion, be not discouraged!
> The LORD, your God, is in your midst, a mighty savior;
> He will rejoice over you with gladness,
>   and renew you in his love,
> He will sing joyfully because of you. (Zep 3:14-17)

23.   The pattern of allusions to the Old Testament continues as Gabriel speaks of the place of Jesus among the descendants of David, and then of the divinity of the Son of Mary. The Old Testament counterpart to the angelic words about the relationship of Jesus to royal David and his eternal rule over the house of Jacob is the prophecy of Nathan addressed to King David a thousand years before: "And when your time comes and you rest with your ancestors, I will raise up your heir after you,

sprung from your loins, and I will make his kingdom firm. It is he who shall build a house for my name. And I will make his royal throne firm forever. I will be a father to him, and he shall be a son to me. And if he does wrong, I will correct him with the rod of men and with human chastisements; but I will not withdraw my favor from him as I withdrew it from your predecessor Saul, whom I removed from my presence. Your house and your kingdom shall endure forever before me; your throne shall stand firm forever" (2 Sm 7:12-16).

24.   In St. Luke's beautifully balanced story, Our Lady's words come next: "How can this be since I do not know man?" Mary's question is evidence of the belief of the early Church that Jesus was virginally conceived, the doctrine usually called the "Virgin Birth." Gabriel's reply to Mary's question leads into the second main part of his message: that the holy Child to be born of Mary will be not only the promised Messiah, but God made man. The angel explains the virginal conception of Jesus as being due to the power of God who has chosen this unique way to send his Son among men as their true brother and Savior. In Jesus, mankind gets a fresh start. The conception of the Son of Mary without a human father is the sign that the Incarnation is the new creation, independent of the will of man or urge of the flesh (Jn 1:13). The merciful Father intervenes in human history to send the new Adam, born of the Virgin Mary through the power of the Spirit.

25.   "Hence, the holy offspring to be born will be called Son of God" (Lk 1:35). The title "Son of God" provides solid ground for us to profess our faith in the divinity of Jesus. Yet Gabriel's words offer an even more subtle and profound reason for affirming that the Son of Mary is truly the Son of God, Emmanuel, God-with-us. Again the key is found in the Old Testament. When the Israelites were wandering through the desert they carried with them the precious "ark of the covenant," a chest made of wood, containing the tables of the law, Aaron's rod, and other sacred objects. They called it "of the covenant" because it reminded them of the alliance between God and Israel. They believed that where the ark of the covenant was, the invisible God was present in a special way. Above the ark and the tent containing it, an overshadowing cloud was the visible sign of God's invisible presence. When the temple was built by Solomon, the ark of the covenant was placed in the Holy of Holies and remained the center of worship and sacrifice. After Jerusalem fell to the Babylonian army in 587 BC, the ark disappeared and has never been found. But its memory still serves Jew and Christian as a symbol of God's protecting presence.

26. One of the many descriptions of the ark and the overshadowing cloud is found in Exodus 40:

Moses did exactly as the Lord commanded him. On the first day of the first month of the second year the Dwelling was erected. It was Moses who erected the Dwelling . . . He took the commandments and put them in the ark; . . . He brought the ark into the Dwelling. . . . Then the cloud covered the meeting tent, and the glory of the Lord filled the Dwelling. Moses could not enter the meeting tent, because the cloud settled down upon it and the glory of the Lord filled the Dwelling. (Ex 40:16-21 and 34-35)

27.   The ark of the covenant and the covering cloud influence St. Luke's narrative. In his account, however, the vivifying power of the unseen Spirit overshadows the Virgin, and God is made visibly present as the Son of Mary. The Mother of Jesus is the new and perfect ark of the covenant, the living tabernacle of the divine presence. The sacred ark that disappeared six centuries before has now returned in a more perfect way. Mary is the living ark of the covenant carrying Jesus. Salvation comes through Mary's flesh, through Mary's faith.

The "ark of the covenant" theme continues in St. Luke's account of Mary's visit to her cousin, Elizabeth. The Old Testament counterpart is provided by the story of the transfer of the ark of the covenant by King David (2 Sm 6). Without elaborating details, we suggest here the parallels between Lk 1 and 2 Sm 6:

(a)   David dances for joy before the ark. The unborn John the Baptist leaps for joy in Elizabeth's womb.
(b)   David calls out: "How can the ark of the Lord come to me?" Elizabeth cries out: "Who am I that the mother of my Lord should come to me?" David's cry of reverential fear was prompted by the sudden death of Uzzah, who had dared to touch the ark; that note of terror is totally absent in the joyous response of Elizabeth.
(c)   "The ark of the Lord remained in the house of Obed-edom the Gittite for three months, and the Lord blessed Obed-edom and his whole house." As St. Luke tells it, Mary remained "about three months" and, clearly, Zachary's whole house received great blessing from the presence of Mary's unborn Son.

28.   The episode of the Annunciation concludes with a double tribute to Mary's faith. The better-known is Mary's word of consent; her maternal "yes" was also her act of faith: "I am the servant of the Lord. Let it be done to me as you say" (Lk 1:38). These words have echoed and re-echoed in Christian liturgy and literature from earliest times. The chapter on Mary in the *Dogmatic Constitution on the Church*

may be regarded as an extended commentary on her consent at the Annunciation. The opening sentence of no. 53 is typical: "At the message of the angel, the Virgin Mary received the Word of God into her heart and her body, and gave life to the world."[6]

29.   Less well-known is the delicate praise of Mary's faith embodied in the final words of Gabriel: "for nothing is impossible with God" (Lk 1:37). This phrase is taken from the Genesis story of Abraham, great Old Testament "man of faith." For Christians, too, Abraham is "our father in faith," as we still call him in Eucharistic Prayer I. The memory of Abraham permeates the opening chapters of St. Luke, as it does the Epistles to the Romans, the Galatians, and the Hebrews, and his name and faith are commemorated repeatedly in Christian liturgical prayer.

30.   There are remarkable likenesses between Abraham and Mary, especially in the accounts of the birth of Isaac, child of promise, and the virginal conception of Jesus, holy Child of Mary. Abraham, Old Testament man of faith, illuminates our understanding of Mary, New Testament woman of faith. Abraham, our father in faith, can teach us much about Mary, our mother in faith.

31.   Mary's "song of poverty," the *Magnificat*, concludes: "He has upheld Israel his servant ever mindful of his mercy; even as he promised our fathers, promised Abraham and his descendants forever" (Lk 1:54-55).

32.   Genesis relates the dramatic story of the son whom God sent to Abraham and Sarah in their old age. In this son, Isaac, all nations will be blessed. Even when Abraham is preparing to sacrifice his child, he still believes that somehow God's promise will be fulfilled. St. Paul reflects: "He is father of us all . . . in the sight of God in whom he believed, the God who restores the dead to life and calls into being those things which had not been. Hoping against hope, Abraham believed . . . Without growing weak in faith, he thought of his own body . . . and of the dead womb of Sarah. Yet he never questioned or doubted God's promise; rather, he was strengthened in faith and gave glory to God, fully persuaded that God could do whatever he had promised" (Rom 4:16-21). When Abraham was told that Isaac was to be born, God strengthened him with the reminder that all things are possible to God (Gn 18:14). That divine reminder runs like a refrain through the many references to Abraham in both Testaments. Sometimes the words are declarative: "All things are possible to God." At other times they form a rhetorical question: "Is there anything God cannot do?" Still again, the divine assurance is simply alluded to: "fully persuaded that God could do whatever he had promised" (Rom 4:21).

33.   Gabriel concludes his message with the unexpected news of Elizabeth's pregnancy, and then repeats the powerful words associated with Abraham in Genesis: "for nothing is impossible with God" (Lk 1:37). St. Luke places Mary, daughter of Abraham, before us as the great Gospel model of faith. He applies to her virginal motherhood the promise made to Abraham, remote ancestor of the Messiah. In the strength of her faith, Mary consents to the merciful Father's invitation, and in the power of the Spirit becomes the Mother of Jesus, Son of God in human flesh.

THE GOSPEL OF ST. JOHN

34.   In the Gospel of St. John, the Mother of Jesus appears at Cana and Calvary, the beginning and the end of her Son's public life. Both times Jesus addresses her as "woman." Each scene turns on a special "hour." At Cana, the hour refers to the beginning of the messianic ministry that "has not yet come" (Jn 2:4), yet which commences in "this first of his signs" that Jesus worked at Mary's request. At Calvary, we have the arrival of the great Johannine hour when Jesus "will be lifted up and draw all men" to himself (Jn 12:32). It is moreover "on the third day" that the wedding feast takes place, and "the third day" is the fulfillment of the sacred time of the Paschal Mystery. What began at Cana achieved its consummation on Calvary.

35.   The words of Jesus to his Mother, "Woman, how does this concern of yours involve me? My hour has not yet come" (Jn 2:4), were an invitation to deepen her faith, to look beyond the failing wine to his messianic career. At the close of the Cana narrative, St. John tells its purpose: "Jesus performed this first of his signs . . . Thus did he reveal his glory and his disciples believed in him" (Jn 2:11). For St. John, the signs (or miracles) of Jesus always have to do with the awakening or strengthening of the faith of his followers. It is striking that no sign is done to help Mary believe. The Mother of Jesus requires no miracle to strengthen her faith. At her Son's word, before "this first of his signs," she shows her faith.

36.   Mary's presence at the wedding feast reveals much about her. We see her quick grasp of the situation, her concern over the embarrassment of the young couple, her willingness to make compassionate intercession. "She was moved by pity, and her intercession brought about the beginning of miracles by Jesus the Messiah."[7] The significance of Mary is also richly ecclesial. At first, Mary is the figure of the synagogue, Daughter of Zion of old, still making use of the imperfect means of the past, the water in the stone jars "as prescribed for Jewish ceremonial washings." But when she says to the waiters, "Do whatever he tells you" (Jn 2:5), she becomes the figure of the new People of God. The change of water into

abundant and very good wine symbolizes the coming of messianic times. Mary is present as figure of the Church, Bride of Christ. On behalf of the Church she greets the messianic Bridegroom. At her request, the new wine is supplied.

37.   The meaning of Mary at Cana is revealed fully when his Mother stands "near the cross of Jesus," and hears him say: "Woman, there is your Son" (Jn 19:26). The Gospel means more than that the dying Jesus is providing for his Mother's care. St. John's thought goes beyond such limited domestic details. The words of Jesus at the Last Supper serve as guide to the meaning of his words on Calvary. The night before he suffered he had said, "When a woman is in labor she is sad that her time has come. When she has borne her child, she no longer remembers her pain for joy that a man has been born into the world" (Jn 16:21). The Old Testament promised that in the messianic age, the Daughter of Zion would bring forth children she had never conceived. Israel's longing for the Messiah was sometimes compared to the pains of labor. The words "Woman, there is your son; there is your mother" contain the solemn announcement that the messianic promise has come true. Mary on Calvary symbolizes the "woman" who is mother Church, the new Israel, the new People of God, the mother of all men, Jew and Gentile. "The Mother of Jesus brings forth in him and with him that whole new people that is to spring from his resurrection; all these children Mary carries in her womb as she once carried Jesus."[8] "The importance of this action is emphasized by the words that follow: 'After this, Jesus, knowing that all was now accomplished. . . .' It is the climax of Jesus' deeds on the cross, the climax of his 'hour,' because it sets the Church on its path, creating the community of love between those he loves."[9]

Chapter Two
THE CHURCH'S UNDERSTANDING OF THE MYSTERY OF MARY

38.   The understanding of Mary in Christian history unfolded along the lines of the Scriptures. The Church saw herself symbolized in the Virgin Mary. The story of Mary, as the Church has come to see her, is at the same time the record of the Church's own self-discovery. The Second Vatican Council quoted St. Ambrose (d. 397): "The Mother of God is a model of the Church in the matter of faith, charity and perfect union with Christ."[10] "As the Church's model and excellent exemplar in faith and charity,"[11] Mary stands out as uniquely virgin and mother within the Church, itself rightly called virgin and mother.[12] As the Virgin Mary conceived and brought forth Jesus, so the Church, virgin in purity of faith, brings forth his brethren at the baptismal font.

39.   The Church appears in the New Testament as the "spotless bride of Christ," as "virgin," and as "mother." Christians early learned to speak of "mother Church." Mary's virginal conception of Jesus, and her lifelong virginal vocation, were taken as the model of the Church's virginal faith. The Church keeps faith with Christ the Bridegroom, who will make his bride spotless, free from every stain.

THE NEW EVE

40.   After the Scriptures, the oldest consideration of the Virgin Mary by Christian writers is that she is the "new Eve." St. Justin (d. 165) contrasts Mary with the first Eve, and St. Irenaeus (d. ca. 202) develops this much further. In writing of the recapitulation of all things in Christ, the new Adam, Irenaeus says:

> If the former, Eve, did disobey God, yet the latter, Mary, was persuaded to be obedient to God in order that the Virgin Mary might become the advocate of the virgin Eve. And thus, as the human race fell into bondage to death by means of a virgin, so it is rescued by a virgin, a virgin's disobedience having been balanced in the scale by virginal obedience.[13]

41.   The early comparisons were between the disobedient Eve and the obedient new Eve. Eve believed the word of deceit; the new Eve heeded Gabriel's message. A woman helped introduce death; Mary became "the cause of salvation" and "advocate of Eve." By St. Jerome's time (d. 420) it was common to hear: "death through Eve, life through Mary."[14] Even more anciently, the Church was regarded as the "new Eve." The Church is the bride of Christ, formed from his side in the sleep of death on the cross, as the first Eve was formed by God from the side of the sleeping Adam. As the first Eve was "mother of the living," the Church becomes the "new mother of the living." In time, some of the maternal characteristics of the Church were seen in Mary, and so St. Epiphanius (d. 403) calls Mary "the mother of the living."[15]

THE VIRGINAL CONCEPTION

42.   We commented briefly above on the virginal conception and birth of Jesus. Here it may be helpful to speak further on this doctrine. Both St. Luke and St. Matthew bear witness to the fact that Jesus had no human father. St. Luke brings this out in relating Mary's question (1:34) and St. Matthew in telling of Joseph's

dream (1:20-25). Some of the Fathers read an allusion to the Virgin birth in St. John's reference to those "begotten not by blood, nor by carnal desire, nor by man's willing it, but by God" (1:13).

43. The Gospel of Mark has no infancy chapters and is silent about the Virgin birth, as is the rest of the New Testament. What is normative in the matter of the Virgin birth is the teaching of the Church. The Bible is read rightly in the Church, whose interpretation is guided by the Holy Spirit. This guidance of the Holy Spirit is experienced at many levels within the Church: (1) in the "sense of the faithful," i.e., the unerring instinct for truth of the Christian people; (2) in the faithful and loving work of Christian theologians; (3) in a very important way in the liturgy and approved prayers of all Christians; (4) and especially in the magisterial teaching of popes and bishops, whether expressed solemnly in ecumenical councils and *ex cathedra* definitions of the pope or through ordinary teaching channels.

44. In the Creed, we profess that Jesus was "born of the Virgin Mary." Our Catholic profession of faith in the Virgin birth is not based on a theoretical acceptance of the possibility of virgin births, which is then applied to the particular fact of the human origin of Jesus. We affirm that "we believe in Jesus Christ, his only Son our Lord, who was conceived by the Holy Spirit and born of the Virgin Mary. . . ." The creedal phrases go together to confess the unique mystery of Jesus the Savior, Son of God, Son of Mary, bound up with the mystery "that we might receive the adoption of sons." The Virgin birth is not merely a symbolical way of describing God's intervention in human history, not just a literary device to convey the divine preexistence of the Word. Nor is the Virgin birth a human construct, as if Christians feared that the divinity of Jesus would be compromised by his having a human father. What really matters here is the manner in which God in fact chose to "send his Son in the fullness of time." We know what God has done, not only from the text of the Bible, taken in isolation, but from the Bible as read, interpreted, and understood by the living Church, guided by the Holy Spirit. Catholic belief in the Virgin birth rests not on the Scriptures alone, but on the constant and consistent faith of the Church. Faith on this precise point has been expressed in many ways from the time of St. Matthew and St. Luke to the present.

45. Many of our beliefs have been taught by the Church without ever having been solemnly defined either by ecumenical councils or by popes invoking their supreme teaching authority. In addition to crisis situations and special needs, the Church has its normal gradual growth in belief and practice. Early Christian writers and creeds repeated the phrase, "born of the Virgin Mary." By the second century, elements of the Apostles' Creed make their appearance in various documents.

Ignatius of Antioch (d. ca. 110) wrote to the Christians of Smyrna of "the Son of God . . . truly born of a virgin." St. Justin in the middle of the second century sees the Isaian prophecy (Is 7:14) fulfilled in the Virgin birth, and calls the Mother of Jesus simply "Virgin Mary." St. Irenaeus looks more deeply into the mystery: "Because an unexpected salvation was to be initiated for men through God's help, an unexpected birth from a Virgin was likewise accomplished. The sign was God-given; the effect was not man-made."[16] Irenaeus's disciple, Hippolytus, records this third-century creed: "I believe in God, the Father Almighty, and in Christ Jesus, Son of God, who was born from the Holy Spirit of Mary the Virgin."[17]

46.   In the understanding of the Church, as well as of Sts. Matthew and Luke, the virginal conception is not accomplished at the expense of the full humanity of Jesus, always insisted upon by Christian faith. If miracles be rejected out of hand, then the Virgin birth will be ruled out as antecedently impossible. Catholic faith, however, does not see God as "a prisoner of his own eternity."[18] In the Virgin birth, he has intervened in a truly unique way. The loving graciousness of God has offered mankind a fresh beginning in Christ, the new Adam. The conception of Jesus is not due to procreation through human love, exalted though this may be, but to the Spirit of divine love.

47.   The Old Testament tells of many marvelous births in preparation for the Messiah, of children sent to elderly couples, as were Isaac, son of Abraham and Sarah, and Samuel, son of Hannah. In the Gospels, there is John the Baptist, son of Zachary and Elizabeth, immediate forerunner of Christ. These unexpected births were signs that salvation comes from God.

48.   The virginal conception of Jesus is the climax and goal of this great series, totally surpassing human hopes and human means. The same God who sanctifies human sexuality and procreation, God the Creator, who made the marriage law of "two in one flesh . . . increase and multiply," has at the dawn of the new creation shown his independence of normal ways. It was prophesied in the Old Testament that the Spirit would revivify all things, would create a new people, renew the face of the earth. The overshadowing Spirit who brings about the virginal conception of the Son of Mary is the same powerful Spirit. The Virgin birth is not simply a privilege affecting only Jesus and Mary, but a sign and means for the Spirit to build the new People of God, the Body of Christ, the Church. The glorious positive sign value of the Virgin birth is the merciful and free saving grace of the Father sending his Son, conceived by the Holy Spirit, born of the Virgin Mary, that we might receive the adoption of sons.

49.   The truth that Mary remained always a virgin, that is, that she had no other children and never used her marital rights, emerges clearly in the Church's consciousness in the fourth century, when "ever-virgin" became a common description of her. This truth was accepted by all Christians until the Reformation. Groups of Christian ascetics were able to form after the peace of Constantine in the early fourth century. Consecrated virgins and celibate monks and hermits gave their lives to the keeping of the evangelical counsels, witnessing to Christ by lives of poverty, obedience, and voluntary virginity. In prayerful reflection and in their own experience of this type of dedication, these Christians discovered in Mary an exemplar of virginal consecration to Christ. This experience, freely chosen by some and held in general honor by the Christian people, provided insights into the mystery of Mary ever-virgin that the Church recognized as guided by the Holy Spirit. In the writings of St. Athanasius of Alexandria (d. 373), of St. Ambrose (d. 397), of St. Augustine (d. 430), and of St. Jerome (d. 420), Our Lady's lifelong virginity is praised. St. Jerome faced the difficulties in such biblical expressions as "brothers of the Lord." He showed that in New Testament Greek this term can mean "cousins" as well as "blood brothers."[19] By the time of the Council of Ephesus, AD 431, belief in the perpetual virginity of Mary was well formulated.

50.   This teaching about Mary's lifelong virginity is an example of the Church's growth in understanding of Christian doctrine. In its ordinary teaching, reflected in catechesis and liturgy, as well as in more formal pronouncements, the Church has here recognized as an aspect of "public Revelation" a belief not clearly demonstrable from the Scriptures. In Mary's virginal dedication to her Son's saving work, the Church sees delineated her own mission to bear witness to values that go beyond the secular city to the city of redeemed man, the Kingdom of God, in its present reality as well as in its future completion. The *Dogmatic Constitution on the Church* repeated this conviction, urging religious to "pattern [themselves] after that manner of virginal and humble life which Christ the Lord elected for himself and which His Virgin Mother also chose."[20]

THE BLESSEDNESS OF MARY

51.   In the Bible, "blessed" is the preferred description of the Mother of Jesus. Considering how infrequently the Gospel writers praise individuals, the insistence on Mary's blessedness is evidence of the veneration in which the early Church held

her. John Macquarrie, Anglican theologian, suggests that the Beatitudes help us understand how the word "blessed" is particularly associated with Mary: "The qualities set forth there are those which we see also in the Blessed Virgin. So the blessedness of the Virgin adumbrates the blessedness of the Church—no earthly happiness, but a 'likeness to God,' which means a participation in God's self-giving love. . . ."[21] The Gospel of St. Luke witnesses to the belief of the primitive Church in Mary's unique holiness: "All ages to come will call me blessed. . . . God who is mighty has done great things for me" (Lk 1:48). In her, above all others, was realized the promise of our Lord "blest are those who hear the word of God and keep it" (Lk 11:28).

52.   The Virgin Mary was called by the Fathers of the Church "all holy," the term beloved to this day by Christians in the East. She was declared to be "free from all stain of sin," "fashioned by the Holy Spirit into a kind of new substance and a new creature." The Second Vatican Council asserts that she was "adorned with the radiance of a singular holiness from the first moment of her conception. . . ."[22] In this statement, the Council calls attention to the doctrine of the Immaculate Conception. In 1854, Pope Pius IX defined as revealed truth "that the Blessed Virgin Mary in the first instant of her conception, by a singular grace and privilege of almighty God, in view of the foreseen merits of Jesus Christ the Savior of the human race, was preserved free from all stain of original sin."[23]

53.   Conceived and born of human parents in the normal way, Mary was especially gifted by God from "the first instant of her conception." The grace that others receive in Baptism, God gave to Mary even before her birth, through the foreseen merits of Christ, to prepare her to be the Mother of the Redeemer. The doctrine of the Immaculate Conception is doubly Christ-centered. It makes clear, first of all, that no one is saved apart from Christ. This is true of all men who have ever lived, even though they were born many centuries before Christ. Secondly, the preservative redemption of Mary is totally and splendidly God's gift to her because she was to be the Mother of Christ.

54.   In one of his first sermons after he became a Catholic, John Henry Newman asserted the great principle contained in our Lord's words, "More blessed is it to do God's will than to be God's Mother." He wrote: "Never say . . . that Catholics forget this passage of Scripture. Whenever they keep the feast of the Immaculate Conception, the Purity, or the like, recollect it is because they make so much of the blessedness of sanctity. . . . For the honor of the Son she [the Church] has ever extolled the glory of the Mother."[24]

55.   As the Council put it, "By thus consenting to the divine utterance, Mary, a daughter of Adam, became the Mother of Jesus. Embracing God's saving will with a full heart and impeded by no sin, she devoted herself totally as a handmaid of the Lord to the person and work of her Son. In subordination to Him and along with Him, by the grace of almighty God she served the mystery of redemption."[25] The Blessed Virgin was eternally predestined, in conjunction with the Incarnation of the divine Word to be the Mother of God" (no. 61, repeating a phrase from Pope Pius IX). For "the Father of Mercies willed that the consent of the predestined mother should precede the Incarnation. . . ."[26] The Mother of the Lord was early regarded by popular piety as singularly holy even in her origin, and a feast of the "conception of holy Mary" was celebrated in some countries as early as the eighth or ninth centuries.[27]

56.   Mary's initial holiness, a totally unmerited gift of God, is a sign of the love of Christ for his Bride, the Church, which, though composed of sinners, is still "holy Church." Mary Immaculate is seen in relation to Christ and the Church. Her privileged origin is the final step in preparing mankind to receive the Redeemer. God's grace triumphed over the power of original sin; the Father chose a perfectly responsive mother for the incarnate Son. The grace of the Immaculate Conception, a charism totally from God, prepared Mary for the motherhood of Jesus, the Savior. The Virgin Mary is "the most excellent fruit of the redemption,"[28] a figure of the spotless Bride of Christ, which is the Church.

THE ASSUMPTION

57.   Another aspect of Our Lady's holiness is brought out in her oldest liturgical feast, the Assumption. The meaning of this doctrine is that Mary is one with the risen Christ in the fullness of her personality, or as we commonly say, "in body and soul." Pope Pius XII solemnly proclaimed on November 1, 1950: "The Immaculate Mother of God, Mary ever-virgin, after her life on earth, was assumed, body and soul, into heavenly glory."[29]

58.   As early as the fifth century, Christians celebrated a "Memorial of Mary," patterned on the "birthday into heaven" of the martyrs' anniversaries. By this, they gave prayer form to their belief in the resurrection of the body and in the special bond between holy Mary and Jesus, the risen Savior. This primitive "Memorial of Mary," sometimes observed on August 15, evolved into the feast of the Dormition (the "falling asleep") of the Virgin. As early as the sixth century, homilies on the

Assumption appear,[30] which bring out the abiding and perfect conformity of the Mother of Jesus with "her Son, the Lord of lords, and the Conqueror of sin and death."[31] An eighth-century prayer, originally an announcement of a procession on August 15, has survived as an entrance prayer in some Western liturgies (e.g., the Carmelite rite until recently): "On this day the holy Mother of God suffered temporal death, but could not be held fast by the bonds of death, who gave birth to our Lord made flesh."

59.   United to the victorious Christ in heaven, Mary is "the image and first-flowering of the Church as she is to be perfected in the world to come." She shines forth "as a sign of sure hope and solace for the pilgrim People of God."[32] In her Assumption, Mary manifests the fullness of redemption, and appears as the "spotless image" of the Church responding in joy to the invitation of the Bridegroom Christ, himself the "first fruits of those who have fallen asleep" (1 Cor 15:20).

60.   Christ has risen from the dead; we need no further assurance of our faith. "Mary assumed into heaven" serves rather as a gracious reminder to the Church that our Lord wishes all whom the Father has given him to be raised with him. In Mary taken to glory, to union with Christ, the Church sees herself answering the invitation of the heavenly Bridegroom.

61.   There is a tender note here that is at the same time profoundly doctrinal, for it is based on the real humanity of the risen Jesus. Archbishop Philip Pocock of Toronto expresses it this way: "Jesus does not wish to be alone, but face-to-face with another in love. Our Lady sharing in the glory of her Son strengthens our hope in the destiny of the entire Church. This was the vision of St. John, when, contemplating the age to come, he saw the holy city, the new Jerusalem, coming down out of heaven from God, made ready as a bride adorned for her husband" (Rv 21:2).[33] The Mother of Jesus stands facing the risen Savior, her Son, a joyful sign to the Church of the answer to its constant prayer, "Come, Lord Jesus." The documents of the Second Vatican Council use several biblical images for the Church. It is called not only the "Body," favored by St. Paul, consisting of Christ as Head and Christians as members, but also "People of God," and "Bride." In a good marriage, their very union perfects the partners as individuals. Similarly, the mystical marriage between Christ and his Church perfects the Bride (and hence each member of the Church) in and through union with the Bridegroom. Mary in her Assumption, as in other aspects of her God-gifted personality, is a figure of the Church as perfected through union with Christ.

62.   In the liturgy "we honor Mary the ever-virgin Mother of Jesus Christ our Lord and God" (Eucharistic Prayer I); "Mary, the virgin Mother of God" (Prayers II and III); and "the Virgin Mary, the Mother of God" (Prayer IV). Cardinal Newman's phrase, "The Glories of Mary for the Sake of Her Son,"[34] is supremely applicable to the title "Mother of God," which was declared to be the faith of the Church at the Third Ecumenical Council, held at Ephesus, in AD 431. The Church's insistence on this title, Mother of God, is understandable, since no other formula makes so evident the intimate link between devotion to the Virgin Mary and belief in the Incarnation. This title was already in use in parts of the Church as early as the third century. The original form of the familiar prayer that begins "We fly to thy patronage, O holy Mother of God" may also be that early.

63.   The term "Mother of God" was used in Christian prayers before the doctrinal controversy that made it a test phrase of Christian faith. In AD 428, the term "Mother of God" was publicly challenged in Constantinople. The Church reacted strongly to this challenge at the Council of Ephesus. At stake was the central Christian truth that the man Jesus, Son of Mary, is truly "Son of God." Mary can be rightly called "Mother of God," not indeed in the blasphemous sense of having existed before God, but as an affirmation of the truth of the Incarnation. The Son of Mary is the one person who is the Son of God, Emmanuel.

64.   St. Cyril of Alexandria spoke for the Church's traditional faith when he wrote: "If we are to confess that Emmanuel is truly God, we must also confess that the Holy Virgin is *Theotokos* [Mother of God]; for she bore according to the flesh the Word of God made flesh." St. Cyril's explanation of the term "Mother of God" shows that the center of attention must be Christ himself: "Nor was he first born of the holy Virgin as an ordinary man, in such a way that the Word only afterwards descended upon him; rather was he united with flesh in the womb itself, and thus is said to have undergone birth according to the flesh, inasmuch as he makes his own the birth of his own flesh. . . . For this reason the holy Fathers have boldly proclaimed the holy Virgin *Theotokos*."[35] Subsequent ecumenical councils, such as Chalcedon, AD 451, and II Constantinople, AD 553, made the meaning of "Mother of God" even more precise.

Chapter Three
MARY, MEDIATRIX AND SPIRITUAL MOTHER

65.   "Mediatrix" is a familiar Catholic term to describe the unique role of the Mother of Jesus in her Son's mission as Mediator. We need to consider the meaning of "mediatrix," since some have the erroneous impression that the Second Vatican Council minimized or even denied the mediation of Mary. Although it used the word "mediatrix" only once, and altogether avoided the words "co-redemptrix" and "dispensatrix," the Council both retained and deepened Catholic understanding of Our Lady's mediatorial role.

66.   For the Council's restricted use of the word "mediatrix" there was a double reason: one ecumenical, the other pastoral. Ecumenically, "mediatrix" has seemed to many who are not Catholics to clash with the biblical insistence on Jesus Christ as our one Mediator (1 Tm 2:5). Pastorally, the bishops were anxious that Catholics understand even better Mary's true place under Christ. As mediatrix, Mary takes away nothing from Christ's all-sufficient mediatorship. It is owing to the Redeemer that all the redeemed are enabled to share in the Savior's work, and to influence the salvation of their brothers and sisters in the Body of Christ. Through her life of faith on earth, and now through her union with the risen Christ, the Mother of Jesus is the supreme example of loving association with the Savior in his mission of redeeming mankind. The manner in which men share in the Savior's redeeming work is similar to the way Christians, both ordained ministers and other believers, share in the priesthood of Christ, and, indeed, to the way all creatures share in the undivided goodness of the Creator.[36]

67.   Pope Paul put it this way: "Since Mary is rightly to be regarded as the way by which we are led to Christ, the person who encounters Mary cannot help but encounter Christ likewise."[37] Fr. Frederick Jelly explains how Mary's mediation, far from being a new role, fosters "immediate union of the faithful with Christ."[38] Fr. Jelly writes: "Mary is not a bridge over the gap that separates us from a remote Christ. . . . Such an approach to Marian devotion and doctrine would minimize the deepest meaning of the Incarnation, the fact that he has become a man like us, and that his sacred humanity has made him the unique mediator between God and us. Mary's greatness is that she brought him close to us, and her mediation continues to create the spiritual climate for our immediate encounter with Christ."[39]

68.   St. Paul saw himself as the herald of Christ Jesus, the one Mediator. Nevertheless, in the same Letter to Timothy in which he extols the unique mediatorship of

Christ, the apostle calls upon all to share in God's saving plan by offering prayers, petitions, intercessions, and thanksgivings (1 Ti 2:1). What St. Paul urges is in fact a sharing in the mission of Christ the Mediator. Mary's mediatorial role, correctly understood, is in perfect accord with the centrality of Christ.

69.   What is the positive value of Mary's role as mediatrix, and how does she exercise it? The Gospels portray her as a woman who walked by faith from the time of the Annunciation to Pentecost. The Virgin of Nazareth belonged to a family circle that was awaiting the consolation of Israel (Lk 2:5). The Mother of Jesus appears as totally responsive to the Father's will, always one with her Son's purposes, led by the Holy Spirit in everything.[40] "Be it done unto me according to your word" (Lk 1:38) was the act of faith of the Lord's Handmaid, a sign of her unwavering service to God in every detail of her life. In the Scriptures, "faith" means surrender of heart and body as well as of mind and intellect. St. Luke writes of Mary "reflecting in her heart" (Lk 2:19,51). St. John records the advice she exemplified in her own life: "Do whatever he tells you" (Jn 2:5). The Gospels provide few details of Mary's life; but they do delineate a remarkable portrait of the woman who gave herself wholeheartedly to her Son and his mission in perfect faith, love, and obedience. What Mary began on earth in association with the saving mission of Jesus, she continues still, in union with the risen Christ.

SPIRITUAL MOTHER

70.   It is a cherished American Catholic custom to call the Mother of Jesus "our Blessed Mother." In many respects this title can be explained in the same way as "mediatrix." Still, it has its own special value. "Mother" belongs to the language of the transmission of life. The reference here is to our life in Christ. St. Paul's familiar comparison likens the Church to a human body, with Christ as Head, and the faithful as its members. Like the Savior's parable of the vine and branches, the image of the Church as "Body of Christ" is a graphic reminder that the same life links members to Head, branches to Vine. From earliest Christian times, the Church was regarded as "Mother Church." Gradually, Mary's relationship to the sons and daughters of the Church came to be regarded also as that of "spiritual mother." Physically mother of Christ the Head, Mary is spiritually mother of the members of Christ. She is mother of all men, for Christ died for all. She is especially the mother of the faithful, or as Pope Paul proclaimed during the Second Vatican Council, she is "Mother of the Church."

71.   It is important to understand what is meant by the title "our Blessed Mother." Mary is not spiritual mother of men solely because she was physical Mother of the Savior. Nonetheless, the full understanding of Mary's motherhood of Jesus contains also the secret of her spiritual motherhood of the brethren of Christ. This secret is the truth already given in the Gospels and constantly stressed ever since in Christian thought and piety: Mary consented *in faith* to become the Mother of Jesus. The Second Vatican Council was in the stream of the constant tradition of the Church when it said that Mary received the Word of God into her heart and her body at the angel's announcement and thereby brought life to the world.[41] She conceived in her heart, with her whole being, before she conceived in her womb. First came Mary's faith, then her motherhood. Faith is the key also to the spiritual motherhood of Mary. By her faith, she became the perfect example of what the Gospels mean by "spiritual motherhood." In the preaching of the Savior, His "mother" is whoever hears God's Word and keeps it. All who truly follow Christ become "mothers" of Christ, for by their faith they bring him to birth in others.

72.   The Council fathers make use of a beautiful passage from St. Augustine, describing Mary as "Mother of the members of Christ . . . since she cooperated out of love so that there might be born in the Church the faithful, who are members of Christ their head."[42] These words were used by Pope Pius XII in his encyclical letter of May 15, 1956, on *The Sacred Heart*. The strength of St. Augustine's words becomes evident when it is realized that he was commenting on two incidents from the public life, the so-called "difficult sayings" of the Lord. The first incident is found in St. Luke. He is the only Evangelist to record the praise of the enthusiastic woman from the crowd: "Blest is the womb that bore you and the breasts that nursed you," and the reply of Jesus: "Rather, blest are they who hear the word of God and keep it" (Lk 11:28). The "true kinsmen" incident is told by Matthew (12:46-50) and Mark (3:31-35), as well as by Luke, who writes (8:19-21): "He was told, 'Your mother and your brothers are standing outside and they wish to see you.' He said in reply, 'My mother and my brothers are those who hear the word of God and act upon it.'"

73.   The passage from St. Augustine quoted above comes from his treatise *On Christian Virginity* (about AD 401). He writes: "More blessed was Mary in receiving the faith of Christ than in conceiving the flesh of Christ. For to her who said, 'Blessed is the womb that bore you and the breasts that nursed you,' he replied, 'Still more blessed are those who hear the word of God and keep it' (Lk 11:27-28). What in fact did their relationship profit his brethren according to the flesh who believed not in him? So too, even the close relationship of motherhood would have

profited Mary nothing had she not also more blessedly borne Christ in her heart than in her flesh. . . .’”

74.   St. Augustine continues: “All holy virgins are, with Mary, mothers of Christ if they do his Father’s will. For in this even Mary is with, greater praise and blessedness Christ’s Mother, according to the sentence, ‘Whoever does the will of my Father who is in heaven, the same is my brother and sister and mother’” (Mt 12:50). Commenting on this passage, Augustine explains: “All these relationships to himself he [Jesus] sets forth spiritually in the people whom he has redeemed. He has as brethren and sisters holy men and holy women, since they are co-heirs with him in the heavenly inheritance (Rom 8:17). The whole Church is his mother, because she it is who brings forth his members, that is, his faithful by the grace of God. His mother too is every good person who does his Father’s will by means of charity, meaning a charity that is in labor for others until Christ be formed in them (Gal 4:15). And therefore Mary in doing God’s will is mother of Christ in the flesh, but spiritually she is both sister and mother . . . She is mother of the members of Christ, which we are, because through love she cooperated in the birth of the faithful in the Church, and they are members of that Head.”

75.   St. Augustine does not restrict spiritual motherhood to the Virgin Mary and to other virgins. For he writes a bit further on: “Both married women of the faith and virgins consecrated to God, by holy lives and by charity ‘from a pure heart and a good conscience and faith unfeigned’ (1 Ti 1:5), are spiritually the mothers of Christ because they do the will of his Father.”[43]

76.   The incidents from the public ministry used by St. Augustine occur frequently in the liturgy. St. Luke’s narrative of the enthusiastic woman is often read at Marian Masses. Our Lord’s reply intensifies the woman’s simple praise: “Still more blessed those who hear the word of God and keep it.” Elizabeth’s words from the first chapter of St. Luke come to mind: “Blest are you among women and blest is the fruit of your womb. . . . Blest is she who trusted that the Lord’s words to her would be fulfilled” (Lk 1:42, 45).

77.   The other incident that refers to Mary is that of “the true kinsmen.” St. Luke relates the event just after the Parable of the Sower and the Seed, in which Jesus likens the rich soil to persons who hear God’s Word “in a spirit of openness, retain it, and bear fruit through perseverance” (Lk 8:15). It is possible that St. Luke deliberately described the visit of the “mother and brothers” of Jesus just after the parable of the sower because of Mary. Mary is the person of noble and generous heart, the

woman of faith who heard the Word and took it to herself and yielded the great harvest through her perseverance, her love, and her faith. Mary put into practice her Son's advice about the Kingdom being above considerations of flesh and blood. Jesus proposed hearing the Word of God and keeping it as the norm of blessedness. His Mother kept the Word so faithfully that her life can be called a "pilgrimage of faith." St. Luke twice calls attention to Mary's "pondering in her heart": when the shepherds relate the experiences that brought them to Bethlehem (Lk 2:19); and in reaction to the mysterious word about "His Father's house" from her twelve-year-old Son (Lk 2:51; cf. Lk 1:29 and 2:33).

78.   As a perfect disciple, the Virgin Mary heard the Word of God and kept it, to the lasting joy of the messianic generations who call her blessed. It is our Catholic conviction that in her present union with the risen Christ, our Blessed Mother is still solicitous for our welfare, still desirous that we become more like Jesus, her first-born. The Mother of Jesus wishes all her other children, all men and all women, to reach the maturity of the fullness of Christ (Eph 4:13; Col 1:28).

79.   Word of God—faith—birth of Christ: this is the pattern for the maternity of Mary and the maternity of the Church. Life is the dominant note in the language of motherhood. Mary brings forth Christ the Life; the Church continually regenerates men in the Christ-life. For both Mary and the Church, their motherhood is virginal, that is, entirely dependent on God, not on man. The Church's mission as "mother of the redeemed" was first realized in the Virgin Mother of Jesus. Open to the overshadowing Spirit, as was the Virgin Mary, the Church receives the Word of God and brings forth life. There are striking likenesses between the Annunciation and Pentecost. From the overshadowing of the Spirit, Christ is conceived; from the Pentecostal outpouring of the Spirit, Christ is born in his members who are the Church. Mary, the great mother figure for the Church, is present not only at the Annunciation, but also praying with her Son's disciples before Pentecost.

80.   Pondering the hidden holiness of Mary, the Church learns to imitate her charity and to carry out in faith the Father's will. Thereby the Church herself becomes a mother, receiving the Word of God in faith. By the ministry of the Word and Baptism, Mother Church brings forth to new life children conceived by the Holy Spirit and born of God. In imitation of the Mother of her Lord, by the power of his Spirit, the Church maintains an integral faith, a firm hope and a sincere charity.[44] In its apostolic work the Church looks to Mary. She conceived, brought forth, and nourished Christ.[45] So too, through the Church, Jesus continues to be born and grow in the hearts of the faithful.[46]

Chapter Four
MARY IN OUR LIFE

MARY'S INTERCESSION:
HER PLACE IN THE COMMUNION OF SAINTS

81.   According to the *Constitution on the Sacred Liturgy*, the Church honors the Mother of God when it celebrates the cycle of Christ's saving mysteries. For "Blessed Mary is joined by an inseparable bond to the saving work of her Son."[47] Deeper biblical insights have increased our awareness of Mary as the model of faithful discipleship; but it is also our purpose here to reinforce our Catholic sense of the Blessed Mother's present concern for us in her union with the risen Christ.

82.   Since early times, but especially after the Council of Ephesus, devotion to Mary in the Church has grown wondrously. The People of God through the ages have shown her veneration and love. They have called upon her in prayer and they imitate her.[48] All these ways of praising Mary draw us closer to Christ. When Mary is honored, her Son is duly acknowledged, loved, and glorified, and his commandments are observed.[49] To venerate Mary correctly means to acknowledge her Son, for she is the Mother of God. To love her means to love Jesus, for she is always the Mother of Jesus. To pray to Our Lady means not to substitute her for Christ, but to glorify her Son who desires us to have loving confidence in his Saints, especially in his Mother. To imitate the "faithful Virgin" means to keep her Son's commandments.

83.   The better we come to know Mary of the Gospels as the Church views her in liturgical celebrations and popular commemorations, the more we will be led to imitate her. We may ask, however, how the two aspects of imitation and prayer are joined in devotion to Mary. Or, to put the question in another way: how are memory of the past and experiences of the present related in our devotion to the Mother of Jesus? Through the Bible, we recall what Mary once was in her earthly association with Jesus; but we also long to know what she means to us now, and why we pray to her. As Catholics, we believe that Mary was once joined to her Son's saving work on earth; but we also believe that she remains inseparably joined to him, associated with the intercession the glorified Jesus makes for us forever at the throne of his Father (Heb 7:25).

84.   All four Eucharistic Prayers contain a prayer of remembrance that names Mary. In Eucharistic Prayer III, after mentioning "Mary, the Virgin Mother of God,

the apostles and martyrs and all your saints," we say that "on their constant intercession we rely for help." Intercession means that the blessed who are one with the risen Christ are still interested in us; they can and do pray for us. It is erroneous to think that the intercession of Mary and the saints is necessary in the sense that we do not have direct access to the merciful Savior. We believe that, having Christ, we have all things together with him. However, it is part of God's loving plan that, even as we help one another on earth by our prayers and deeds, so we can rely on the blessed in heaven, above all the Blessed Virgin Mary, to assist us by their prayers.

85.   There is little doubt that we are passing through a period marked by a lack of interest in the saints. Much more is involved here than devotion to the saints, even St. Mary. What is at stake is the reality of the humanity of the risen Jesus. There is danger of so spiritualizing the risen Christ that we diminish awareness of his humanity. It is our Christian belief that, as man, Jesus has taken his seat at the right hand of the Father; as man, Christ rose from the dead and ascended to heaven; as man, he lives forever to make intercession for us. When he was asked about the decline of Marian devotion, the German Jesuit Fr. Karl Rahner declared that the special temptation that affects Christians today, Catholics and Protestants alike, is the temptation to turn the central truths of the faith into abstractions, and abstractions have no need of mothers (quoted by Cardinal Suenens at Zagreb, August 1971).[50]

86.   The seventh chapter of the *Dogmatic Constitution on the Church*[51] concerns the relationship of the pilgrim Church to the Church in heaven, or, more familiarly, treats the "Communion of Saints." This strongly scriptural chapter has been even more neglected than the chapter on our Blessed Lady. The Council reminds us of our Catholic belief that we are still united with our brothers and sisters who have fallen asleep in the peace of Christ. Far from being interrupted, our union with them is strengthened by a sharing of spiritual goods.

87.   Fr. Herbert McCabe, OP, explains: "Prayer for the dead is first of all an expression of our presence in Christ, not merely to our contemporaries, but to the men and women of the past . . . Because Christ is risen and present to us we are more present to each other." In the risen Christ "we establish a deep and mysterious union with our fellow-men."[52] Christians live together in the Spirit of Christ; death cannot break this living community. Belief in the Resurrection does not mean that we think of Christ simply as a person from the past whom we still remember; belief in the risen Christ means that we are somehow in personal contact with him, that the glorified Jesus is present to us.

88.   For the same reason, Fr. McCabe adds, all "who have 'died in Christ' are also not merely objects of memory . . . in him they are really present to us and in him they will share the future we hope for." The Church has recognized that certain holy people, led by the Mother of the Lord, are already in glory. When we celebrate the memory of Mary in the liturgy, we join together in a present liturgical "moment" the past and the future—what Mary once was on earth, as the Gospels show her, and the future, our reunion with Mary and the saints, including the uncanonized saints of our own families, reunited in the risen Lord. The saints "have been received into their heavenly home and are present to the Lord. Through him, with him and in him, they do not cease to intercede with the Father for us."[53] Through their fraternal concern, our pilgrim weakness is greatly alleviated. We seek from the saints for our greater good and that of the Church "example in their way of life, fellowship in their communion, and aid by their intercession,"[54] as a new Preface says.[55]

89.   The *Constitution on the Sacred Liturgy* states: "In the earthly liturgy, by way of foretaste we share in that heavenly liturgy which is celebrated in the holy city of Jerusalem toward which we journey as pilgrims, and in which Christ is sitting at the right hand of God. . . ."[56] Celebrating the Eucharistic sacrifice, we are most closely joined with the worship of the heavenly Church, as we unite to honor the memory first of all of "the ever-virgin Mother of Jesus Christ our Lord and God,"[57] of Mary who is the "image and first-flowering of the Church as she is to be perfected in the world to come."[58]

90.   In speaking of Catholic devotion to Mary, we must not neglect to mention the special honor paid to Our Lady in the liturgy and theology of the Eastern rites. Some of the most beautiful and profound passages concerning the Mother of God were written by the Eastern Fathers of the Church. Even today, in almost every liturgical service, we find repeated use of three glorious titles for the Mother of the Lord: she is called "the all-holy one," "the one without even the slightest stain," and "the one blessed beyond all others."[59]

MARY IN CHRISTIAN DEVOTION

91. What is the place of Our Lady in Catholic prayer life? Many Catholics today are forgetful of the saints and have little sense of being one with the blessed when they celebrate the liturgy and in their other prayers and devotions. From an age of novenas to Our Lady under many titles, and to certain favorite saints (one thinks readily of St. Anne, St. Francis Xavier, and St. Therese of Lisieux), we have passed

abruptly to near silence about these friends of Christ. In spite of the urging of the *Constitution on the Sacred Liturgy* that we celebrate the feasts of Our Lady and deepen the sense of her association in the central saving mysteries of Jesus the Savior, the Church is suffering a malaise with respect to the commemoration of Mary. Two numbers, 66-67, in the chapter on Our Lady deal with the cult of Mary, and are filled with practical suggestions, e.g., let the liturgy provide the lead, even for non-liturgical devotions, which are encouraged, especially those that have enjoyed the Church's favor for a long time. A middle way is recommended between the extremes of too much and too little.[60]

92.   As we write this pastoral letter, our concern about Our Lady is most keenly felt in the area of devotion. No survey is needed to show that all over the country many forms of Marian devotion have fallen into disuse, and others are taking an uncertain course. In an age avid for symbols (the peace medals and other signs of the young are evidence of this), the use of Catholic Marian symbols, such as the scapular and the Miraculous Medal, has noticeably diminished. Only a few years ago, use of the rosary was a common mark of a Catholic, and it was customarily taught to children, both at home and in courses in religious instruction. Adults in every walk of life found strength in this familiar prayer that is biblically based and is filled with the thought of Jesus and his Mother in the "mysteries." The praying of the rosary has declined. Some Catholics feel that there has even been a campaign to strip the churches of statues of Our Lady and the saints. Admittedly, many churches were in need of artistic reform; but one wonders at the severity of judgment that would find no place for a fitting image of the Mother of the Lord.

93.   We view with great sympathy the distress our people feel over the loss of devotion to Our Lady and we share their concern that the young be taught a deep and true love for the Mother of God. We bishops of the United States wish to affirm with all our strength the lucid statements of the Second Vatican Council on the permanent importance of authentic devotion to the Blessed Virgin, not only in the liturgy, where the Church accords her a most special place under Jesus her Son, but also in the beloved devotions that have been repeatedly approved and encouraged by the Church and that are still filled with meaning for Catholics. As Pope Paul has reminded us, the rosary and the scapular are among these tested forms of devotion that bring us closer to Christ through the example and protection of his Holy Mother.

94. In this sensitive area, where it is not possible to assess and comment on all the individual aspects of concern or to enter into local differences of viewpoint, we offer to the faithful some suggestions to increase love and devotion to the Blessed Virgin.

Above all, the renewed liturgy offers immense riches with respect to the Mother of the Lord. Having the liturgy in English increases these possibilities even more. Far from having minimized the place of Our Lady, the present lectionary contains more readings than we had before, from Old Testament and New, arranged for Our Lady's feasts and commemorations. In the current calendar, there are more optional days on which a Marian votive Mass may be celebrated, on Saturdays in particular. Pope Paul's missal of 1970 has many excellent new prayers for Mary's feasts, based on the Bible and in the spirit of the Council. Among the more than eighty prefaces of the Sacramentary, there are four of Our Lady: two for regular use, one for the Immaculate Conception, and another for the Assumption.

95. Our bond with the saints, and St. Mary at their head, has its noblest expression in the liturgy, where we praise with joy the Majesty of God. "Celebrating the Eucharistic sacrifice, therefore, we are most closely united to the worshipping Church in Heaven as we join with and venerate the memory first of all of the glorious ever-virgin Mary, of blessed Joseph and the blessed Apostles and martyrs and of all the saints."[61]

96. Besides her place in the liturgy, Our Lady has been honored by an amazingly rich variety of extra-liturgical devotional forms. Some of these have a long history. In particular, the Dominican rosary of fifteen decades links Our Lady to her Son's salvific career, from the Annunciation and the joyful events of the infancy and childhood of Jesus, through the sorrowful mysteries of his suffering and death, to his Resurrection and Ascension, and the sending of the Spirit to the Apostles at Pentecost, and concluding with the Mother's reunion with her Son in the mysteries of Assumption and Coronation. It is unwise to reject the rosary without a trial simply because of the accusation that it comes from the past, that it is repetitious and ill-suited to sophisticated moderns. The scriptural riches of the rosary are of permanent value. Its prayers, in addition to the opening Apostles' Creed and the occasional repetition of the ancient and simple Doxology (Glory Be to the Father), are the Our Father and the Hail Mary. The words of the first half of the Hail Mary are taken from St. Luke. The second half, "Holy Mary, Mother of God, pray for us sinners, now and at the hour of our death," is in the mainstream of prayers that go back to the early centuries of Christian devotion.[62]

97. The recommended saying of the rosary does not consist merely in "telling the beads" by racing through a string of familiar prayers. Interwoven with the prayers are the "mysteries." Almost all of these relate saving events in the life of

Jesus, episodes in which the Mother of Jesus shared. Nor is rhythmic prayer alien to modern man, as is shown by the attraction of Eastern religions for many young people today. Besides the precise rosary pattern long known to Catholics, we can freely experiment. New sets of mysteries are possible. We have customarily gone from the childhood of Jesus to his Passion, bypassing the whole public life. There is rich matter here for rosary meditation, such as the wedding feast of Cana, and incidents from the public life where Mary's presence and Mary's name serve as occasions for her Son to give us a lesson in discipleship: "Still more blessed are they who hear the word of God and keep it" (Lk 11:28). Rosary vigils have already been introduced in some places, with an instructive use of readings, from Old Testament as well as New, and with recitation of a decade or two, if not all five. In a public celebration of the rosary, hymns can be introduced as well, and time allowed for periods of silent prayer.

98.   The rosary suggestions here sketched can be applied to other devotional practices as well. In these changing times, great inventiveness on the part of the whole Catholic people is needed. Under the guidance of the Holy Father and the bishops, we must revitalize old forms and devise new devotions corresponding to current needs and desires. The liturgical season should set the tone for Marian prayers at each particular time of the year, e.g., May devotions should reflect Paschal and Pentecostal orientations.[63] Advent provides a unique opportunity for the consideration of Mary, in whom all Old Testament hopes culminated. Following her example, the Church awaits the Lord, not only in his coming at Bethlehem, but also in his second coming, and indeed in that daily presence to which the Church as Bride must ever be sensitive.

99.   We turn our reflections now to the authenticated appearances of Our Lady and their influence on Catholic devotion, especially in the years since the Apparition at Lourdes, in 1858. Other nineteenth-century events of this kind were the experiences of St. Catherine Laboure in 1830 (the "Miraculous Medal"), and the apparition at La Salette in 1846. In our own hemisphere, we recall the apparition in 1531 of Our Lady of Guadalupe, "Queen of the Americas." Best known of the twentieth-century appearances of the Mother of the Lord is that at Fatima, in 1917.

100. These providential happenings serve as reminders to us of basic Christian themes: prayer, penance, and the necessity of the sacraments. After due investigation, the Church has approved the pilgrimages and other devotions associated with certain private revelations. She has also at times certified the holiness of their recipients by beatification and canonization, for example, St. Bernadette of Lourdes and

St. Catherine Laboure. The Church judges the devotions that have sprung from these extraordinary events in terms of its own traditional standards. Catholics are encouraged to practice such devotions when they are in conformity with authentic devotion to Mary. Even when a "private revelation" has spread to the entire world, as in the case of Our Lady of Lourdes, and has been recognized in the liturgical calendar, the Church does not make mandatory the acceptance either of the original story or of particular forms of piety springing from it. With the Vatican Council, we remind true lovers of Our Lady of the danger of superficial sentiment and vain credulity.[64] Our faith does not seek new Gospels, but leads us to know the excellence of the Mother of God and moves us to a filial love toward our Mother and to the imitation of her virtues.[65]

THE BLESSED VIRGIN AND ECUMENISM

101. We live in a new era of friendly relations between Catholics and members of other Christian Churches, Orthodox, Anglican, and Protestant. Often in the past, even fairly recently, the matter of Mary caused acrimonious differences between Catholics and Protestants. The dialogues of recent years, thanks to initiatives taken on both sides (on the Catholic side especially through the Second Vatican Council), have brought Christians to consider the difficulties of doctrine about and devotion to Mary openly and with charity. It would be naive to suggest that openness and mutual love can suddenly break down barriers erected on both sides over centuries. Yet encouraging signs appear. Catholics have been spurred on by the Second Vatican Council to "return to the Bible" for a profounder understanding of the Mother of Jesus as woman of faith. Br. Max Thurian, of the French Calvinist monastery of Taize, has put all Christians in his debt with a valuable book on the Mary of the Gospels: *Mary, Mother of the Lord, Figure of the Church.*[66]

102. Taking their cue from the Council's careful language, and profiting from its advice to "painstakingly guard against any word or deed which could lead separated brethren or anyone else into error regarding the true doctrine of the Church"[67] about Our Lady, Catholic theology and piety of the last few years have been more discriminating in the use of such words as "mediatrix." This term, as we mentioned before, was used only once by the fathers of Vatican II. Of ecumenical import also are Catholic efforts to show that such beliefs about the Mother of the Lord as her initial freedom from Original Sin (the Immaculate Conception) and her final union with the risen Christ (the Assumption) are not isolated privileges, but mysteries filled with meaning for the whole Church.

103. For too long Mary's place in Catholic doctrine and, even more, in Catholic devotion has been a sharp point of difference with other Christians of the West. What began in the Reformation as a reaction against certain abuses soon led in some quarters to forbidding all invocation of the saints, even of St. Mary, and to a diminished sense of the Communion of Saints. Throughout the Reformation and Counter-Reformation, excesses abounded on both sides. Protestant polemicists made a battle cry of the supposedly fatal choices: Christ or Mary, Scripture or Tradition, grace or freedom, God or man, as if Catholics did not also accept Christ and the Bible and the supremacy of grace and God as central to the faith.

104. The Catholic counterattack exalted and extolled Mary as "conqueror of all heresy." It seemed to many Protestants that the Roman Catholic Church had moved even farther away from Christ the Center, when Pope Pius IX defined the Immaculate Conception of Mary in 1854, and Pope Pius XII her Assumption in 1950. Karl Barth was fully in the Reformed tradition in his strong rejection of what he called "the Mariological dogma." He saw this as the sign *par excellence* of the Roman Church, which was to him "that church of man who, prompted by the grace of God, cooperates with grace and merits salvation."[68]

105. The role of the Mother of Jesus remains one of our many persisting religious differences, even though we are now better able to speak openly and charitably, putting aside old prejudices in common efforts to seek out what we share jointly in our Christian heritage and also where and why we differ.

106. We are convinced that all Christians share a basic reverence for the Mother of Jesus, a veneration deeper than doctrinal differences and theological disputes. We share a common past. Together we accept the Gospel respect for the Mother of Jesus, Handmaid of the Lord, woman of faith, model of prayer, servant of the Spirit. The faith of the Church is anchored in history, and Mary is part of that anchor. Mentioned with Pontius Pilate in the Creed (but for a greatly different reason!), she attests to the historicity of Jesus Christ. In the early Church and in the first ecumenical councils, attention was focused on Jesus Christ, truly man and truly God. The phrase, "born of the Virgin Mary," was used in the second century to defend the reality of Jesus' humanity. At Ephesus, in AD 431, the divine motherhood was defined in defense of the divinity of the Son of Mary. The title, "Mother of God" became a permanent part of the creeds and liturgies of the entire Church. We have seen above how the Church recognized many aspects of herself in the Mother of Jesus—as virgin, as mother, as holy. The Middle Ages explored still further the likenesses between Mary and the Church. The emphasis on the heavenly intercession

of the Mother of God strengthened the sense of community between the pilgrim Church on earth and the Church triumphant in heaven. With St. Luke as a basis, earlier times had made much of the Annunciation. The Middle Ages pondered Mary's compassion on Calvary, leading to the familiar representations of the *Pietà*.

107. We ask our brothers in other Christian churches to reexamine with us Mary's place in our common patrimony. To an encouraging degree, this is already being done in Bible studies and in the return to the study of the Fathers. The generally favorable reaction outside the Catholic Church to the Council's document on the Blessed Virgin Mary is encouraging indeed. Our Christian brothers have shown sensitivity to the conciliar use of Scripture and of the early Christian authors. They have also expressed appreciation of the restraint exercised by the Council with regard to the difficult term "mediatrix." Perhaps most encouraging of all, they have paid notice to the reference in the *Decree on Ecumenism* to "the hierarchy of truths," which "vary in their relationship to the foundation of the Christian faith."[69]

108. The document on ecumenism brings out this "hierarchy of truths" with regard to the differences that still divide Western Christians, in spite of our common formula of Trinitarian and Christological faith. "Our thoughts are concerned first of all with those Christians who openly confess Jesus Christ as God and Lord and as the sole Mediator between God and man, unto the glory of the one God, Father, Son, and the Holy Spirit. We are indeed aware that among them views are held considerably different from the doctrine of the Catholic Church even concerning Christ, God's Word made flesh, and the work of redemption, and thus concerning the mystery and ministry of the Church, and the role of Mary in the work of salvation."[70]

109. No sound ecumenism can ignore the question of Mary. "Marian truths cannot be pushed to one side, because there are no such things as isolated Christian truths which concern Mary alone."[71] She no more stands alone without Christ now than she did in the Scriptures or at Ephesus or in the liturgy, as it has been celebrated through the ages in the Eastern and Western rites. Christ is at the center of our faith; but he did not come among men without the *Theotokos*. Nor is he in glory now without his Mother, *Theotokos* still.

110. Another difficulty among Christians is the relationship between Scripture, Tradition, and the Church's teaching role. How have Catholics come to regard as revealed truth such doctrines as Mary's Immaculate Conception and Assumption, in the absence of clear biblical evidence? And, most difficult of all, is the problem:

what can man do under the power of grace? The chief reason why "silence about Mary" is an ecumenically destructive policy is that one's attitude toward the mystery of Mary shows his position on this important question.[72]

111. What the Church has said about the effects of redemption in Mary, she has affirmed in other ways and at other times of us all. The Immaculate Conception and the Assumption, as we sought to show earlier in this letter, are basically affirmations about the nature of human salvation. "Mary is today, even as at Ephesus, a witness to the Incarnation. She was then a pointer to the truly historical reality of Jesus Christ who is God. Today she must be seen as indicating the full implications of the Incarnation for our understanding of being human."[73]

112. Another matter we might profitably explore together as Christians is the bond between Mary and the Holy Spirit. Christ sent his Spirit as the new Advocate, as the Intercessor who comes to help us in our weakness. Any correct understanding of Mary's role must be seen in connection with the predominant role of the Holy Spirit. The Bible provides us with a starting point:. St. Luke presents Mary as the humble woman overshadowed by the Holy Spirit in order that Christ be formed. "God sent his Son born of a woman . . . that we might receive the adoption of sons" (Gal 4:4).[74]

Chapter Five

MARY, MOTHER OF THE CHURCH

113. The title, "Mother of the Church," was announced by Pope Paul VI during the Council. The proclamation came after the promulgation of the *Dogmatic Constitution on the Church*, November 21, 1964. The pope chose the occasion to give Mary a title "that expresses with wonderful brevity the exalted place in the Church which the Church recognizes as proper to the Mother of God."[75] The Holy Father desired to state in a single phrase the spiritual motherhood that the Mother of Jesus exercises toward the members of the "Mystical Body," the Church, of which Christ is Head. The Council set out to show forth the true beauty of the face of the Church, Spouse of Christ, and our teacher and mother. What the Council said about Mary's role in the mystery of Christ and his Church harmonized perfectly with this aim, and Pope Paul hoped that the title, "Mother of the Church" would call attention to the Council's teaching.

114.   In this title, the "Church," of which Mary is Mother, is seen as comprising both shepherds and flocks, both pastors and people. As a believing disciple of Jesus, Mary can be called *daughter* of the Church, and our *sister* as well. For, like us, she has been redeemed by Christ, although in an eminent and privileged way.[76] What is the special significance of the title "Mother of the Church"? It is based on Mary's being the Mother of God. By God's call and her free response in the power of his grace, Mary became the Mother of Jesus, Son of God made man, and thus truly "Mother of God."

115.   She remained joined to her Son's saving work in the new economy in which he freed men from sin by the mysteries of his flesh.[77] On Calvary, Jesus gave John into Mary's care and thus designated her Mother of the human race that the beloved disciple represented. At the Annunciation, Mary conceived Christ by the power of the Holy Spirit. After Christ's Resurrection, surrounded by his disciples, Mary prayed for the coming of that same Spirit, in order that the Church, the Body of her Son, might be born on Pentecost. Through her faith and love, Mary's maternity reached out to include all the members of her Son's Mystical Body.

116.   Her union with the risen Lord has added to Mary's motherhood of the Church a new effectiveness, as she shares in the everlasting intercession of our great High Priest. In calling Mary "Mother of the Church," we are reminded that she is also the Mother of unity, sharing her Son's desire and prayer that his Body be truly one. It is encouraging to note that some members of other Christian Churches, for example, John Macquarrie, found in Pope Paul's title, Mother of the Church, a sign of ecumenical hope.[78]

117.   The basic reason Mary is Mother of the Church is that she is Mother of God, and the associate of Christ in his saving work. Another great reason is that the Mother of Jesus "shines as the model of virtues for the whole community of the elect."[79] As Pope Paul put it, "Jesus gave us Mary as our Mother, and proposed her as a model to be imitated."[80] The Mother of Jesus exemplified in her own life the Beatitudes preached by her Son, and so the Church, in and through the many activities of its various members and vocations, rightly regards Mary, Mother of the Church, as the perfect model of the imitation of Christ."[81]

118.   The role of the Holy Spirit in the life of Mary is especially pertinent to our time. Mary of the *Magnificat* is, after Jesus himself, the supreme New Testament example of one who is led by the Holy Spirit. Not only the *Magnificat*, but Mary's whole life was a song of love inspired by the Holy Spirit. "Led by the Holy Spirit,

she devoted herself entirely to the mystery of man's redemption."[82] She brought forth Jesus by the power of the Spirit. So too, Jesus is brought forth and lives in us through the Spirit.

MARY AND THE PRIESTHOOD

119. All the members of the People of God share in the priesthood of Christ and join in the offering of the Eucharist. Nevertheless, there is a difference not only in degree, but in essence between the common priesthood of the faithful and the ministerial priesthood of those who have received Holy Orders.[83]

120. At ordination, "by the anointing of the Holy Spirit," the priest is "marked with a special character," and is "so configured to Christ the priest that he can act in the person of Christ the Head."[84] His distinct calling to be fellow worker with Christ bears a resemblance to Mary's unique association in the saving work of Jesus. Our Lady's relationship to Christ the eternal High Priest overflows into her spiritual motherhood of all priests in their call to holiness and ministry. As Our Lady's *fiat* at the Annunciation was consummated in her total surrender to the Father's will at the foot of the cross, so too through Mary's inspiration and intercession the priest is offered the grace of Christ to give of himself, in union with the Eucharistic victim, for the salvation of his fellow men.

121. In the Latin Rite, the priest freely accepts the solemn obligation of celibacy out of love for Christ. The spotless purity of Mary is a constant source of inspiration and strength to him in living his celibate life. Having sacrificed for the Kingdom of God the natural right to marriage and a family of his own, he feels himself more closely bound to the Mother of the Savior for whose sake he has made this sacrifice. There will be inevitable loneliness in the life of the good priest, accepted out of love for the suffering Christ. The sorrowful mysteries of the rosary have special meaning to the priest as he walks with the Mother of Jesus along the way of the cross.

122. In Mary, Mother of the Church, the priest has the model of his own devotion to her Son. He looks to her, the woman of faith, for that faith and charity that will make fruitful his own human sharing in the priesthood of the Savior. And as Mary was faithful to the end, so he too is confident that he will persevere in the work God began in him by his ordination.

123. In a family where love rules, the mother has a special affection for each child. Mary, Mother of the Church, is universal mother. In the community of faith, religious men and women hold a special place, and for them also Mary is Mother and model in a particular way. These religious, who have consecrated their lives to the Church, know from experience the tension between their vocation of prayer and the demands of the apostolate. Mary was the perfect contemplative, totally committed to "the one thing necessary," yet fully attentive to the needs of others, e.g., Elizabeth, the Cana couple, the disciples praying for Pentecost.

124. The special vocation of religious is to bear witness to the Kingdom of God, both present and to come, by living in the spirit of the three vows that they publicly profess in answer to the Savior's evangelical counsels. Religious give up great human goods: the control of their possessions, the joy and companionship of married life, and free disposition of their personal talents. Catholic people rightly understand that the giving up of such human experiences, out of a desire to follow Christ, does honor also to the Christian vocations of the laity and supplies strength to the rest of the Church.

125. Their vows put religious at the disposal of their brothers and sisters in the wider Christian family, both for an apostolate free from family ties and for total dedication to prayer for the Church and world by cloistered monks and nuns. The goal of religious life is the Christian ideal of love of God and neighbor, not only in our present time-conditioned existence, but as a sign to the world of eternal union with the risen Christ, to which all men are called.

126. Again, it is the loving faith of Mary that makes her a perfect model for the religious. She is the greatest among the "lowly and poor of the Lord," whose trust in him brings the abundant harvest. Humanly speaking, her virginity seemed to exclude her maternity; yet God made her Mother of the Messiah. Her poverty seemed to exclude her Son from the Davidic inheritance; but Jesus was the promised "Son of David." Her humble circumstances left little choice but to accept what life brought; but her splendid obedience made her an associate of her Son's saving work.

127. Mary's life testified to the Kingdom her Son preached, which was inaugurated by his death and Resurrection and the sending of his Spirit. "Temple of the Holy Spirit,"[85] she continues to exercise a special influence on religious men and women

today, whose lives proclaim that the risen Christ reigns, and that union with him, now and forever, is man's true vocation.

128. The founders and other holy members of religious congregations, past and present, have shown by example that true devotion to the Mother of Jesus is an indispensable element in maturing in the life of Christ. Now, as throughout the history of the Church, religious women find special inspiration in the Virgin Mother of Jesus. To both cloistered nuns and the sisters active in schools and hospitals and other works of mercy and service, Mary remains the model of following Jesus.

MARY AND FAMILY LIFE

129. What does "Holy Mary" say to struggling humanity in a sinful world? How does the example of her virtues touch laymen and women in the pilgrim Church? In her faithful discipleship, her union with Christ, her openness to the Spirit, Mary stands in contrast to all the sin, all the evil in the world.

130. We say "Holy Mary, Mother of God, pray for us sinners, now and at the hour of our death," confessing that we have added to the evil in the world by our own sins, and asking God's forgiveness. Yet our prayer is filled with confidence. For we find strength for the "now" not only in the constant loving intercession of the Mother of God, but also in the memory of how Our Lady of the Gospels lived the life of faith. The Mother of Jesus is the great exemplar to the whole Church; but she is model also to each individual in the Church, at every stage of human life and in every particular Christian vocation. No one ever followed Jesus so well as Mary his Mother. No one can help us more, by her example and by her intercession.

131. What does Mary mean to today's family? Mother of the Holy Family at Nazareth, Mary is mother and queen of every Christian family. When Mary conceived and gave birth to Jesus, human motherhood reached its greatest achievement. From the time of the Annunciation, she was the living chalice of the Son of God made man. In the tradition of her people she recognized that God gives life and watches over its growth. "Just as you do not know the way of the wind or the mysteries of a woman with child, no more do you know the work of God who is behind it all" (Eccl 11:5; see also Ps 138 (139):13; 2 Mc 7:22).

132. Reverence for human life as sacred from the beginning is bound up with the correct understanding and use of sexual love. Abortion arouses in the Christian the

same horror as the slaughter of the innocents in St. Matthew's Gospel. Defenders of unborn life do well to appeal to the first part of the Hail Mary. Elizabeth's words, "Blessed is the fruit of your womb," are true in a real sense of every unborn child.

133. God called Mary and Joseph to sublimate the consummation of their married love in exclusive dedication to the holy Child, conceived not by a human father but by the Holy Spirit. When Mary said to Gabriel, "How can this be since I do not know man?" (Lk 1:34), the angel told her of the virginal conception. Joseph received the same message in a dream. Christian tradition from early times has seen St. Joseph as protector of the Christ Child and of his wife's consecrated virginity throughout their married life.

134. Christian marriage is a sign of the union between Christ and his Church. Man and wife in mutual love, and in the children they welcome from God and care for, are a witness to the world of love of God and of their fellow men. The offering of the bride's bouquet at Our Lady's statue is an American Catholic custom that invites the Blessed Virgin into the life of the newlyweds. The conjugal chastity of a holy marriage is an answer to the neo-pagan degradation of human sexuality by pornography and by the glorification of promiscuity, divorce, and perversions. Parents and children will find renewed strength in the grace of Christ and in the example and assistance of the Blessed Virgin, model of perfect purity and of self-surrender to God and neighbor. Christ was "Man of Sorrows," tortured and executed for the sins of men. Mary was "Mother of Sorrows" sharing her Son's sufferings even to Calvary. But there were also the joyous years at Nazareth, as her Son grew to adulthood, and something of the happiness of the Holy Family comes through in the Gospel preaching of Jesus with his tender examples from home life.

135. Because she is seen as the Mother of all the living, Mary is viewed properly as the guardian of the child in the womb, as well as of the child that enters this earth alive. More than any other person, the Blessed Mother understood that the beginning of human life is attributable to God's creative love, as well as to the parents' action. When God became man within Mary, the Incarnation began. When Mary accepted the message from the angel and the Holy Spirit overshadowed her, the Divine Word, the God-man began to live. Entrusted with this precious life of her Child, Mary loved it, and defended it against all dangers. She protected Jesus before and after he was born.

136. So too, the Blessed Mother protects human life today from the moment of conception through birth (the beginning of our pilgrimage of faith), until all

mankind realizes its goal in the Beatific Vision. Abortion, the deliberate killing of an unborn fetus, is a heinous crime and a serious sin. We, the Catholic bishops of the United States, denounce abortion as an affront to the human race, as an unspeakable crime and a serious sin. We call upon all people of good will who reverence life to join in a crusade to protect life on all levels. No court, no matter how prestigious, can make acceptable what is obviously totally opposed to the Law of God and the best interests of our society.

137. Mary is Queen of the home. As a woman of faith, she inspires all mothers to transmit the Christian faith to their children. In the setting of family love, children should learn free and loving obedience, inspired by Mary's obedience to God. Her example of concern for others, as shown at the wedding feast of Cana, will exercise its gentle influence. "He went down with them . . . and was obedient to them . . . [Jesus] progressed steadily in wisdom and age and grace before God and men" (Lk 2:51-52). This obedience of Jesus is emphasized throughout the New Testament: at Nazareth, throughout his ministry in which he sought only to do his Father's will, even unto death. The Gospel makes clear also Mary's obedience to the law and to the traditional prayer life of her people. This is evident, for example, in her annual trip to Jerusalem for the Passover. Faithful to the Law of Moses, the holy couple brought Jesus to the temple, his Father's house, for the presentation. Such obedience was the flower of Mary's faith. Because of it, God found her worthy to be the Mother of his Son.

138. In her appearances during the public life, Mary showed the same generous response to the will of the Father made manifest in her Son. At the marriage feast of Cana, after her Son's mysterious reference to the "hour not yet come," Mary's reaction was to advise the waiters, "Do whatever he tells you" (Jn 2:5). Family love builds on the Fourth Commandment, and in Jesus, Mary, and Joseph, parents and children have a powerful example of obedience to the will of God.

139. Family prayer, in whatever form it takes—meal prayers, night prayers, the family rosary, attending Mass together—provides opportunities for prayer to the Blessed Virgin. Children forget many things when they grow up. They do not forget the manly piety of the father, the gentle devotion of the mother, and love of Jesus and Mary as the support of the home, in sorrow and in joy.

140. Here we may recall the words of the joint pastoral letter of 1968, *Human Life in Our Day*: "Because of the primacy of the spiritual in all that makes for renewal, we give top priority to whatever may produce a sound 'family spirituality': family

prayer, above all that which derives its content and spirit from the liturgy and other devotions, particularly the rosary."[86]

141. According to the Gospels, Christ showed an enlightened attitude toward women: in his conversation with the Samaritan woman at the well; in his friendship with Martha and Mary, especially in his defense of Mary's preference to listen to his words, rather than wait upon him; in his behavior toward the Syrophenician woman with the sick daughter (Mk 7:29); and in his appearance as risen Lord to Mary Magdalene, whom he sends to announce the Good News to his Apostles. These incidents, interpreted in their cultural context, give us a basis for a genuine emancipation and liberation of womanhood.

142. The dignity that Christ's redemption won for all women was fulfilled uniquely in Mary as the model of all real feminine freedom. The Mother of Jesus is portrayed in the Gospels as: *intelligent* (the Annunciation, "How can this be?"); *apostolic* (the visit to Elizabeth); *inquiring and contemplative* (the Child lost in the temple); *responsive and creative* (at Cana); *compassionate and courageous* (at Calvary); a woman of *great faith*. These implications in the lives of Jesus and Mary need to be elaborated into a sound theology on the role of Christian women in contemporary Church and society.

MARY AND YOUTH

143. Young people, adolescents in particular, will find in Mary the totally unselfish person, the brave young woman who could face and accept the hidden future bound up with being Virgin Mother of the Messiah. According to the customs of her time and people, Mary was probably no more than fourteen when her parents arranged her marriage, and Joseph probably about eighteen. God asked great things of them both, and they responded to his call with dedicated love.

144. So too, many young people today are eager to make the world into a better place, where justice and peace and love will prevail. The great obstacles still remain human greed and selfishness, all the deadly sins that bring turmoil and agony to so many suffering human beings. The succession of wars that grow in horror as technology improves, the oppression of underprivileged people at home and abroad, the imbalance between rich and poor countries are evils that become even more intolerable when men would seem to have such great potential and when modern communications have so shrunk the information world. Only God can change men's

hearts; only with the help of his grace can the enemies of mankind be conquered. Only those men and women will make an impact on society and change the world for the better, who make themselves powerful, effective instruments of God by lives of faith, hope, and love, giving themselves completely to God in order that in and through them he may accomplish his great designs.

MARY AND SINGLE LIFE

145. Mary is model also for women who live a single life in the world. This can be a true vocation from God, freely chosen under the inspiration of grace, bringing with it the fruits of joy, personal holiness, and unselfish service of others. Many a young girl, on the death of her mother, has generously taken on herself the care of younger brothers and sisters to train them in the love of God. Others dedicate their lives to the service of their fellow men as nurses, teachers, and social workers. Many exercise an apostolate through personal example and influence, and through their work in Catholic lay organizations. All these devoted women share in the spiritual motherhood of the Mother Jesus and, like her, find true happiness and fulfillment in doing God's will.

CONCLUSION

146. As we conclude these pastoral reflections on the Virgin Mary, Mother of Jesus and Mother of the Church, we commend our efforts to her loving protection. For we are deeply convinced that the correct appreciation of the "mystery of Mary" leads to deep and perfect understanding of the mystery of Christ and his Church. We have contemplated Our Lady with joy, pondering her holiness, her generosity, her hope, her burning love, her whole-hearted dedication in faith to the saving work of her Son. For we believe the Father gave her to us as a "model of virtues for the whole community of the elect." May her pilgrimage of faith strengthen us in our individual Christian vocations. May her loving desire that her Son's words be heeded hasten Christian unity. May her motherly intercession make us worthy of the promises of Christ.

MARY'S PLACE IN AMERICAN CATHOLIC HISTORY

Devotion to the Mother of God is well-illustrated in American history, from early explorations through the colonial period and the founding of the Republic, soon to celebrate its bicentenary. Christopher Columbus's flagship was the *Santa Maria*. His successors planted the Christian cross with the Spanish flag across many territories that now fall within the United States. The names these pioneers gave to many cities in the South and West are an indication of their love of Mary. For example, they gave Los Angeles the full name St. Mary Queen of the Angels of the Portiuncola. When Menendez landed in Florida in 1565 and founded the city of St. Augustine, the oldest city in the United States, one of his first acts was to have the chaplain, Fr. Mendoza, offer Mass in honor of Our Lady's Nativity. Our Lady of La Leche is still venerated there. In New Mexico, the conquistadores paid tribute to the greater and fairer La Conquistadora, brought to Santa Fe in 1625.

The French missionaries came from the north, down the St. Lawrence, and our maps still bear traces of their devotion to our Lady. Père Marquette explored the Mississippi with Louis Joliet in 1673 and called it River of the Immaculate Conception. Before him, St. Isaac Jogues (d. 1646) and his companions had brought the Christian faith and devotion to Mary to the region around the Great Lakes. Our Lady of the Martyrs' Shrine at Auriesville commemorates their witness.

The England of penal times was an unlikely point of origin for an American colony where religious toleration would prevail and Catholics could publicly profess their faith, even their devotion to St. Mary. Yet George Calvert, a convert to Catholicism and the first Lord Baltimore, was given a charter to found the crown colony of Maryland, where religious freedom would be guaranteed. When he died in 1632, his sons carried the project through. Their two ships, *The Ark* and *The Dove*, landed in Maryland (named for the queen), March 1634. Their chaplain, Fr. Andrew White, SJ, recorded how the Catholics of the group consecrated the future colony to Our Lady of the Immaculate Conception. They called their first settlement and capital St. Mary's City, and they named the Chesapeake, St. Mary's Bay.

A son of Maryland, John Carroll, was the first bishop of the new United States. Consecrated bishop in 1790 on the feast of the Assumption, he placed his newly founded diocese of Baltimore under the patronage of Mary. In his first pastoral in 1792, he wrote: "Having chosen Her the special patroness of this Diocese, you are placed, of course, under Her powerful protection and it becomes your duty to be careful to deserve its continuance by a zealous imitation of Her virtues, and reliance on Her motherly superintendence." The Cathedral of Baltimore, which Bishop Carroll began, was dedicated at its completion in honor of the Assumption of Our Lady.

The worldwide movement that resulted in the definition of the Immaculate Conception by Pope Pius IX in 1854 had its influence on the American Church. The sixth provincial Council of Baltimore was held in 1846 under the presidency of Archbishop Samuel Eccleston, SS, of Baltimore, with twenty-three of the country's twenty-six bishops in attendance. Their first decision (May 13, 1846) was to request of the Holy See that Mary under the title of the Immaculate Conception be named patroness of the United States. This petition was granted by Pope Pius IX in the following year. In their pastoral of 1846, the bishops wrote: "We take this occasion, brethren, to communicate to you the determination, unanimously adopted by us, to place ourselves, and all entrusted to our charge throughout the United States under the special patronage of the holy Mother of God, whose Immaculate Conception is venerated by the piety of the faithful throughout the Catholic Church."

The example of devotion to Mary set by the pioneers led to a pattern among American Catholics. Cathedrals and churches and chapels too many to enumerate carry Mary's titles across the country. From St. Mary's Seminary, Baltimore, founded in 1791, to the present, the institutions of higher learning bearing Mary's name are manifold. Notre Dame and all its lovely variants have become titles for many institutions and for every sort of Catholic apostolic enterprise, e.g., Sodalities, Legion of Mary, and the Family Rosary, which has spread from America to all the world.

In 1913, Bishop Thomas J. Shahan, fourth rector of the Catholic University of America, suggested the building of a national Shrine of the Immaculate Conception. This, he hoped, would be "a large and beautiful church in honor of our Blessed Mother, erected by nationwide cooperation at the nation's capital . . . a great hymn in stone." Most of the crypt area and the foundations of the upper church were built by 1931. In 1954, work began on the upper church and was sufficiently well along to permit the solemn dedication on November 20, 1959. Since then, much more has been done and the shrine, open daily and the scene of many religious celebrations, is still being completed. Contributions of Catholics countrywide maintain the magnificent church, as their offerings paid for its building, in testimony to the place the Mother of God, Mary Immaculate, holds in the hearts and religious life of American Catholics. Along with the many Washington visitors of all faiths who visit the shrine, in touring the capital city, more and more groups are coming on pilgrimage, even from distant dioceses, and focusing on Mary's Shrine as a place of prayer and inspiration.

From this brief survey, it is evident that a loyal and loving devotion to our Lady has been, from the very beginning, an important part of American Catholicism. It is up to the American Catholics of today to cherish and to pass on to succeeding generations of Catholics this rich heritage of devotion to Mary, the Mother of God and Mother of the Church.

NOTES

With a few exceptions, scriptural quotations are from the *New American Bible* © 1970, Confraternity of Christian Doctrine, Washington, D.C. Scriptural references are given parenthetically, immediately after the text; the abbreviations are those of the *New American Bible*. Other quotations are followed by a superior number directing the reader to these references.

After the Sacred Scriptures, the most frequently quoted source is the Second Vatican Council of 1962-1965. The texts of conciliar pronouncements used by the editors of this letter are excerpts from *The Documents of Vatican II*, Walter J. Abbott, SJ, General Editor, copyright © 1966, by permission of New Century Publishers, Inc., Piscataway, New Jersey 08854. For reference purposes, the title of this source will be given as DVII. The conciliar document most frequently drawn upon is *The Dogmatic Constitution on the Church*, the Latin title of which is *Lumen Gentium*. For reference purposes this text is given as DCC, followed by the number of the paragraph from which the quotation comes and the page number of the Abbott edition. On the relatively few occasions on which reference is made to another conciliar document (e.g., *The Constitution on the Sacred Liturgy*), the title of the document is given in full.

Introduction:
1.   Pope Paul VI, Address of November 21, 1964, *The Pope Speaks* X (1965), 137-138.
2.   Ibid.
3.   DCC, no. 63, Abbott, 92.
4.   *The Pope Speaks* X (1965), 140.

Chapter One:
1.   DCC, no. 58, Abbott, 89.
2.   DCC, no. 55, Abbott, 87.
3.   DCC, no. 56, Abbott, 88.
4.   Ibid.
5.   DCC, no. 55, Abbott, 87.
6.   DCC, no. 53, Abbott, 86.
7.   DCC, no. 58, Abbott, 89.
8.   Pierre Benoit, OP, *The Passion and Resurrection of Jesus Christ* (New York: Herder and Herder, 1969), 141.
9.   Henry Wansbrough, "The Resurrection," *The Way* xii:2 (April 1972): 144.

Chapter Two:
10.   DCC, no. 63, Abbott, 92.
11.   DCC, no. 53, Abbott, 86.
12.   DCC, no. 63, Abbott, 92.
13.   St. Irenaeus, *Adversus haereses*, lib. v, ch. xix, no. l, in Migne, PG, vii, col. 1175.

14. DCC, no. 56, Abbott, 88.
15. Ibid.
16. St. Irenaeus, loc. cit.
17. St. Hippolytus, quoted in Gregory Dix, ed., *Treatise on the Apostolic Tradition* (New York: Macmillan, 1937), xxi, nos. 15-16.
18. Joseph Ratzinger, *Introduction to Christianity* (NY: Herder and Herder, 1970), 211.
19. St. Jerome, "Against Helvidius," in *Dogmatic and Polemical Works* (The Fathers of the Church Series, vol. 53), trans. and ed. John N. Hritzu (Washington, DC: The Catholic University of America Press, 1965), 19.
20. DCC, no. 46, Abbott, 77.
21. John Macquarrie, *Principles of Christian Theology* (New York: Scribner, 1966), 355.
22. DCC, no. 56. Here the translation is taken from *The Pope Speaks* X (1965), 396.
23. Pope Pius IX, Bull *Ineffabilis Deus*, December 8, 1854.
24. John Henry Newman, *Faith and Prejudice and Other Unpublished Essays*, ed. C. S. Dessain (New York: Longmans, 1956), 88.
25. DCC, no. 56, Abbott, 88.
26. DCC, no. 56, Abbott, 87.
27. "Immaculate Conception of BVM," in *Oxford Dictionary of the Christian Church*, ed. F. L. Cross (London: Oxford, 1957), 681.
28. DVII, *Constitution on the Sacred Liturgy*, no. 103, Abbott, 168.
29. Pope Pius XII, Apostolic Constitution *Munificentissimus*, November 1, 1950, AAS 42 (1950), 770.
30. "Assumption of BVM," in *Oxford Dictionary of the Christian Church*, 97.
31. DCC, no. 59, Abbott, 90.
32. DCC, no. 68, Abbott, 95.
33. Archbishop Philip Pocock, "Pastoral Letter," *The Ecumenist* ii (May-June 1964): 73.
34. This is the title of one of Newman's "Sermons to Mixed Congregations." Text in C. F. Harrold, ed., *Sermons and Discourses, 1830-1857* (New York: Longmans Green, 1949), 247.
35. St. Cyril of Alexandria, in Denzinger, *Enchiridion*, 250-251.

Chapter Three:
36. DCC, no. 62, Abbott, 92.
37. Pope Paul VI, *Mensi Maio*, English trans. in *The Pope Speaks* X, 3 (1965), 220.
38. DCC, no. 60, Abbott, 91.
39. Frederick Jelly, OP, "Mary and the Eucharistic Liturgy," *Our Lady's Digest* XXVII (May-June 1972): 21.
40. DVII, *Decree on the Ministry and Life of Priests*, no. 18, Abbott, 570.
41. DCC, no. 53, Abbott, 86.
42. Ibid.
43. St. Augustine, "*De Sancta Virginitate*," in *St. Augustine: Treatises on Marriage and Other Subjects* (The Fathers of the Church Series, vol. 27), English trans. John McQuade, SM, ed. Charles Wilcox and others (New York: 1955), 148-150, passim.

Chapter Four:
44. DCC, no. 64, Abbott, 93.
45. DCC, no. 61, Abbott, 91.
46. DCC, no. 65, Abbott, 93. See also DVII, *Decree on the Apostolate of the Laity*, no. 4, Abbott, 495.
47. DVII, *Constitution on the Sacred Liturgy*, no. 103, Abbott, 168.
48. DCC, no. 66, Abbott, 94.
49. Ibid.
50. Cardinal Leon Suenens, "Mary and the World of Today." *L'Osservatore Romano*, English edition (June 15, 1972).
51. Abbott, 78-85.
52. Herbert McCabe, OP, Editorial in *New Blackfriars* 52 (November 1971): 482.
53. DCC, no. 49, Abbott, 81.

54. DCC, no. 51, Abbott, 84.
55. Ibid.
56. DVII, *Constitution on the Sacred Liturgy*, no. 8, Abbott, 141.
57. Eucharistic Prayer I.
58. DCC, no. 68, Abbott, 95.
59. Ibid., Abbott, 96.
60. Abbott, 94-95.
61. DCC, no. 50, Abbott, 83.
62. Donald Attwater, ed., *A Dictionary of Mariology* (New York: Kenedy, 1956), 279.
63. DVII, *Constitution on the Sacred Liturgy*, no. 13, Abbott, 143.
64. DCC, no. 67, Abbott, 94-95.
65. Ibid.
66. Max Thurian, *Mary, Mother of the Lord, Figure of the Church* (London: Faith Press, 1963). Also published with title *Mary, Mother of All Christians* (New York: Herder and Herder, 1964).
67. DCC, no. 67, Abbott, 95.
68. Karl Barth, *Church Dogmatics*, vol. 1, part 2 (London: Allenson, 1936), 143.
69. DVII, *Decree on Ecumenism*, no. 11, Abbott, 354.
70. Op. cit., no. 20, Abbott, 362.
71. Donal Flanagan, "Mary in the Ecumenical Discussion," *Irish Theological Quarterly*, vol. XL (July 1973): 227-249.
72. Yves Congar, OP, *Christ, Mary and the Church* (Westminster, MD: 1957).
73. Flanagan, op. cit.
74. DCC no. 52, Abbott, 85.

Chapter Five:
75. Macquarrie, op. cit., 122.
76. Pope Paul VI, Address of February 2, 1965, *The Pope Speaks* X (1965), 103.
77. DCC, no. 55, Abbott, 87.
78. Macquarrie, op. cit., 122.
79. DCC, no. 65, Abbott, 93.
80. Pope Paul VI, "Mary, Mother of the Church," May 13, 1967, *The Pope Speaks* XII (1967), 285.
81. Pope Paul VI, Address of November 21, 1964, *The Pope Speaks* X (1965), 139.
82. DVII, *Decree on the Ministry and Life of Priests*, no. 18, Abbott, 570.
83. DCC, no. 10, Abbott, 27.
84. DVII, *Decree on the Ministry and Life of Priests*, no. 2, Abbott, 535.
85. DCC, no. 53, Abbott, 86.
86. Pastoral letter *Human Life in Our Day*, in *Pastoral Letters of the American Hierarchy, 1792-1970*, ed. Hugh J. Nolan (Huntington, IN: Our Sunday Visitor Press, 1972), 679-705.

MARIALIS CULTUS:
FOR THE RIGHT ORDERING AND DEVELOPMENT OF DEVOTION TO THE BLESSED VIRGIN MARY

An Apostolic Exhortation of His Holiness Pope Paul VI

FEBRUARY 2, 1974

INTRODUCTION: OCCASION AND PURPOSE

Venerable Brothers:
Health and the Apostolic Blessing:

From the moment when we were called to the See of Peter, we have constantly striven to enhance devotion to the Blessed Virgin Mary, not only with the intention of interpreting the sentiments of the Church and our own personal inclination but also because, as is well known, this devotion forms a very noble part of the whole sphere of that sacred worship in which there intermingle the highest expressions of wisdom and of religion[1] and which is therefore the primary task of the People of God.

Precisely with a view to this task, we have always favored and encouraged the great work of liturgical reform promoted by the Second Vatican Ecumenical Council; and it has certainly come about not without a particular design of divine Providence that the first conciliar document which together with the venerable Fathers we approved and signed in *Spiritu Sancto* was the Constitution *Sacrosanctum Concilium*. The purpose of this document was precisely to restore and enhance the liturgy and to make more fruitful the participation of the faithful in the sacred mysteries.[2] From that time onwards, many acts of our Pontificate have been directed towards the improvement of divine worship, as is demonstrated by the fact that we have promulgated in these recent years numerous books of the Roman Rite, restored according to the principles and norms of the same Council. For this we profoundly thank the Lord, the giver of all good things, and we are grateful to the episcopal conferences and individual bishops who in various ways have collaborated with us in the preparation of these books.

We contemplate with joy and gratitude the work so far accomplished and the first positive results of the liturgical renewal, destined as they are to increase as this renewal comes to be understood in its basic purposes and correctly applied. At the same time we do not cease with vigilant solicitude to concern ourself with whatever can give orderly fulfillment to the renewal of the worship with which the Church in spirit and truth (cf. Jn 4:24) adores the Father and the Son and the Holy Spirit, "venerates with special love Mary the most holy Mother of God"[3] and honors with religious devotion the memory of the martyrs and the other saints.

The development, desired by us, of devotion to the Blessed Virgin Mary is an indication of the Church's genuine piety. This devotion fits—as we have indicated above—into the only worship that is rightly called "Christian," because it takes its origin and effectiveness from Christ, finds its complete expression in Christ, and leads through Christ in the Spirit to the Father. In the sphere of worship this devotion necessarily reflects God's redemptive plan, in which a special form of veneration is appropriate to the singular place which Mary occupies in that plan.[4] Indeed every authentic development of Christian worship is necessarily followed by a fitting increase of veneration for the Mother of the Lord. Moreover, the history of piety shows how "the various forms of devotion towards the Mother of God that the Church has approved within the limits of wholesome and orthodox doctrine"[5] have developed in harmonious subordination to the worship of Christ, and have gravitated towards this worship as to their natural and necessary point of reference. The same is happening in our own time. The Church's reflection today on the mystery of Christ and on her own nature has led her to find at the root of the former and as a culmination of the latter the same figure of a Woman: the Virgin Mary, the Mother of Christ and the Mother of the Church. And the increased knowledge of Mary's mission has become joyful veneration of her and adoring respect for the wise plan of God, who has placed within his Family (the Church), as in every home, the figure of a Woman, who in a hidden manner and in a spirit of service watches over that Family "and carefully looks after it until the glorious day of the Lord."[6]

In our time, the changes that have occurred in social behavior, people's sensibilities, manners of expression in art and letters and in the forms of social communication have also influenced the manifestations of religious sentiment. Certain practices of piety that not long ago seemed suitable for expressing the religious sentiment of individuals and of Christian communities seem today inadequate or unsuitable because they are linked with social and cultural patterns of the past. On the other hand, in many places people are seeking new ways of expressing the unchangeable relationship of creatures with their Creator, of children with their Father. In some people this may cause temporary confusion. But anyone who with trust in God reflects upon these phenomena discovers that many tendencies of modern piety (for example, the interiorization of religious sentiment) are meant to play their part in the development of Christian piety in general and devotion to the Blessed Virgin in particular. Thus our own time, faithfully attentive to tradition and to the progress of theology and the sciences, will make its contribution of praise to her whom, according to her own prophetical words, all generations will call blessed (cf. Lk 1:48).

We therefore judge it in keeping with our apostolic service, venerable Brothers, to deal, in a sort of dialogue, with a number of themes connected with the place that the Blessed Virgin occupies in the Church's worship. These themes have already been partly touched upon by the Second Vatican Council[7] and also by ourself,[8] but it is useful to return to them in order to remove doubts and, especially, to help the development of that devotion to the Blessed Virgin which in the Church is motivated by the Word of God and practiced in the Spirit of Christ.

We therefore wish to dwell upon a number of questions concerning the relationship between the sacred liturgy and devotion to the Blessed Virgin (I), to offer considerations and directives suitable for favoring the development of that devotion (II) and finally to put forward a number of reflections intended to encourage the restoration, in a dynamic and more informed manner, of the recitation of the Rosary, the practice of which was so strongly recommended by our predecessors and is so widely diffused among the Christian people (III).

Part One
DEVOTION TO THE BLESSED VIRGIN MARY IN THE LITURGY

1.   As we prepare to discuss the place which the Blessed Virgin Mary occupies in Christian worship, we must first turn our attention to the sacred liturgy. In addition to its rich doctrinal content, the liturgy has an incomparable pastoral effectiveness and a recognized exemplary value for the other forms of worship. We would have liked to take into consideration the various liturgies of the East and the West, but

for the purpose of this document we shall dwell almost exclusively on the books of the Roman Rite. In fact, in accordance with the practical norms issued by the Second Vatican Council,[9] it is this Rite alone which has been the object of profound renewal. This is true also in regard to expressions of veneration for Mary. This Rite therefore deserves to be carefully considered and evaluated.

SECTION 1. THE BLESSED VIRGIN IN THE REVISED ROMAN LITURGY

2.   The reform of the Roman liturgy presupposed a careful restoration of its *General Calendar*. This Calendar is arranged in such a way as to give fitting prominence to the celebration on appropriate days of the work of salvation. It distributes throughout the year the whole mystery of Christ, from the Incarnation to the expectation of his return in glory,[10] and thus makes it possible in a more organic and closely-knit fashion to include the commemoration of Christ's Mother in the annual cycle of the mysteries of her Son.

3.   For example, during Advent there are many liturgical references to Mary besides the Solemnity of December 8, which is a joint celebration of the Immaculate Conception of Mary, of the basic preparation (cf. Is 11:1, 10) for the coming of the Savior and of the happy beginning of the Church without spot or wrinkle.[11] Such liturgical references are found especially on the days from December 17 to 24, and more particularly on the Sunday before Christmas, which recalls the ancient prophecies concerning the Virgin Mother and the Messiah[12] and includes readings from the Gospel concerning the imminent birth of Christ and His precursor.[13]

4.   In this way the faithful, living in the liturgy the spirit of Advent, by thinking about the inexpressible love with which the Virgin Mother awaited her Son,[14] are invited to take her as a model and to prepare themselves to meet the Savior who is to come. They must be "vigilant in prayer and joyful in . . . praise."[15] We would also remark that the Advent liturgy, by linking the awaiting of the Messiah and the awaiting of the glorious return of Christ with the admirable commemoration of His Mother, presents a happy balance in worship. This balance can be taken as a norm for preventing any tendency (as has happened at times in certain forms of popular piety) to separate devotion to the Blessed Virgin from its necessary point of reference—Christ. It also ensures that this season, as liturgy experts have noted, should be considered as a time particularly suited to devotion to the Mother of the Lord. This is an orientation that we confirm and which we hope to see accepted and followed everywhere.

5.   The Christmas season is a prolonged commemoration of the divine, virginal and salvific motherhood of her whose "inviolate virginity brought the Savior into the world."[16] In fact, on the Solemnity of the Birth of Christ the Church both adores the Savior and venerates His glorious Mother. On the Epiphany, when she celebrates the universal call to salvation, the Church contemplates the Blessed Virgin, the true Seat of Wisdom and true Mother of the King, who presents to the Wise Men, for their adoration, the Redeemer of all peoples (cf. Mt 2:11). On the Feast of the Holy Family of Jesus, Mary and Joseph (the Sunday within the octave of Christmas) the Church meditates with profound reverence upon the holy life led in the house at Nazareth by Jesus, the Son of God and Son of Man, Mary His Mother, and Joseph the just man (cf. Mt 1:19).

In the revised ordering of the Christmas period it seems to us that the attention of all should be directed towards the restored Solemnity of Mary the holy Mother of God. This celebration, placed on January 1 in conformity with the ancient indication of the liturgy of the City of Rome, is meant to commemorate the part played by Mary in this mystery of salvation. It is meant also to exalt the singular dignity which this mystery brings to the "holy Mother . . . through whom we were found worthy to receive the Author of life."[17] It is likewise a fitting occasion for renewing adoration of the newborn Prince of Peace, for listening once more to the glad tidings of the angels (cf. Lk 2:14), and for imploring from God, through the Queen of Peace, the supreme gift of peace. It is for this reason that, in the happy concurrence of the Octave of Christmas and the first day of the year, we have instituted the World Day of Peace, an occasion that is gaining increasing support and already bringing forth fruits of peace in the hearts of many.

6.   To the two solemnities already mentioned (the Immaculate Conception and the Divine Motherhood) should be added the ancient and venerable celebrations of March 25 and August 15.

For the Solemnity of the Incarnation of the Word, in the Roman Calendar the ancient title—the Annunciation of the Lord—has been deliberately restored, but the feast was and is a joint one of Christ and of the Blessed Virgin: of the Word, who becomes "Son of Mary" (Mk 6:3), and of the Virgin, who becomes Mother of God. With regard to Christ, the East and the West, in the inexhaustible riches of their liturgies, celebrate this solemnity as the commemoration of the salvific "fiat" of the Incarnate Word, who, entering the world, said: "God, here I am! I am coming to obey Your will" (cf. Heb 10:7; Ps 39:8-9). They commemorate it as the beginning of the redemption and of the indissoluble and wedded union of the divine nature with human nature in the one Person of the Word. With regard to Mary, these liturgies celebrate it as a feast of the new Eve, the obedient and faithful virgin, who with her generous "fiat" (cf. Lk 1:38) became through the working of the Spirit the Mother of God, but also the true Mother of the living, and, by receiving into her womb the one Mediator (cf. 1 Tm 2:5), became the true Ark of the Covenant and true Temple of God. These liturgies celebrate it as a culminating moment in the salvific dialogue between God and man, and as a commemoration of the Blessed Virgin's free consent and cooperation in the plan of redemption. The solemnity of August 15 celebrates the glorious Assumption of Mary into heaven. It is a feast of her destiny of fullness and blessedness, of the glorification of her immaculate soul and of her virginal body, of her perfect configuration to the Risen Christ, a feast that sets before the eyes of the Church and of all mankind the image and the consoling proof of the fulfillment of their final hope, namely, that this full glorification is the destiny of all those whom Christ has made His brothers, having "flesh and blood in common with them" (Heb 2:14; cf. Gal 4:4). The Solemnity of the Assumption is prolonged in the celebration of the Queenship of the Blessed Virgin Mary, which occurs seven days later. On this occasion we contemplate her who, seated beside the King of ages, shines forth as Queen and intercedes as Mother.[18] These four solemnities, therefore, mark with the highest liturgical rank the main dogmatic truths concerning the handmaid of the Lord.

7.   After the solemnities just mentioned, particular consideration must be given to those celebrations that commemorate salvific events in which the Blessed Virgin was closely associated with her Son. Such are the feasts of the Nativity of Our Lady (September 8), "the hope of the entire world and the dawn of salvation"[19]; and the Visitation (May 31), in which the liturgy recalls the "Blessed Virgin Mary carrying her Son within her,"[20] and visiting Elizabeth to offer charitable assistance and to proclaim the mercy of God the Savior.[21] Then there is the commemoration of Our Lady of Sorrows (September 15), a fitting occasion for reliving a decisive moment in the history of salvation and for venerating, together with the Son "lifted up on the cross, His suffering Mother."[22]

The feast of February 2, which has been given back its ancient name, the Presentation of the Lord, should also be considered as a joint commemoration of the Son and of the Mother, if we are fully to appreciate its rich content. It is the celebration of a mystery of salvation accomplished by Christ, a mystery with which the Blessed Virgin was intimately associated as the Mother of the Suffering Servant of Yahweh, as the one who performs a mission belonging to ancient Israel, and as the model for the new People of God, which is ever being tested in its faith and hope by suffering and persecution (cf. Lk 2:21-35).

8.   The restored Roman Calendar gives particular prominence to the celebrations listed above, but it also includes other kinds of commemorations connected
with local devotions and which have acquired a wider popularity and interest (e.g.,
February 11, Our Lady of Lourdes; August 5, the Dedication of the Basilica of
St. Mary Major). Then there are others, originally celebrated by particular religious
families but which today, by reason of the popularity they have gained, can truly be
considered ecclesial (e.g., July 16, Our Lady of Mount Carmel; October 7, Our
Lady of the Rosary). There are still others which, apart from their apocryphal content, present lofty and exemplary values and carry on venerable traditions having
their origin especially in the East (e.g., the Immaculate Heart of the Blessed Virgin,
celebrated on the Saturday following the second Sunday after Pentecost).

9.   Nor must one forget that the General Roman Calendar does not include all
celebrations in honor of the Blessed Virgin. Rather, it is for individual Calendars to
include, with fidelity to liturgical norms but with sincere endorsement, the Marian
feasts proper to the different local Churches. Lastly, it should be noted that frequent commemorations of the Blessed Virgin are possible through the use of the
Saturday Masses of our Lady. This is an ancient and simple commemoration and
one that is made very adaptable and varied by the flexibility of the modern
Calendar and the number of formulas provided by the Missal.

10.   In this Apostolic Exhortation we do not intend to examine the whole content
of the new *Roman Missal*. But by reason of the work of evaluation that we have
undertaken to carry out in regard to the revised books of the Roman Rite,[23] we
would like to mention some of the aspects and themes of the Missal. In the first
place, we are pleased to note how the Eucharistic Prayers of the Missal, in admirable
harmony with the Eastern liturgies,[24] contain a significant commemoration of the
Blessed Virgin. For example, the ancient Roman Canon, which commemorates the
Mother of the Lord in terms full of doctrine and devotional inspiration: "In union
with the whole Church we honor Mary, the ever-virgin Mother of Jesus Christ our
Lord and God." In a similar way the recent Eucharistic Prayer III expresses with
intense supplication the desire of those praying to share with the Mother the inheritance of sons: "May he make us an everlasting gift to you [the Father] and enable
us to share in the inheritance of your saints, with Mary, the Virgin Mother of God."
This daily commemoration, by reason of its place at the heart of the divine Sacrifice,
should be considered a particularly expressive form of the veneration that the
Church pays to the "Blessed of the Most High" (cf. Lk 1:28).

11.   As we examine the texts of the revised Missal we see how the great Marian themes of the Roman prayerbook have been accepted in perfect doctrinal continuity with the past. Thus, for example, we have the themes of Mary's Immaculate Conception and fullness of grace, the divine motherhood, the unblemished and fruitful virginity, the Temple of the Holy Spirit, Mary's cooperation in the work of her Son, her exemplary sanctity, merciful intercession, Assumption into heaven, maternal Queenship and many other themes. We also see how other themes, in a certain sense new ones, have been introduced in equally perfect harmony with the theological developments of the present day. Thus, for example, we have the theme of Mary and the Church, which has been inserted into the texts of the Missal in a variety of aspects, a variety that matches the many and varied relations that exist between the Mother of Christ and the Church. For example, in the celebration of the Immaculate Conception which texts recognize the beginning of the Church, the spotless Bride of Christ.[25] In the Assumption they recognize the beginning that has already been made and the image of what, for the whole Church, must still come to pass.[26] In the mystery of Mary's motherhood they confess that she is the Mother of the Head and of the members—the holy Mother of God and therefore the provident Mother of the Church.[27]

When the liturgy turns its gaze either to the primitive Church or to the Church of our own days it always finds Mary. In the primitive Church she is seen praying with the apostles;[28] in our own day she is actively present, and the Church desires to live the mystery of Christ with her: "Grant that your Church which with Mary shared Christ's passion may be worthy to share also in his resurrection."[29] She is also seen represented as a voice of praise in unison with which the Church wishes to give glory to God: ". . . with her [Mary] may we always praise you."[30] And since the liturgy is worship that requires a way of living consistent with it, it asks that devotion to the Blessed Virgin should become a concrete and deeply-felt love for the Church, as is wonderfully expressed in the prayer after Communion in the Mass of September 15: ". . . that as we recall the sufferings shared by the Blessed Virgin Mary, we may with the Church fulfill in ourselves what is lacking in the sufferings of Christ."

12.   The *Lectionary* is one of the books of the Roman Rite that has greatly benefited from the post-conciliar reform, by reason both of its added texts and of the intrinsic value of these texts, which contain the ever-living and efficacious word of God (cf. Heb 4:12). This rich collection of biblical texts has made it possible to arrange the whole history of salvation in an orderly three-year cycle and to set forth more completely the mystery of Christ. The logical consequence has been that the

Lectionary contains a larger number of Old and New Testament readings concerning the Blessed Virgin. This numerical increase has not however been based on random choice: only those readings have been accepted which in different ways and degrees can be considered Marian, either from the evidence of their content or from the results of careful exegesis, supported by the teachings of the magisterium or by solid Tradition. It is also right to observe that these readings occur not only on feasts of the Blessed Virgin but are read on many other occasions, for example on certain Sundays during the liturgical year,[31] in the celebration of rites that deeply concern the Christian's sacramental life and the choices confronting him,[32] as also in the joyful or sad experiences of his life on earth.[33]

13.   The Liturgy of the Hours, the revised book of the Office, also contains outstanding examples of devotion to the Mother of the Lord. These are to be found in the hymns—which include several masterpieces of universal literature, such as Dante's sublime prayer to the Blessed Virgin[34]—and in the antiphons that complete the daily Office. To these lyrical invocations there has been added the well-known prayer *Sub tuum praesidium*, venerable for its antiquity and admirable for its content. Other examples occur in the prayers of intercession at Lauds and Vespers, prayers which frequently express trusting recourse to the Mother of mercy. Finally there are selections from the vast treasury of writings on our Lady composed by authors of the first Christian centuries, of the Middle Ages and of modern times.

14.   The commemoration of the Blessed Virgin occurs often in the Missal, the *Lectionary* and the Liturgy of the Hours—the hinges of the liturgical prayer of the Roman Rite. In the other revised liturgical books also expressions of love and suppliant veneration addressed to the *Theotokos* are not lacking. Thus the Church invokes her, the Mother of grace, before immersing candidates in the saving waters of baptism;[35] the Church invokes her intercession for mothers who, full of gratitude for the gift of motherhood, come to church to express their joy;[36] the Church holds her up as a model to those who follow Christ by embracing the religious life[37] or who receive the Consecration of Virgins.[38] For these people the Church asks Mary's motherly assistance.[39] The Church prays fervently to Mary on behalf of her children who have come to the hour of their death.[40] The Church asks Mary's intercession for those who have closed their eyes to the light of this world and appeared before Christ, the eternal Light;[41] and the Church, through Mary's prayers, invokes comfort upon those who in sorrow mourn with faith the departure of their loved ones.[42]

15.   The examination of the revised liturgical books leads us to the comforting observation that the post-conciliar renewal has, as was previously desired by the

liturgical movement, properly considered the Blessed Virgin in the mystery of Christ, and, in harmony with tradition, has recognized the singular place that belongs to her in Christian worship as the holy Mother of God and the worthy Associate of the Redeemer.

It could not have been otherwise. If one studies the history of Christian worship, in fact, one notes that both in the East and in the West the highest and purest expressions of devotion to the Blessed Virgin have sprung from the liturgy or have been incorporated into it.

We wish to emphasize the fact that the veneration which the universal Church today accords to blessed Mary is a derivation from and an extension and unceasing increase of the devotion that the Church of every age has paid to her, with careful attention to truth and with an ever watchful nobility of expression. From perennial Tradition kept alive by reason of the uninterrupted presence of the Spirit and continual attention to the Word, the Church of our time draws motives, arguments and incentives for the veneration that she pays to the Blessed Virgin. And the liturgy, which receives approval and strength from the magisterium, is a most lofty expression and an evident proof of this living Tradition.

SECTION II. THE BLESSED VIRGIN AS A MODEL OF THE CHURCH IN DIVINE WORSHIP

16.   In accordance with some of the guidelines of the Council's teaching on Mary and the Church, we now wish to examine more closely a particular aspect of the relationship between Mary and the liturgy—namely, Mary as a model of the spiritual attitude with which the Church celebrates and lives the divine mysteries. That the Blessed Virgin is an exemplar in this field derives from the fact that she is recognized as a most excellent exemplar of the Church in the order of faith, charity and perfect union with Christ,[43] that is, of that interior disposition with which the Church, the beloved spouse, closely associated with her Lord, invokes Christ and through Him worships the eternal Father.[44]

17.   Mary is the attentive Virgin, who receives the word of God with faith, that faith which in her case was the gateway and path to divine motherhood, for, as St. Augustine realized, "Blessed Mary by believing conceived Him [Jesus] whom believing she brought forth."[45] In fact, when she received from the angel the answer to her doubt (cf. Lk 1:34-37), "full of faith, and conceiving Christ in her mind

before conceiving Him in her womb, she said, 'I am the handmaid of the Lord, let what you have said be done to me' (Lk 1:38)."[46] It was faith that was for her the cause of blessedness and certainty in the fulfillment of the promise: "Blessed is she who believed that the promise made her by the Lord would be fulfilled" (Lk 1:45). Similarly, it was faith with which she, who played a part in the Incarnation and was a unique witness to it, thinking back on the events of the infancy of Christ, meditated upon these events in her heart (cf. Lk 2:19, 51). The Church also acts in this way, especially in the liturgy, when with faith she listens, accepts, proclaims and venerates the word of God, distributes it to the faithful as the bread of life[47] and in the light of that word examines the signs of the times and interprets and lives the events of history.

18.   Mary is also the Virgin in prayer. She appears as such in the visit to the mother of the precursor, when she pours out her soul in expressions glorifying God, and expressions of humility, faith and hope. This prayer is the Magnificat (cf. Lk 1:46-55), Mary's prayer par excellence, the song of the messianic times in which there mingles the joy of the ancient and the new Israel. As St. Irenaeus seems to suggest, it is in Mary's canticle that there was heard once more the rejoicing of Abraham who foresaw the Messiah (cf. Jn 8:56)[48] and there rang out in prophetic anticipation the voice of the Church: "In her exultation Mary prophetically declared in the name of the Church: 'My soul proclaims the glory of the Lord. . . .'"[49] And in fact Mary's hymn has spread far and wide and has become the prayer of the whole Church in all ages.

At Cana, Mary appears once more as the Virgin in prayer: when she tactfully told her Son of a temporal need, she also obtained an effect of grace, namely, that Jesus, in working the first of His "signs," confirmed His disciples' faith in Him (cf. Jn 2:1-12).

Likewise, the last description of Mary's life presents her as praying. The apostles "joined in continuous prayer, together with several women, including Mary the mother of Jesus, and with his brothers" (Acts 1:14). We have here the prayerful presence of Mary in the early Church and in the Church throughout all ages, for, having been assumed into heaven, she has not abandoned her mission of intercession and salvation.[50] The title Virgin in prayer also fits the Church, which day by day presents to the Father the needs of her children, "praises the Lord unceasingly and intercedes for the salvation of the world."[51]

19.   Mary is also the Virgin-Mother—she who "believing and obeying . . . brought forth on earth the Father's Son. This she did, not knowing man but overshadowed

by the Holy Spirit."[52] This was a miraculous motherhood, set up by God as the type and exemplar of the fruitfulness of the Virgin-Church, which "becomes herself a mother. . . . For by her preaching and by baptism she brings forth to a new and immortal life children who are conceived by the power of the Holy Spirit and born of God."[53] The ancient Fathers rightly taught that the Church prolongs in the sacrament of Baptism the virginal motherhood of Mary. Among such references we like to recall that of our illustrious predecessor, St. Leo the Great, who in a Christmas homily says: "The origin which [Christ] took in the womb of the Virgin He has given to the baptismal font: He has given to water what He had given to His Mother—the power of the Most High and the overshadowing of the Holy Spirit (cf. Lk 1:35), which was responsible for Mary's bringing forth the Savior, has the same effect, so that water may regenerate the believer."[54] If we wished to go to liturgical sources, we could quote the beautiful *Illatio* of the Mozarabic liturgy: "The former [Mary] carried Life in her womb; the latter [the Church] bears Life in the waters of baptism. In Mary's members Christ was formed; in the waters of the Church Christ is put on."[55]

20.   Mary is, finally, the Virgin presenting offerings. In the episode of the Presentation of Jesus in the Temple (cf. Lk 2:22-35), the Church, guided by the Spirit, has detected, over and above the fulfillment of the laws regarding the offering of the firstborn (cf. Ex 13:11-16) and the purification of the mother (cf. Lv 12:6-8), a mystery of salvation related to the history of salvation. That is, she has noted the continuity of the fundamental offering that the Incarnate Word made to the Father when He entered the world (cf. Heb 15:5-7). The Church has seen the universal nature of salvation proclaimed, for Simeon, greeting in the Child the light to enlighten the peoples and the glory of the people Israel (cf. Lk 2:32), recognized in Him the Messiah, the Savior of all. The Church has understood the prophetic reference to the Passion of Christ: the fact that Simeon's words, which linked in one prophecy the Son as "the sign of contradiction" (Lk 2:34) and the Mother, whose soul would be pierced by a sword (cf. Lk 2:35), came true on Calvary. A mystery of salvation, therefore, that in its various aspects orients the episode of the Presentation in the Temple to the salvific event of the cross. But the Church herself, in particular from the Middle Ages onwards, has detected in the heart of the Virgin taking her Son to Jerusalem to present Him to the Lord (cf. Lk 2:22) a desire to make an offering, a desire that exceeds the ordinary meaning of the rite. A witness to this intuition is found in the loving prayer of St. Bernard: "Offer your Son, holy Virgin, and present to the Lord the blessed fruit of your womb. Offer for the reconciliation of us all the holy Victim which is pleasing to God."[56]

This union of the Mother and the Son in the work of redemption[57] reaches its climax on Calvary, where Christ "offered himself as the perfect sacrifice to God" (Heb 9:14) and where Mary stood by the cross (cf. Jn 19:25), "suffering grievously with her only-begotten Son. There she united herself with a maternal heart to His sacrifice, and lovingly consented to the immolation of this victim which she herself had brought forth"[58] and also was offering to the eternal Father.[59] To perpetuate down the centuries the Sacrifice of the Cross, the divine Savior instituted the Eucharistic Sacrifice, the memorial of His death and resurrection, and entrusted it to His spouse the Church,[60] which, especially on Sundays, calls the faithful together to celebrate the Passover of the Lord until He comes again.[61] This the Church does in union with the saints in heaven and in particular with the Blessed Virgin,[62] whose burning charity and unshakeable faith she imitates.

21. Mary is not only an example for the whole Church in the exercise of divine worship but is also, clearly, a teacher of the spiritual life for individual Christians. The faithful at a very early date began to look to Mary and to imitate her in making their lives an act of worship of God and making their worship a commitment of their lives. As early as the fourth century, St. Ambrose, speaking to the people, expressed the hope that each of them would have the spirit of Mary in order to glorify God: "May the heart of Mary be in each Christian to proclaim the greatness of the Lord; may her spirit be in everyone to exult in God."[63] But Mary is above all the example of that worship that consists in making one's life an offering to God. This is an ancient and ever new doctrine that each individual can hear again by heeding the Church's teaching, but also by heeding the very voice of the Virgin as she, anticipating in herself the wonderful petition of the Lord's Prayer—"Your will be done" (Mt 6:10)—replied to God's messenger: "I am the handmaid of the Lord. Let what you have said be done to me" (Lk 1:38). And Mary's "yes" is for all Christians a lesson and example of obedience to the will of the Father, which is the way and means of one's own sanctification.

22.   It is also important to note how the Church expresses in various effective attitudes of devotion the many relationships that bind her to Mary: in profound veneration, when she reflects on the singular dignity of the Virgin who, through the action of the Holy Spirit, has become Mother of the Incarnate Word, in burning love, when she considers the spiritual motherhood of Mary towards all members of the Mystical Body; in trusting invocation, when she experiences the intercession of her advocate and helper;[64] in loving service, when she sees in the humble handmaid of the Lord the queen of mercy and the mother of grace; in zealous imitation, when she contemplates the holiness and virtues of her who is "full of grace"

(Lk 1:28); in profound wonder, when she sees in her, "as in a faultless model, that which she herself wholly desires and hopes to be";[65] in attentive study, when she recognizes in the associate of the Redeemer, who already shares fully in the fruits of the Paschal Mystery, the prophetic fulfillment of her own future, until the day on which, when she has been purified of every spot and wrinkle (cf. Eph 5:27), she will become like a bride arrayed for the bridegroom, Jesus Christ (cf. Rev 21:2).

23.   Therefore, venerable Brothers, as we consider the piety that the liturgical Tradition of the universal Church and the renewed Roman Rite expresses towards the holy Mother of God, and as we remember that the liturgy through its pre-eminent value as worship constitutes the golden norm for Christian piety, and finally as we observe how the Church when she celebrates the sacred mysteries assumes an attitude of faith and love similar to that of the Virgin, we realize the rightness of the exhortation that the Second Vatican Council addresses to all the children of the Church, namely "that the cult, especially the liturgical cult, of the Blessed Virgin be generously fostered."[66] This is an exhortation that we would like to see accepted everywhere without reservation and put into zealous practice.

Part Two
THE RENEWAL OF DEVOTION TO MARY

24.   The Second Vatican Council also exhorts us to promote other forms of piety side by side with liturgical worship, especially those recommended by the magisterium.[67] However, as is well known, the piety of the faithful and their veneration of the Mother of God has taken on many forms according to circumstances of time and place the different sensibilities of peoples and their different cultural traditions. Hence it is that the forms in which this devotion is expressed, being subject to the ravages of time, show the need for a renewal that will permit them to substitute elements that are transient, to emphasize the elements that are ever new and to incorporate the doctrinal data obtained from theological reflection and the proposals of the Church's magisterium. This shows the need for episcopal conferences, local churches, religious families and communities of the faithful to promote a genuine creative activity and at the same time to proceed to a careful revision of expressions and exercises of piety directed towards the Blessed Virgin. We would like this revision to be respectful of wholesome tradition and open to the legitimate requests of the people of our time. It seems fitting therefore, venerable Brothers, to put forward some principles for action in this field.

SECTION I. TRINITARIAN, CHRISTOLOGICAL, AND ECCLESIAL ASPECTS OF DEVOTION TO THE BLESSED VIRGIN

25.   In the first place it is supremely fitting that exercises of piety directed towards the Virgin Mary should clearly express the Trinitarian and Christological note that is intrinsic and essential to them. Christian worship in fact is of itself worship offered to the Father and to the Son and to the Holy Spirit, or, as the liturgy puts it, to the Father through Christ in the Spirit. From this point of view worship is rightly extended, though in a substantially different way, first and foremost and in a special manner, to the Mother of the Lord and then to the saints, in whom the Church proclaims the Paschal Mystery, for they have suffered with Christ and have been glorified with Him.[68] In the Virgin Mary everything is relative to Christ and dependent upon Him. It was with a view to Christ that God the Father from all eternity chose her to be the all-holy Mother and adorned her with gifts of the Spirit granted to no one else. Certainly genuine Christian piety has never failed to high-light the indissoluble link and essential relationship of the Virgin to the divine Savior.[69] Yet it seems to us particularly in conformity with the spiritual orientation of our time, which is dominated and absorbed by the "question of Christ,"[70] that in the expressions of devotion to the Virgin the Christological aspect should have par-ticular prominence. It likewise seems to us fitting that these expressions of devotion should reflect God's plan, which laid down "with one single decree the origin of Mary and the Incarnation of the divine Wisdom."[71] This will without doubt con-tribute to making piety towards the Mother of Jesus more solid, and to making it an effective instrument for attaining to full "knowledge of the Son of God, until we become the perfect man, fully mature with the fullness of Christ himself" (Eph 4:13). It will also contribute to increasing the worship due to Christ Himself, since, accord-ing to the perennial mind of the Church authoritatively repeated in our own day,[72] "what is given to the handmaid is referred to the Lord; thus what is given to the Mother redounds to the Son; . . . and thus what is given as humble tribute to the Queen becomes honor rendered to the King."[73]

26.   It seems to us useful to add to this mention of the Christological orientation of devotion to the Blessed Virgin a reminder of the fittingness of giving prominence in this devotion to one of the essential facts of the Faith: the Person and work of the Holy Spirit. Theological reflection and the liturgy have in fact noted how the sanctifying intervention of the Spirit in the Virgin of Nazareth was a culminating moment of the Spirit's action in the history of salvation. Thus, for example, some Fathers and writers of the Church attributed to the work of the Spirit the original holiness of Mary, who was as it were "fashioned by the Holy Spirit into a kind of

new substance and new creature."[74] Reflecting on the Gospel texts—"The Holy Spirit will come upon you and the power of the Most High will cover you with his shadow" (Lk 1:35) and "[Mary] was found to be with child through the Holy Spirit. . . . She has conceived what is in her by the Holy Spirit" (Mt 1:18, 20)—they saw in the Spirit's intervention an action that consecrated and made fruitful Mary's virginity[75] and transformed her into the "Abode of the King" or "Bridal Chamber of the Word,"[76] the "Temple" or "Tabernacle of the Lord,"[77] the "Ark of the Covenant" or "the Ark of Holiness,"[78] titles rich in biblical echoes. Examining more deeply still the mystery of the Incarnation, they saw in the mysterious relationship between the Spirit and Mary an aspect redolent of marriage, poetically portrayed by Prudentius: "The unwed Virgin espoused the Spirit,"[79] and they called her the "Temple of the Holy Spirit,"[80] an expression that emphasizes the sacred character of the Virgin, now the permanent dwelling of the Spirit of God. Delving deeply into the doctrine of the Paraclete, they saw that from Him as from a spring there flowed forth the fullness of grace (cf. Lk 1:28) and the abundance of gifts that adorned her. Thus they attributed to the Spirit the faith, hope and charity that animated the Virgin's heart, the strength that sustained her acceptance of the will of God, and the vigor that upheld her in her suffering at the foot of the cross.[81] In Mary's prophetic canticle (cf. Lk 1:46-55) they saw a special working of the Spirit who had spoken through the mouths of the prophets.[82] Considering, finally, the presence of the Mother of Jesus in the Upper Room, where the Spirit came down upon the infant Church (cf. Acts 1:12-14; 2:1-4), they enriched with new developments the ancient theme of Mary and the Church.[83] Above all they had recourse to the Virgin's intercession in order to obtain from the Spirit the capacity for engendering Christ in their own soul, as is attested to by St. Ildephonsus in a prayer of supplication, amazing in its doctrine and prayerful power: "I beg you, holy Virgin, that I may have Jesus from the Holy Spirit, by whom you brought Jesus forth. May my soul receive Jesus through the Holy Spirit by whom your flesh conceived Jesus. . . . May I love Jesus in the Holy Spirit in whom you adore Jesus as Lord and gaze upon Him as your Son."[84]

27. It is sometimes said that many spiritual writings today do not sufficiently reflect the whole doctrine concerning the Holy Spirit. It is the task of specialists to verify and weigh the truth of this assertion, but it is our task to exhort everyone, especially those in the pastoral ministry and also theologians, to meditate more deeply on the working of the Holy Spirit in the history of salvation, and to ensure that Christian spiritual writings give due prominence to His life-giving action. Such a study will bring out in particular the hidden relationship between the Spirit of God and the Virgin of Nazareth, and show the influence they exert on the Church. From a more profound meditation on the truths of the Faith will flow a more vital piety.

28.   It is also necessary that exercises of piety with which the faithful honor the Mother of the Lord should clearly show the place she occupies in the Church: "the highest place and the closest to us after Christ."[85] The liturgical buildings of Byzantine rite, both in the architectural structure itself and in the use of images, show clearly Mary's place in the Church. On the central door of the iconostasis there is a representation of the annunciation and in the apse an image of the glorious *Theotokos*. In this way one perceives how through the assent of the humble handmaid of the Lord mankind begins its return to God and sees in the glory of the all-holy Virgin the goal towards which it is journeying. The symbolism by which a church building demonstrates Mary's place in the mystery of the Church is full of significance and gives grounds for hoping that the different forms of devotion to the Blessed Virgin may everywhere be open to ecclesial perspectives.

The faithful will be able to appreciate more easily Mary's mission in the mystery of the Church and her preeminent place in the communion of saints if attention is drawn to the Second Vatican Council's references to the fundamental concepts of the nature of the Church as the Family of God, the People of God, the Kingdom of God and the Mystical Body of Christ.[86] This will also bring the faithful to a deeper realization of the brotherhood which unites all of them as sons and daughters of the Virgin Mary, "who with a mother's love has cooperated in their rebirth and spiritual formation,"[87] and as sons and daughters of the Church, since "we are born from the Church's womb we are nurtured by the Church's milk, we are given life by the Church's Spirit."[88] They will also realize that both the Church and Mary collaborate to give birth to the Mystical Body of Christ since "both of them are the Mother of Christ, but neither brings forth the whole [body] independently of the other."[89] Similarly the faithful will appreciate more clearly that the action of the Church in the world can be likened to an extension of Mary's concern. The active love she showed at Nazareth, in the house of Elizabeth, at Cana and on Golgotha—all salvific episodes having vast ecclesial importance—finds its extension in the Church's maternal concern that all men should come to knowledge of the truth (cf. 1 Tm 2:4), in the Church's concern for people in lowly circumstances and for the poor and weak, and in her constant commitment to peace and social harmony, as well as in her untiring efforts to ensure that all men will share in the salvation which was merited for them by Christ's death. Thus love for the Church will become love for Mary, and vice versa, since the one cannot exist without the other, as St. Chromatius of Aquileia observed with keen discernment: "The Church was united . . . in the Upper Room with Mary the Mother of Jesus and with His brethren. The Church therefore cannot be referred to as such unless it includes Mary the Mother of our Lord, together with His brethren."[90] In conclusion, therefore, we repeat that devotion to the Blessed Virgin must explicitly show its intrinsic and ecclesiological content: thus it will be enabled to revise its forms and texts in a fitting way.

SECTION II. FOUR GUIDELINES FOR DEVOTION TO THE BLESSED VIRGIN: BIBLICAL, LITURGICAL, ECUMENICAL, AND ANTHROPOLOGICAL

29.   The above considerations spring from an examination of the Virgin Mary's relationship with God—the Father and the Son and the Holy Spirit—and with the Church. Following the path traced by conciliar teaching,[91] we wish to add some further guidelines from Scripture, liturgy, ecumenism and anthropology. These are to be borne in mind in any revision of exercises of piety or in the creation of new ones, in order to emphasize and accentuate the bond which unites us to her who is the Mother of Christ and our Mother in the communion of saints.

30.   Today it is recognized as a general need of Christian piety that every form of worship should have a biblical imprint. The progress made in biblical studies, the increasing dissemination of the Sacred Scriptures, and above all the example of Tradition and the interior action of the Holy Spirit are tending to cause the modern Christian to use the Bible ever increasingly as the basic prayer book, and to draw from it genuine inspiration and unsurpassable examples. Devotion to the Blessed Virgin cannot be exempt from this general orientation of Christian piety;[92] indeed it should draw inspiration in a special way from this orientation in order to gain new vigor and sure help. In its wonderful presentation of God's plan for man's salvation, the Bible is replete with the mystery of the Savior, and from Genesis to the Book of Revelation, also contains clear references to her who was the Mother and associate of the Savior. We would not, however, wish this biblical imprint to be merely a diligent use of texts and symbols skillfully selected from the Sacred Scriptures. More than this is necessary. What is needed is that texts of prayers and chants should draw their inspiration and their wording from the Bible, and above all that devotion to the Virgin should be imbued with the great themes of the Christian message. This will ensure that, as they venerate the Seat of Wisdom, the faithful in their turn will be enlightened by the divine word, and be inspired to live their lives in accordance with the precepts of Incarnate Wisdom.

31.   We have already spoken of the veneration which the Church gives to the Mother of God in the celebration of the sacred liturgy. However, speaking of the

other forms of devotion and of the criteria on which they should be based we wish to recall the norm laid down in the Constitution *Sacrosanctum Concilium*. This document, while wholeheartedly approving of the practices of piety of the Christian people, goes on to say: ". . . it is necessary however that such devotions with consideration for the liturgical seasons should be so arranged as to be in harmony with the sacred liturgy. They should somehow derive their inspiration from it, and because of its pre-eminence they should orient the Christian people towards it."[93] Although this is a wise and clear rule, its application is not an easy matter, especially in regard to Marian devotions, which are so varied in their formal expressions. What is needed on the part of the leaders of the local communities is effort, pastoral sensitivity and perseverance, while the faithful on their part must show a willingness to accept guidelines and ideas drawn from the true nature of Christian worship; this sometimes makes it necessary to change long-standing customs wherein the real nature of this Christian worship has become somewhat obscured.

In this context we wish to mention two attitudes which in pastoral practice could nullify the norm of the Second Vatican Council. In the first place there are certain persons concerned with the care of souls who scorn, *a priori*, devotions of piety which, in their correct forms, have been recommended by the magisterium, who leave them aside and in this way create a vacuum which they do not fill. They forget that the Council has said that devotions of piety should harmonize with the liturgy, not be suppressed. Secondly there are those who, without wholesome liturgical and pastoral criteria, mix practices of piety and liturgical acts in hybrid celebrations. It sometimes happens that novenas or similar practices of piety are inserted into the very celebration of the Eucharistic Sacrifice. This creates the danger that the Lord's Memorial Rite, instead of being the culmination of the meeting of the Christian community, becomes the occasion, as it were, for devotional practices. For those who act in this way we wish to recall the rule laid down by the Council prescribing that exercises of piety should be harmonized with the liturgy, not merged into it. Wise pastoral action should, on the one hand, point out and emphasize the proper nature of the liturgical acts, while on the other hand it should enhance the value of practices of piety in order to adapt them to the needs of individual communities in the Church and to make them valuable aids to the liturgy.

32.   Because of its ecclesial character, devotion to the Blessed Virgin reflects the preoccupations of the Church herself. Among these especially in our day is her anxiety for the re-establishment of Christian unity. In this way devotion to the Mother of the Lord is in accord with the deep desires and aims of the ecumenical movement, that is, it acquires an ecumenical aspect. This is so for a number of reasons.

In the first place, in venerating with particular love the glorious *Theotokos* and in acclaiming her as the "Hope of Christians,"[94] Catholics unite themselves with their brethren of the Orthodox Churches, in which devotion to the Blessed Virgin finds its expression in a beautiful lyricism and in solid doctrine. Catholics are also united with Anglicans, whose classical theologians have already drawn attention to the sound scriptural basis for devotion to the Mother of our Lord, while those of the present day increasingly underline the importance of Mary's place in the Christian life. Praising God with the very words of the Virgin (cf. Lk 1:46-55), they are united, too, with their brethren in the Churches of the Reform, where love for the Sacred Scriptures flourishes.

For Catholics, devotion to the Mother of Christ and Mother of Christians is also a natural and frequent opportunity for seeking her intercession with her Son in order to obtain the union of all the baptized within a single People of God.[95] Yet again, the ecumenical aspect of Marian devotion is shown in the Catholic Church's desire that, without in any way detracting from the unique character of this devotion,[96] every care should be taken to avoid any exaggeration which could mislead other Christian brethren about the true doctrine of the Catholic Church.[97] Similarly, the Church desires that any manifestation of cult which is opposed to correct Catholic practice should be eliminated.

Finally, since it is natural that in true devotion to the Blessed Virgin "the Son should be duly known, loved and glorified . . .when the Mother is honored,"[98] such devotion is an approach to Christ, the source and center of ecclesiastical communion, in which all who openly confess that He is God and Lord, Savior and sole Mediator (cf. 1 Tm 2:5) are called to be one, with one another, with Christ and with the Father in the unity of the Holy Spirit.[99]

33.   We realize that there exist important differences between the thought of many of our brethren in other Churches and ecclesial communities and the Catholic doctrine on "Mary's role in the work of salvation."[100] In consequence there are likewise differences of opinion on the devotion which should be shown to her. Nevertheless, since it is the same power of the Most High which overshadowed the Virgin of Nazareth (cf. Lk 1:35) and which today is at work within the ecumenical movement and making it fruitful, we wish to express our confidence that devotion to the humble handmaid of the Lord, in whom the Almighty has done great things (cf. Lk 1:49), will become, even if only slowly, not an obstacle but a path and a rallying point for the union of all who believe in Christ. We are glad to see that, in fact, a better understanding of Mary's place in the mystery of Christ and

of the Church on the part also of our separated brethren is smoothing the path to union. Just as at Cana the Blessed Virgin's intervention resulted in Christ's performing His first miracle (cf. Jn 2:1-12), so today her intercession can help to bring to realization the time when the disciples of Christ will again find full communion in faith. This hope of ours is strengthened by a remark of our predecessor Leo XIII, who wrote that the cause of Christian unity "properly pertains to the role of Mary's spiritual motherhood. For Mary did not and cannot engender those who belong to Christ, except in one faith and one love: for 'Is Christ divided?' (1 Cor 1:13). We must all live together the life of Christ, so that in one and the same body 'we may bear fruit for God' (Rom 7:4)."[101]

34.   Devotion to the Blessed Virgin must also pay close attention to certain findings of the human sciences. This will help to eliminate one of the causes of the difficulties experienced in devotion to the Mother of the Lord, namely, the discrepancy existing between some aspects of this devotion and modern anthropological discoveries and the profound changes which have occurred in the psycho-sociological field in which modern man lives and works. The picture of the Blessed Virgin presented in a certain type of devotional literature cannot easily be reconciled with today's life-style, especially the way women live today. In the home, woman's equality and co-responsibility with man in the running of the family are being justly recognized by laws and the evolution of customs. In the sphere of politics women have in many countries gained a position in public life equal to that of men. In the social field women are at work in a whole range of different employments, getting further away every day from the restricted surroundings of the home. In the cultural field new possibilities are opening up for women in scientific research and intellectual activities.

In consequence of these phenomena some people are becoming disenchanted with devotion to the Blessed Virgin and finding it difficult to take as an example Mary of Nazareth because the horizons of her life, so they say, seem rather restricted in comparison with the vast spheres of activity open to mankind today. In this regard we exhort theologians, those responsible for the local Christian communities and the faithful themselves to examine these difficulties with due care. At the same time we wish to take the opportunity of offering our own contribution to their solution by making a few observations.

35.   First, the Virgin Mary has always been proposed to the faithful by the Church as an example to be imitated, not precisely in the type of life she led, and much less for the socio-cultural background in which she lived and which today scarcely exists anywhere. She is held up as an example to the faithful rather for the way in

which, in her own particular life, she fully and responsibly accepted the will of God (cf. Lk 1:38), because she heard the word of God and acted on it, and because charity and a spirit of service were the driving force of her actions. She is worthy of imitation because she was the first and the most perfect of Christ's disciples. All of this has a permanent and universal exemplary value.

36.   Secondly, we would like to point out that the difficulties alluded to above are closely related to certain aspects of the image of Mary found in popular writings. They are not connected with the Gospel image of Mary nor with the doctrinal data which have been made explicit through a slow and conscientious process of drawing from Revelation. It should be considered quite normal for succeeding generations of Christians in differing socio-cultural contexts to have expressed their sentiments about the Mother of Jesus in a way and manner which reflected their own age. In contemplating Mary and her mission these different generations of Christians, looking on her as the New Woman and perfect Christian, found in her as a virgin, wife and mother the outstanding type of womanhood and the preeminent exemplar of life lived in accordance with the Gospels and summing up the most characteristic situations in the life of a woman. When the Church considers the long history of Marian devotion she rejoices at the continuity of the element of cult which it shows, but she does not bind herself to any particular expression of an individual cultural epoch or to the particular anthropological ideas underlying such expressions. The Church understands that certain outward religious expressions, while perfectly valid in themselves, may be less suitable to men and women of different ages and cultures.

37.   Finally, we wish to point out that our own time, no less than former times, is called upon to verify its knowledge of reality with the word of God, and, keeping to the matter at present under consideration, to compare its anthropological ideas and the problems springing therefrom with the figure of the Virgin Mary as presented by the Gospel. The reading of the divine Scriptures, carried out under the guidance of the Holy Spirit, and with the discoveries of the human sciences and the different situations in the world today being taken into account, will help us to see how Mary can be considered a mirror of the expectations of the men and women of our time. Thus, the modern woman, anxious to participate with decision-making power in the affairs of the community, will contemplate with intimate joy Mary who, taken into dialogue with God, gives her active and responsible consent,[102] not to the solution of a contingent problem, but to that "event of world importance," as the Incarnation of the Word has been rightly called.[103] The modern woman will appreciate that Mary's choice of the state of virginity, which in God's plan prepared her

for the mystery of the Incarnation, was not a rejection of any of the values of the married state but a courageous choice which she made in order to consecrate herself totally to the love of God. The modern woman will note with pleasant surprise that Mary of Nazareth, while completely devoted to the will of God, was far from being a timidly submissive woman or one whose piety was repellent to others; on the contrary, she was a woman who did not hesitate to proclaim that God vindicates the humble and the oppressed, and removes the powerful people of this world from their privileged positions (cf. Lk 1:51-53). The modern woman will recognize in Mary, who "stands out among the poor and humble of the Lord,"[104] a woman of strength, who experienced poverty and suffering, flight and exile (cf. Mt 2:13-23). These are situations that cannot escape the attention of those who wish to support, with the Gospel spirit, the liberating energies of man and of society. And Mary will appear not as a Mother exclusively concerned with her own divine Son, but rather as a woman whose action helped to strengthen the apostolic community's faith in Christ (cf. Jn 2:1-12), and whose maternal role was extended and became universal on Calvary.[105] These are but examples, but examples which show clearly that the figure of the Blessed Virgin does not disillusion any of the profound expectations of the men and women of our time but offers them the perfect model of the disciple of the Lord: the disciple who builds up the earthly and temporal city while being a diligent pilgrim towards the heavenly and eternal city; the disciple who works for that justice which sets free the oppressed and for that charity which assists the needy; but above all, the disciple who is the active witness of that love which builds up Christ in people's hearts.

38.   Having offered these directives, which are intended to favor the harmonious development of devotion to the Mother of the Lord, we consider it opportune to draw attention to certain attitudes of piety which are incorrect. The Second Vatican Council has already authoritatively denounced both the exaggeration of content and form which even falsifies doctrine and likewise the small-mindedness which obscures the figure and mission of Mary. The Council has also denounced certain devotional deviations, such as vain credulity, which substitutes reliance on merely external practices for serious commitment. Another deviation is sterile and ephemeral sentimentality, so alien to the spirit of the Gospel that demands persevering and practical action.[106] We reaffirm the Council's reprobation of such attitudes and practices. They are not in harmony with the Catholic Faith and therefore they must have no place in Catholic worship. Careful defense against these errors and deviations will render devotion to the Blessed Virgin more vigorous and more authentic. It will make this devotion solidly based, with the consequence that study of the sources of Revelation and attention to the documents of the

magisterium will prevail over the exaggerated search for novelties or extraordinary phenomena. It will ensure that this devotion is objective in its historical setting, and for this reason everything that is obviously legendary or false must be eliminated. It will ensure that this devotion matches its doctrinal content—hence the necessity of avoiding a one-sided presentation of the figure of Mary, which by overstressing one element compromises the overall picture given by the Gospel. It will make this devotion clear in its motivation; hence every unworthy self-interest is to be carefully banned from the area of what is sacred.

39.   Finally, insofar as it may be necessary we would like to repeat that the ultimate purpose of devotion to the Blessed Virgin is to glorify God and to lead Christians to commit themselves to a life which is in absolute conformity with His will. When the children of the Church unite their voices with the voice of the unknown woman in the Gospel and glorify the Mother of Jesus by saying to Him: "Blessed is the womb that bore you and the breasts that you sucked" (Lk 11:27), they will be led to ponder the Divine Master's serious reply: "Blessed rather are those who hear the word of God and keep it!" (Lk 11:28). While it is true that this reply is in itself lively praise of Mary, as various Fathers of the Church interpreted it[107] and the Second Vatican Council has confirmed,[108] it is also an admonition to us to live our lives in accordance with God's commandments. It is also an echo of other words of the Savior: "Not every one who says to me 'Lord, Lord,' will enter the kingdom of heaven, but he who does the will of my Father who is in heaven" (Mt 7:21); and again: "You are my friends if you do what I command you" (Jn 15:14).

Part Three
OBSERVATIONS ON TWO EXERCISES OF PIETY: THE *ANGELUS* AND THE ROSARY

40.   We have indicated a number of principles which can help to give fresh vigor to devotion to the Mother of the Lord. It is now up to episcopal conferences, to those in charge of local communities and to the various religious congregations prudently to revise practices and exercises of piety in honor of the Blessed Virgin, and to encourage the creative impulse of those who through genuine religious inspiration or pastoral sensitivity wish to establish new forms of piety. For different reasons we nevertheless feel it is opportune to consider here two practices which are widespread in the West, and with which this Apostolic See has concerned itself on various occasions: the Angelus and the Rosary.

THE *ANGELUS*

41.   What we have to say about the Angelus is meant to be only a simple but earnest exhortation to continue its traditional recitation wherever and whenever possible. The Angelus does not need to be revised, because of its simple structure, its biblical character, its historical origin which links it to the prayer for peace and safety, and its quasi-liturgical rhythm which sanctifies different moments during the day, and because it reminds us of the Paschal Mystery, in which recalling the Incarnation of the Son of God we pray that we may be led "through his passion and cross to the glory of his resurrection."[109] These factors ensure that the Angelus despite the passing of centuries retains an unaltered value and an intact freshness. It is true that certain customs traditionally linked with the recitation of the Angelus have disappeared or can continue only with difficulty in modern life. But these are marginal elements. The value of contemplation on the mystery of the Incarnation of the Word, of the greeting to the Virgin, and of recourse to her merciful intercession remains unchanged. And despite the changed conditions of the times, for the majority of people there remain unaltered the characteristic periods of the day— morning, noon and evening—which mark the periods of their activity and constitute an invitation to pause in prayer.

THE ROSARY

42.   We wish now, venerable Brothers, to dwell for a moment on the renewal of the pious practice which has been called "the compendium of the entire Gospel":[110] the Rosary. To this our predecessors have devoted close attention and care. On many occasions they have recommended its frequent recitation, encouraged its diffusion, explained its nature, recognized its suitability for fostering contemplative prayer—prayer of both praise and petition—and recalled its intrinsic effectiveness for promoting Christian life and apostolic commitment.

We, too, from the first general audience of our pontificate on July 13, 1963, have shown our great esteem for the pious practice of the Rosary.[111] Since that time we have underlined its value on many different occasions, some ordinary, some grave. Thus, at a moment of anguish and uncertainty, we published the Letter *Christi Matri* (September 15, 1966), in order to obtain prayers to Our Lady of the Rosary and to implore from God the supreme benefit of peace.[112] We renewed this appeal in our Apostolic Exhortation *Recurrens mensis October* (October 7, 1969), in which we also commemorated the fourth centenary of the Apostolic Letter *Consueverunt*

Romani pontifices of our predecessor St. Pius V, who in that document explained and in a certain sense established the traditional form of the Rosary.[113]

43.   Our assiduous and affectionate interest in the Rosary has led us to follow very attentively the numerous meetings which in recent years have been devoted to the pastoral role of the Rosary in the modern world, meetings arranged by associations and individuals profoundly attached to the Rosary and attended by bishops, priests, religious and lay people of proven experience and recognized ecclesial awareness. Among these people special mention should be made of the sons of St. Dominic, by tradition the guardians and promoters of this very salutary practice. Parallel with such meetings has been the research work of historians, work aimed not at defining in a sort of archaeological fashion the primitive form of the Rosary but at uncovering the original inspiration and driving force behind it and its essential structure. The fundamental characteristics of the Rosary, its essential elements and their mutual relationship have all emerged more clearly from these congresses and from the research carried out.

44.   Thus, for instance, the Gospel inspiration of the Rosary has appeared more clearly: the Rosary draws from the Gospel the presentation of the mysteries and its main formulas. As it moves from the angel's joyful greeting and the Virgin's pious assent, the Rosary takes its inspiration from the Gospel to suggest the attitude with which the faithful should recite it. In the harmonious succession of Hail Mary's the Rosary puts before us once more a fundamental mystery of the Gospel— the Incarnation of the Word, contemplated at the decisive moment of the Annunciation to Mary. The Rosary is thus a Gospel prayer, as pastors and scholars like to define it, more today perhaps than in the past.

45.   It has also been more easily seen how the orderly and gradual unfolding of the Rosary reflects the very way in which the Word of God, mercifully entering into human affairs, brought about the Redemption. The Rosary considers in harmonious succession the principal salvific events accomplished in Christ, from His virginal conception and the mysteries of His childhood to the culminating moments of the Passover—the blessed passion and the glorious resurrection—and to the effects of this on the infant Church on the day of Pentecost, and on the Virgin Mary when at the end of her earthly life she was assumed body and soul into her heavenly home. It has also been observed that the division of the mysteries of the Rosary into three parts not only adheres strictly to the chronological order of the facts but above all reflects the plan of the original proclamation of the Faith and sets forth once more the mystery of Christ in the very way in which it is seen by St. Paul in

the celebrated "hymn" of the Letter to the Philippians—kenosis, death and exaltation (cf. 2:6-11).

46. As a Gospel prayer, centered on the mystery of the redemptive Incarnation, the Rosary is therefore a prayer with a clearly Christological orientation. Its most characteristic element, in fact, the litany-like succession of Hail Mary's, becomes in itself an unceasing praise of Christ, who is the ultimate object both of the angel's announcement and of the greeting of the mother of John the Baptist: "Blessed is the fruit of your womb" (Lk 1:42). We would go further and say that the succession of Hail Mary's constitutes the warp on which is woven the contemplation of the mysteries. The Jesus that each Hail Mary recalls is the same Jesus whom the succession of the mysteries proposes to us—now as the Son of God, now as the Son of the Virgin—at His birth in a stable at Bethlehem, at His presentation by His Mother in the Temple, as a youth full of zeal for His Father's affairs, as the Redeemer in agony in the garden, scourged and crowned with thorns, carrying the cross and dying on Calvary; risen from the dead and ascended to the glory of the Father to send forth the gift of the Spirit. As is well known, at one time there was a custom, still preserved in certain places, of adding to the name of Jesus in each Hail Mary a reference to the mystery being contemplated. And this was done precisely in order to help contemplation and to make the mind and the voice act in unison.

47. There has also been felt with greater urgency the need to point out once more the importance of a further essential element in the Rosary, in addition to the value of the elements of praise and petition, namely the element of contemplation. Without this the Rosary is a body without a soul, and its recitation is in danger of becoming a mechanical repetition of formulas and of going counter to the warning of Christ: "And in praying do not heap up empty phrases as the Gentiles do; for they think that they will be heard for their many words" (Mt 6:7). By its nature the recitation of the Rosary calls for a quiet rhythm and a lingering pace, helping the individual to meditate on the mysteries of the Lord's life as seen through the eyes of her who was closest to the Lord. In this way the unfathomable riches of these mysteries are unfolded.

48. Finally, as a result of modern reflection the relationships between the liturgy and the Rosary have been more clearly understood. On the one hand it has been emphasized that the Rosary is, as it were, a branch sprung from the ancient trunk of the Christian liturgy, the Psalter of the Blessed Virgin, whereby the humble were associated in the Church's hymn of praise and universal intercession. On the other hand it has been noted that this development occurred at a time—the last period

of the Middle Ages—when the liturgical spirit was in decline and the faithful were turning from the liturgy towards a devotion to Christ's humanity and to the Blessed Virgin Mary, a devotion favoring a certain external sentiment of piety. Not many years ago some people began to express the desire to see the Rosary included among the rites of the liturgy, while other people, anxious to avoid repetition of former pastoral mistakes, unjustifiably disregarded the Rosary. Today the problem can easily be solved in the light of the principles of the Constitution *Sacrosanctum Concilium*. Liturgical celebrations and the pious practice of the Rosary must be neither set in opposition to one another nor considered as being identical.[114] The more an expression of prayer preserves its own true nature and individual characteristics the more fruitful it becomes. Once the pre-eminent value of liturgical rites has been reaffirmed it will not be difficult to appreciate the fact that the Rosary is a practice of piety which easily harmonizes with the liturgy. In fact, like the liturgy, it is of a community nature, draws its inspiration from Sacred Scripture and is oriented towards the mystery of Christ. The commemoration in the liturgy and the contemplative remembrance proper to the Rosary, although existing on essentially different planes of reality, have as their object the same salvific events wrought by Christ. The former presents anew, under the veil of signs and operative in a hidden way, the great mysteries of our Redemption. The latter, by means of devout contemplation, recalls these same mysteries to the mind of the person praying and stimulates the will to draw from them the norms of living. Once this substantial difference has been established, it is not difficult to understand that the Rosary is an exercise of piety that draws its motivating force from the liturgy and leads naturally back to it, if practiced in conformity with its original inspiration. It does not, however, become part of the liturgy. In fact, meditation on the mysteries of the Rosary, by familiarizing the hearts and minds of the faithful with the mysteries of Christ, can be an excellent preparation for the celebration of those same mysteries in the liturgical action and can also become a continuing echo thereof. However, it is a mistake to recite the Rosary during the celebration of the liturgy, though unfortunately this practice still persists here and there.

49.   The Rosary of the Blessed Virgin Mary, according to the tradition accepted by our predecessor St. Pius V and authoritatively taught by him, consists of various elements disposed in an organic fashion:

(a)   Contemplation in communion with Mary, of a series of mysteries of salvation, wisely distributed into three cycles. These mysteries express the joy of the messianic times, the salvific suffering of Christ and the glory of the Risen Lord which fills the Church. This contemplation by its very nature encourages practical reflection and provides stimulating norms for living.

(b)   The Lord's Prayer, or Our Father, which by reason of its immense value is at the basis of Christian prayer and ennobles that prayer in its various expressions.

(c)   The litany-like succession of the Hail Mary, which is made up of the angel's greeting to the Virgin (cf. Lk 1:28), and of Elizabeth's greeting (cf. Lk 1:42), followed by the ecclesial supplication Holy Mary. The continued series of Hail Marys is the special characteristic of the Rosary, and their number, in the full and typical number of one hundred and fifty, presents a certain analogy with the Psalter and is an element that goes back to the very origin of the exercise of piety. But this number, divided, according to a well-tried custom, into decades attached to the individual mysteries, is distributed in the three cycles already mentioned, thus giving rise to the Rosary of fifty Hail Marys as we know it. This latter has entered into use as the normal measure of the pious exercise and as such has been adopted by popular piety and approved by papal authority, which also enriched it with numerous indulgences.

(d)   The doxology Glory be to the Father which, in conformity with an orienta-tion common to Christian piety, concludes the prayer with the glorifying of God who is one and three, from whom, through whom and in whom all things have their being (cf. Rom 11:36).

50.   These are the elements of the Rosary. Each has its own particular character which, wisely understood and appreciated, should be reflected in the recitation in order that the Rosary may express all its richness and variety. Thus the recitation will be grave and suppliant during the Lord's Prayer, lyrical and full of praise during the tranquil succession of Hail Marys, contemplative in the recollected meditation on the mysteries and full of adoration during the doxology. This applies to all the ways in which the Rosary is usually recited: privately, in intimate recollection with the Lord; in community, in the family or in groups of the faithful gathered together to ensure the special presence of the Lord (cf. Mt 18:20); or publicly, in assemblies to which the ecclesial community is invited.

51.   In recent times certain exercises of piety have been created which take their inspiration from the Rosary. Among such exercises we wish to draw attention to and recommend those which insert into the ordinary celebration of the word of God some elements of the Rosary, such as meditation on the mysteries and litany-like repetition of the angel's greeting to Mary. In this way these elements gain in importance, since they are found in the context of Bible readings, illustrated with a homily, accompanied by silent pauses and emphasized with song. We are happy to know that such practices have helped to promote a more complete understanding

of the spiritual riches of the Rosary itself and have served to restore esteem for its recitation among youth associations and movements.

52.   We now desire, as a continuation of the thought of our predecessors, to recommend strongly the recitation of the family Rosary. The Second Vatican Council has pointed out how the family, the primary and vital cell of society, "shows itself to be the domestic sanctuary of the Church through the mutual affection of its members and the common prayer they offer to God."[115] The Christian family is thus seen to be a domestic Church[116] if its members, each according to his proper place and tasks, all together promote justice, practice works of mercy, devote themselves to helping their brethren, take part in the apostolate of the wider local community and play their part in its liturgical worship.[117] This will be all the more true if together they offer up prayers to God. If this element of common prayer were missing, the family would lack its very character as a domestic Church. Thus there must logically follow a concrete effort to reinstate communal prayer in family life if there is to be a restoration of the theological concept of the family as the domestic Church.

53.   In accordance with the directives of the Council the *Institutio Generalis de Liturgia Horarum* rightly numbers the family among the groups in which the Divine Office can suitably be celebrated in community: "It is fitting . . . that the family, as a domestic sanctuary of the Church, should not only offer prayers to God in common, but also, according to circumstances, should recite parts of the Liturgy of the Hours, in order to be more intimately linked with the Church."[118] No avenue should be left unexplored to ensure that this clear and practical recommendation finds within Christian families growing and joyful acceptance.

54.   But there is no doubt that, after the celebration of the Liturgy of the Hours, the high point which family prayer can reach, the Rosary should be considered as one of the best and most efficacious prayers in common that the Christian family is invited to recite. We like to think, and sincerely hope, that when the family gathering becomes a time of prayer, the Rosary is a frequent and favored manner of praying. We are well aware that the changed conditions of life today do not make family gatherings easy, and that even when such a gathering is possible many circumstances make it difficult to turn it into an occasion of prayer. There is no doubt of the difficulty. But it is characteristic of the Christian in his manner of life not to give in to circumstances but to overcome them, not to succumb but to make an effort. Families which want to live in full measure the vocation and spirituality proper to the Christian family must therefore devote all their energies to overcoming the pressures that hinder family gatherings and prayer in common.

55.   In concluding these observations, which give proof of the concern and esteem which the Apostolic See has for the Rosary of the Blessed Virgin, we desire at the same time to recommend that this very worthy devotion should not be propagated in a way that is too one-sided or exclusive. The Rosary is an excellent prayer, but the faithful should feel serenely free in its regard. They should be drawn to its calm recitation by its intrinsic appeal.

Conclusion

THEOLOGICAL AND PASTORAL VALUE OF DEVOTION TO THE BLESSED VIRGIN

56 v 57

56.   Venerable Brothers, as we come to the end of this our Apostolic Exhortation we wish to sum up and emphasize the theological value of devotion to the Blessed Virgin and to recall briefly its pastoral effectiveness for renewing the Christian way of life.

Third draft

The Church's devotion to the Blessed Virgin is an intrinsic element of Christian worship. The honor which the Church has always and everywhere shown to the Mother of the Lord, from the blessing with which Elizabeth greeted Mary (cf. Lk 1:42-45) right up to the expressions of praise and petition used today, is a very strong witness to the Church's norm of prayer and an invitation to become more deeply conscious of her norm of faith. And the converse is likewise true. The Church's norm of faith requires that her norm of prayer should everywhere blossom forth with regard to the Mother of Christ. Such devotion to the Blessed Virgin is firmly rooted in the revealed word and has solid dogmatic foundations. It is based on the singular dignity of Mary, "Mother of the Son of God, and therefore beloved daughter of the Father and Temple of the Holy Spirit—Mary, who, because of this extraordinary grace, is far greater than any other creature on earth or in heaven."[119] This devotion takes into account the part she played at decisive moments in the history of the salvation which her Son accomplished, and her holiness, already full at her Immaculate Conception yet increasing all the time as she obeyed the will of the Father and accepted the path of suffering (cf. Lk 2:34-35, 41-52; Jn 19:25-27), growing constantly in faith, hope and charity. Devotion to Mary recalls too her mission and the special position she holds within the People of God, of which she is the preeminent member, a shining example and the loving Mother; it recalls her unceasing and efficacious intercession which, although she is assumed into heaven, draws her close to those who ask her help, including those who do not realize that they are her children. It recalls Mary's glory which ennobles the whole of mankind, as the outstanding phrase of Dante recalls: "You have so ennobled human nature that its very Creator did not disdain to share in it."[120] Mary, in fact, is one of our race, a true daughter of Eve—though free of that mother's sin—and truly our sister, who as a poor and humble woman fully shared our lot.

We would add further that devotion to the Blessed Virgin finds its ultimate justification in the unfathomable and free will of God who, being eternal and divine charity (cf. 1 Jn 4:7-8, 16), accomplishes all things according to a loving design. He loved her and did great things for her (cf. Lk 1:49). He loved her for His own sake, and He loved her for our sake, too; He gave her to Himself and He gave her also to us.

57.   Christ is the only way to the Father (cf. Jn 14:4-11), and the ultimate example to whom the disciple must conform his own conduct (cf. Jn 13:15), to the extent of sharing Christ's sentiments (cf. Phil 2:5), living His life and possessing His Spirit (cf. Gal 2:20; Rom. 8:10-11). The Church has always taught this and nothing in pastoral activity should obscure this doctrine. But the Church, taught by the Holy Spirit and benefiting from centuries of experience, recognizes that devotion to the Blessed Virgin, subordinated to worship of the divine Savior and in connection with it, also has a great pastoral effectiveness and constitutes a force for renewing Christian living. It is easy to see the reason for this effectiveness. Mary's many-sided mission to the People of God is a supernatural reality which operates and bears fruit within the body of the Church. One finds cause for joy in considering the different aspects of this mission, and seeing how each of these aspects with its individual effectiveness is directed towards the same end, namely, producing in the children the spiritual characteristics of the first-born Son. The Virgin's maternal intercession, her exemplary holiness and the divine grace which is in her become for the human race a reason for divine hope.

The Blessed Virgin's role as Mother leads the People of God to turn with filial confidence to her who is ever ready to listen with a mother's affection and efficacious assistance.[121] Thus the People of God have learned to call on her as the Consoler of the afflicted, the Health of the sick, and the Refuge of sinners, that they may find comfort in tribulation, relief in sickness and liberating strength in guilt. For she, who is free from sin, leads her children to combat sin with energy and resoluteness.[122] This liberation from sin and evil (cf. Mt 6:13)—it must be repeated—is the necessary premise for any renewal of Christian living.

The Blessed Virgin's exemplary holiness encourages the faithful to "raise their eyes to Mary who shines forth before the whole community of the elect as a model of the virtues."[123] It is a question of solid, evangelical virtues: faith and the docile acceptance of the Word of God (cf. Lk 1:26-38, 1:45, 11:27-28; Jn 2:5); generous obedience (cf. Lk 1:38); genuine humility (cf. Lk 1:48); solicitous charity (cf. Lk 1:39-56); profound wisdom (cf. Lk 1:29, 34; 2:19, 33, 51); worship of God manifested in alacrity in the fulfillment of religious duties (cf. Lk 2:21-41), in gratitude for gifts received (cf. Lk 1:46-49), in her offering in the Temple (cf. Lk 2:22-24) and in her prayer in the midst of the apostolic community (cf. Acts 1:12-14); her fortitude in exile (cf. Mt 2:13-23) and in suffering (cf. Lk 2:34-35, 49; Jn 19:25); her poverty reflecting dignity and trust in God (cf. Lk 1:48, 2:24); her attentive care for her Son, from His humble birth to the ignominy of the cross (cf. Lk 2:1-7; Jn 19:25-27); her delicate forethought (cf. Jn 2:1-11); her virginal purity (cf. Mt 1:18-25; Lk 1:26-38); her strong and chaste married love. These virtues of the Mother will also adorn her children who steadfastly study her example in order to reflect it in their own lives. And this progress in virtue will appear as the consequence and the already mature fruit of that pastoral zeal which springs from devotion to the Blessed Virgin.

Devotion to the Mother of the Lord becomes for the faithful an opportunity for growing in divine grace, and this is the ultimate aim of all pastoral activity. For it is impossible to honor her who is "full of grace" (Lk 1:28) without thereby honoring in oneself the state of grace, which is friendship with God, communion with Him and the indwelling of the Holy Spirit. It is this divine grace which takes possession of the whole man and conforms him to the image of the Son of God (cf. Rom 8:29; Col 1:18). The Catholic Church, endowed with centuries of experience, recognizes in devotion to the Blessed Virgin a powerful aid for man as he strives for fulfillment. Mary, the New Woman, stands at the side of Christ, the New Man, within whose mystery the mystery of man[124] alone finds true light; she is given to us as a pledge and guarantee that God's plan in Christ for the salvation of the whole man has already achieved realization in a creature: in her. Contemplated in the episodes of the Gospels and in the reality which she already possesses in the City of God, the Blessed Virgin Mary offers a calm vision and a reassuring word to modern man, torn as he often is between anguish and hope, defeated by the sense of his own limitations and assailed by limitless aspirations, troubled in his mind and divided in his heart, uncertain before the riddle of death, oppressed by loneliness while yearning for fellowship, a prey to boredom and disgust. She shows forth the victory of hope over anguish, of fellowship over solitude, of peace over anxiety, of joy and beauty over boredom and disgust, of eternal visions over earthly ones, of life over death.

Let the very words that she spoke to the servants at the marriage feast of Cana, "Do whatever he tells you" (Jn 2:5), be a seal on our Exhortation and a further reason in favor of the pastoral value of devotion to the Blessed Virgin as a means of leading men to Christ. Those words, which at first sight were limited to the desire to remedy an embarrassment at the feast, are seen in the context of St. John's Gospel to re-echo the words used by the people of Israel to give approval to the Covenant at Sinai (cf. Ex 19:8, 24:3, 7; Dt 5:27) and to renew their commitments (cf. Jos 24:24; Ezr 10:12; Neh 5:12). And they are words which harmonize wonderfully with those spoken by the Father at the theophany on Mount Tabor: "Listen to him" (Mt 17:5).

EPILOGUE

58.   Venerable Brothers, we have dealt at length with an integral element of Christian worship: devotion to the Mother of the Lord. This has been called for by the nature of the subject, one which in these recent years has been the object of study and revision and at times the cause of some perplexity. We are consoled to think that the work done by this Apostolic See and by yourselves in order to carry out the norms of the Council—particularly the liturgical reform—is a stepping-stone to an ever more lively and adoring worship of God, the Father and the Son and the Holy Spirit, and to an increase of the Christian life of the faithful. We are filled with confidence when we note that the renewed Roman liturgy, also taken as a whole, is a splendid illustration of the Church's devotion to the Blessed Virgin. We are upheld by the hope that the directives issued in order to render this devotion ever more pure and vigorous will be applied with sincerity. We rejoice that the Lord has given us the opportunity of putting forward some points for reflection in order to renew and confirm esteem for the practice of the rosary. Comfort, confidence, hope and joy are the sentiments which we wish to transform into fervent praise and thanksgiving to the Lord as we unite our voice with that of the Blessed Virgin in accordance with the prayer of the Roman Liturgy.[125]

Dear Brothers, while we express the hope that, thanks to your generous commitment, there will be among the clergy and among the people entrusted to your care a salutary increase of devotion to Mary with undoubted profit for the Church and for society, we cordially impart our special apostolic blessing to yourselves and to all the faithful people to whom you devote your pastoral zeal.

Given in Rome, at St. Peter's, on the second day of February, the Feast of the Presentation of the Lord, in the year 1974, the eleventh of our Pontificate.

1. Cf. Lactantius, *Divinae Institutiones* IV, 3, 6-10: CSEL 19, p. 279.
2. Cf. Second Vatican Council, Constitution on the Sacred Liturgy, *Sacrosanctum Concilium*, 1-3, 11, 21, 48: AAS 56 (1964), pp. 97-98, 102-103, 105-l06, 113.
3. Second Vatican Council, Constitution on the Sacred Liturgy, *Sacrosanctum Concilium*, 103: AAS 56 (1964), p. 125.
4. Cf. Second Vatican Council, Dogmatic Constitution on the Church, *Lumen Gentium*, 66: AAS 57 (1965), p. 65.
5. Ibid.
6. Votive Mass of the Blessed Virgin Mary, Mother of the Church, Preface.
7. Cf. Second Vatican Council, Dogmatic Constitution of the Church, *Lumen Gentium*, 66-67: AAS 57 (1965), pp. 65-66, Constitution on the Sacred Liturgy, *Sacrosanctum Concilium*, 103: AAS 56 (1964), p. 125.
8. Apostolic Exhortation, *Signum Magnum*: AAS 59 (1967), pp. 465-475.
9. Cf. Second Vatican Council, Constitution on the Sacred Liturgy, *Sacrosanctum Concilium*, 3: AAS 56 (1964), p. 98.
10. Cf. Second Vatican Council, ibid., 102: AAS 56 (1964), p. 125.
11. Cf. *Roman Missal* restored by Decree of the Sacred Ecumenical II Vatican Council, promulgated by authority of Pope Paul VI typical edition, MCMLXX, 8 December, Preface.
12. *Roman Missal*, restored by Decree of the Sacred Ecumenical II Vatican Council promulgated by authority of Pope Paul VI, *Ordo Lectionum Missae*. typical edition, MCMLXIX, p. 8, First Reading (Year A: Is 7:10-14: "Behold a Virgin shall conceive"; Year B: 2 Sam 7:1-15; 8b-11, 16: "The throne of David shall be established for ever before the face of the Lord"; Year C: Mic 5:2-5a [Heb 1-4a]: "Out of you will be born for me the one who is to rule over Israel").
13. Ibid., p. 8, Gospel (Year A: Mt 1:18-24: "Jesus is born of Mary who was espoused to Joseph, the son of David"; Year B: Lk 1:26-38: "You are to conceive and bear a son"; Year C: Lk 1:39-45: "Why should I be honoured with a visit from the Mother of my Lord?").
14. Cf. *Roman Missal*, Advent Preface, II.
15. *Roman Missal*, ibid.
16. *Roman Missal*, Eucharistic Prayer I, Communicantes for Christmas and its octave.
17. *Roman Missal*, January 1, Entry antiphon and Collect.
18. Cf. *Roman Missal*, August 22, Collect.
19. *Roman Missal*, September 8, Prayer after Communion .
20. *Roman Missal*, May 31, Collect.
21. Cf. ibid., Collect and Prayer over the gifts.
22. Cf. *Roman Missal*, September 15, Collect.
23. Cf. 1, p. 15.
24. From among the many anaphoras cf. the following which are held in special honor by the Eastern rites: *Anaphora Marci Evangelistae: Prex Eucharistica*, ed. A. Hanggi-l. Pahl, Fribourg, Editions Universitaires, 1968, p. 107; *Anaphora Iacobi fratris Domini graeca* ibid., p. 257; *Anaphora Iaonnis Chrysostomi*, ibid., p. 229.
25. Cf. *Roman Missal*, December 8, Preface.
26. Cf. *Roman Missal*, August 15, Preface.
27. Cf. *Roman Missal*, January 1, Prayer after Communion.
28. Cf. *Roman Missal*, Common of the Blessed Virgin Mary, 6, Paschaltide, Collect.
29. *Roman Missal*, September 15, Collect.
30. *Roman Missal*, May 31, Collect. On the same lines is the Preface of the Blessed Virgin Mary, II: "We do well . . . in celebrating the memory of the Virgin Mary . . . to glorify your love for us in the words of her song of thanksgiving."

31. Cf. *Lectionary*, III Sunday of Advent (Year C: Zeph 3:14-18a); IV Sunday of Advent (cf. above footnote 12); Sunday within the octave of Christmas (Year A, Mt 2:13-15; 19-23; Year B: Lk 2:22-40; Year C: Lk 2:41-52); II Sunday after Christmas (Jn 1:1-18); VII Sunday after Easter (Year A: Acts 1:12-14); II Sunday of the Year C: Jn 1:1-12); X Sunday of the Year (Year B: Gen 3:9-15); XIV Sunday of the Year (Year B: Mk 6:1-6).

32. Cf. *Lectionary*, the Catechumenate and Baptism of Adults the Lord's Prayer (Second Reading, 2, Gal 4:4-7); Christian Initiation Outside the Easter Vigil (Gospel, 7, Jn 1:1-5; 9-14; 16-18); Nuptial Mass (Gospel, 7, Jn 2:1-11); Consecration of Virgins and Religious Profession (First Reading 7, Is 61:9-11; Gospel, 6, Mk 3:31-35; Lk 1:26-38 [cf. *Ordo Consecrationis Virginum*, 130; *Ordo Professionis Religiosae, Pars Altera*, 145]).

33. Cf. *Lectionary*, For Refugees and Exiles (Gospel, 1, Mt 2:13-15, 19-23); In Thanksgiving (First Reading, 4, Zeph 3:14-15).

34. Cf. *La Divina Commedia*, Paradiso XXXIII, 1-9, cf. Liturgy of the Hours, Remembrance of Our Lady on Saturdays, Office of Reading, Hymn.

35. *Ordo Baptismi Parvulorum*, 48: *Ordo Initiationis Christianae Adultorum*, 214.

36. Cf. *Rituale Romanum*, Tit. VII, cap. III, *De Benedictione Mulieris Post Partum*.

37. Cf. *Ordo Professionis Religiosae, Pars Prior*, 57 and 67.

38. Cf. *Ordo Consecrationis Virginum*, 16.

39. Cf. *Ordo Professionis Religiosae, Pars Prior*, 62 and 142; *Pars Altera*, 67 and 158; *Ordo Consecrationis Virginum*, 18 and 20.

40. Cf. *Ordo Unctionis Infirmorum Eorumque Pastoralis Curae*, 143, 146, 147, 150.

41. Cf. *Roman Missal*, Masses for the Dead, For Dead Brothers and Sisters, Relations and Benefactors, Collect.

42. Cf. *Ordo Exsequiarum*, 226.

43. Cf. Second Vatican Council, Dogmatic Constitution on the Church, *Lumen Gentium*, 63: AAS 57 (1965), p. 64.

44. Cf. Second Vatican Council, Constitution on the Sacred Liturgy, *Sacrosanctum Concilium*, 7: AAS 56 (1964), pp. 100; 101.

45. *Sermo* 215, 4: PL 38, 1074.

46. Ibid.

47. Cf. Second Vatican Council, Dogmatic Constitution on Divine Revelation, *Dei Verbum*, 21: AAS 58 (1966), pp. 827-828.

48. Cf. *Adversus Haereses IV*, 7, 1: PG 7, 1, 990-991; S. Ch. 100, t. II, pp. 454-458.

49. Cf. *Adversus Haereses III*, 10, 2: PG 7, 1, 873; S. Ch. 34, p. 164.

50. Cf. Second Vatican Council, Dogmatic Constitution on the Church, *Lumen Gentium*, 62: AAS 57 (1965), p. 63.

51. Second Vatican Council, Constitution on the Sacred Liturgy, *Sacrosanctum Concilium*, 83: AAS 56 (1964), p. 121.

52. Second Vatican Council, Dogmatic Constitution on the Church, *Lumen Gentium*, 63: AAS 57 (1965), p. 64.

53. Ibid., 64: AAS 57 (1965), p. 64.

54. *Tractatus XXV* (*In Nativitate Domini*), 5: CCL 138, p. 123; S. Ch. 22 bis, p. 132; cf. also *Tractatus XXIX* (*In Nativitate Domini*), I: CCL ibid., p. 147; S. Ch ibid., p. 178; *Tractatus LXIII* (*De Passione Domini*) 6: CCL ibid., p. 386; S. Ch. 74, p. 82.

55. M. Ferotin, *Le Liber Mozarabicus Sacramentorum*, col. 56.

56. *In Purificatione B. Mariae, Sermo III*, 2: PL 183, 370; *Sancti Bernardi Opera*, ed. J. Leclercq-H. Rochais, vol. IV, Rome 1966, p. 342.

57. Cf. Second Vatican Council, Dogmatic Constitution on the Church, *Lumen Gentium*, 57. AAS 57 (1965), p. 61.

58. Ibid., 58: AAS 57 (1965), p. 61.

59. Cf. Pope Pius XII, Encyclical Letter *Mystici Corporis*: AAS 35 (1943), p. 247.

60. Cf. Second Vatican Council, Constitution on the Sacred Liturgy, *Sacrosanctum Concilium*, 47: AAS 56 (1964), p. 113.

61. Ibid., 102, 106: AAS 56 (1964), pp. 125, 126.
62. ". . . deign to remember all who have been pleasing to you throughout the ages, the holy Fathers, the Patriarchs, Prophets, Apostles . . . and the holy and glorious Mother of God and all the saints . . . may they remember our misery and poverty, and together with us may they offer you this great and unbloody sacrifice": *Anaphora Iacobi Fratris Domini Syriaca: Prex Eucharistica*, ed. A. Hanggi-l. Pahl, Fribourg, Editions Universitaires, 1968, p. 274.
63. *Expositio Evangelii Secundum Lucam*, 11, 26: CSEL 32, IV, p. 55; S. Ch. 45, pp. 83-84.
64. Cf. Second Vatican Council, Dogmatic Constitution on the Church, *Lumen Gentium*, 62: AAS 57 (1965), p. 63.
65. Second Vatican Council, Constitution on the Sacred Liturgy *Sacrosanctum Concilium*, 103: AAS 56 (1964), p. 125.
66. Second Vatican Council, Dogmatic Constitution on the Church, *Lumen Gentium*, 67: AAS 57 (1965), pp. 65-66.
67. Cf. ibid.
68. Cf. Second Vatican Council, Constitution on the Sacred Liturgy, *Sacrosanctum Concilium*, 104: AAS 56 (1964), pp. 125-126.
69. Cf. Second Vatican Council, Dogmatic Constitution on the Church, *Lumen Gentium*, 66: AAS 57 (1965), p. 65.
70. Cf. Pope Paul VI, Talk of April 24, 1970, in the church of Our Lady of Bonaria in Cagliari: AAS 62 (1970), p. 300.
71. Pius IX, Apostolic Letter *Ineffabilis Deus: Pii IX Pontificis Maximi Acta I*, 1 Rome 1854, p. 599. Cf. also V. Sardi, *La Solenne Definizione del Dogma dell'Immacolato Concepimento di Maria Sanctissima. Atti e documenti* . . . Rome 1904-1905, vol. II, p. 302.
72. Cf. Second Vatican Council, Dogmatic Constitution on the Church, *Lumen Gentium*, 66: AAS 57 (1965), p. 65.
73. S. Ildephonsus, *De Virginitate Perpetua Sanctae Mariae*, chapter XII: PL 96, 108.
74. Cf. Second Vatican Council, Dogmatic Constitution on the Church, *Lumen Gentium*, 56: AAS 57 (1965), p. 60 and the authors mentioned in note 176 of the document.
75. Cf. St. Ambrose, *De Spiritu Sancto II*, 37-38; CSEL 79 pp. 100-101; Cassian, *De Incarnatione Domini II*, chapter II: CSEL 17, pp. 247-249; St. Bede, *Homilia I*, 3: CCL 122, p. 18 and p. 20.
76. Cf. St. Ambrose, *De Institutione Virginis*, chapter XII, 79: PL 16 (ed. 1880), 339; *Epistula 30*, 3 and *Epistula 42*, 7: ibid., 1107 and 1175 *Expositio Evangelii Secundum Lucam X*, 132 S. Ch. 52 p. 200; S. Proctus of Constantinople, *Oratio I*, 1 and *Oratio V*, 3: PG 65, 681 and 720: St. Basil of Seleucia, *Oratio XXXIX*, 3: PG 85, 433; St. Andrew of Crete, *Oratio IV*: PG 97, 868; St. Germanus of Constantinople, *Oratio III*, 15: PG 98, 305.
77. Cf. St. Jerome, *Adversus Lovinianum I*, 33: PL 23, 267; St. Ambrose, *Epistula 63*, 33: PL 16 (ed. 1880), 1249; *De Institutione Virginis*, chapter XVII, 105: ibid. 346; *De Spiritu Sancto III*, 79-80: CSEL 79, pp. 182-183; Sedulius, Hymn "A Solis Ortus Cardine", verses 13-14: CSEL 10, p. 164; *Hymnus Acathistos*, Str. 23; ed. 1. B. Pitra, *Analecta Sacra I*, p. 261; St. Proctus of Constantinople, *Oratio I*, 3: PG 65, 648: *Oratio II*, 6: Ibid., 700; St. Basil of Seleucia, *Oratio IV, In Nativitatem B. Mariae*: PG 97, 868; St. John Damascene, *Oratio IV*, 10: PG 96, 677.
78. Cf. Severus of Anthioch, *Homilia 57*; PO 8, pp. 357-358; Hesychius of Jerusalem, *Homilia de Sancta Maria Deipara*, PG 93, 1464; Chrysippus of Jerusalem, *Oratio in Sanctam Mariam Deiparam*, 2 PO 19, p. 338; St. Andrew of Crete, *Oratio V*: PG 97, 896: St. John Damascene, *Oratio VI*, 6: PG 96, 972.
79. *Liber Apotheosis*, verses 571-572: CCL 126, p. 97. 80) Cf. S. Isidore, *De Ortu et Obitu Patrum*, chapter LXVII, 111: PL 83, 148; St. Ildephonsus, *De Virginitate Perpetua Sanctae Mariae*, chapter X: PL 96, 95; St. Bernard, *In Assumptione B. Virginis Mariae: Sermo IV*, 4: PL 183, 428; *In Nativitate B. Virginis Mariae*: II, *Oratio ad Deum Filium*: PL 145, 921; Antiphon "Beata Dei Genetrix Maria": *Corpus Antiphonalium Officii*, ed. R. J. Hesbert, Rome 1970, vol. IV, n. 6314, p. 80.
81. Cf. Paulus Diaconus, *Homilia I, In Assumptione B. Mariae Virginis*: PL 95, 1567; *De Assumptione Sanctae Mariae Virginis: Paschasio Radherto Trib.*, 31, 42, 57, 83: ed. A. Ripberger, in "Spicilegium Friburgense", 9, 1962, pp. 72, 76, 84, 96-97; Eadmer of Canterbury, *De Excellentia Virginis Mariae*, chapters IV-V: PL 159, 562-567: St. Bernard, *In Laudibus Virginis Matris, Homilia IV*, 3: *Sancti Bernardi Opera*, ed. J. Leclercq-H. Rochais, IV Rome 1966, pp. 49-50.

82. Cf. Origen, *In Lucam Homilia VII*, 3: PG 13, 1817; S. Ch. 87, p. 156; St. Cyril of Alexandria, *Commentarius in Aggacum Prophetam*, chapter XIX: PG 71, 1060; St. Ambrose, *De fide IV* 9, 113-114: CSEL 78, pp. 197-198: *Expositio Evangelii Secundum; Lucam II*, 23 and 27-28: CSEL 32, IV, pp. 53-54 and 55-56; Severianus Galbalensis, *In Mundi Creationem, Oratio VI*, 10: PG 56, 497-498; Antipater of Bostra, *Homilia in Sanctissimae Deiparae Annuntiationem*, 16: PG 85, 1785.

83. Cf. Eadmer of Canterbury, *De Excellentia Virginis Mariae*, chapter VII: PL 159, 571: St. Amedeus of Lausanne, *De Maria Virginea Matre, Homilia VII*: PL 188, 1337; S. Ch. 72, p. 184.

84. *De Virginitate Perpetua Sanctae Mariae*, chapter XII: PL 96, 106.

85. Second Vatican Council, Dogmatic Constitution on the Church, *Lumen Gentium*, 54: AAS 57 (1965), p. 59. Cf. Pope Paul VI, *Allocutio ad Patres Conciliares Habita, Altera Exacta Concilii Oecumenici Vaticani Secundi Sessione*, December 4, 1963: AAS 56 (1964), p. 57.

86. Cf. Second Vatican Council, Dogmatic Constitution of the Church, *Lumen Gentium*, 6, 7-8. 9-11: AAS 57 (1965), pp. 8-9, 9-12, 12-21.

87. Ibid., 63: AAS 57 (1965), p. 64.

88. St. Cyprian, *De Catholicae Ecclesiae Unitate*, 5: CSEL 3, p. 214.

89. Isaac de Stella, *Sermo LI, In Assumptione B. Mariae*: PL 194, 1863.

90. *Sermo XXX*, 1: S. Ch. 164, p. 134.

91. Cf. Second Vatican Council, Dogmatic Constitution on the Church, *Lumen Gentium*, 66-69: AAS 57 (1965), pp. 65-67.

92. Cf. Second Vatican Council, Dogmatic Constitution on Divine Revelation, *Dei Verbum*, 25: AAS 58 (1966), pp. 829-830.

93. Op cit., 13: AAS 50 (1964), p. 103.

94. Cf. *Officum Magni Canonis Paracletici, Magnum Orologion*, Athens 1963, p. 558; passim in liturgical canons and prayers: cf. Sophronius Eustradiadou, *Theotokarion, Chennevieres, sur Marne* 1931, pp. 9, 19.

95. Cf. Second Vatican Council, Dogmatic Constitution on the Church, *Lumen Gentium*, 69: AAS 57 (1965), pp. 66-67

96. Cf. ibid., 66: AAS 57 (1965), p. 65; Constitution on the Sacred Liturgy, *Sacrosanctum Concilium*, 103: AAS 56 (1964), p. 125.

97. Cf. Second Vatican Council, Dogmatic Constitution on the Church, *Lumen Gentium*, 67: AAS 57 (1965), pp. 65-66.

98. Ibid., 66: AAS 57 (1965), p. 65.

99. Cf. Pope Paul VI, Address in the Vatican Basilica to the Fathers of the Council, November 21, 1964: AAS 56 (1964), p. 1017.

100. Cf. Second Vatican Council, Decree on Ecumenism, *Unitatis Redintegratio*, 20: AAS 57 (1965), p. 105.

101. Encyclical Letter, *Adiutricem Populi*: ASS 28 (1895-1896), p. 135.

102. Cf. Second Vatican Council, Dogmatic Constitution on the Church, *Lumen Gentium*, 56: AAS 57 (1965), p. 60.

103. Cf. St. Peter Chrysologus, *Sermo CXLIII*: PL 52, 583.

104. Second Vatican Council, Dogmatic Constitution on the Church, *Lumen Gentium*, 55: AAS 57 (1965), pp. 59-60.

105. Cf. Pope Paul VI, Apostolic Constitution, *Signum Magnum*, I: AAS 59 (1967), pp. 467-468: *Roman Missal*, September 15, Prayer over the gifts.

106. Cf. Dogmatic Constitution on the Church, *Lumen Gentium*, 67: AAS 57 (1965), pp. 65-66.

107. St. Augustine, *In Johannis Evangelium Tractatus X*, 3: CCL 36, pp. 101-102; *Epistula 243, Ad Laetum*, 9: CSEL 57, pp. 575-576; St. Bede, *In Lucae Evangelium Expositio*, IV, XI, 28: CCL 120, p. 237; *Homilia I*, 4: CCL 122, pp. 26-27.

108. Cf. Second Vatican Council, Dogmatic Constitution on the Church, *Lumen Gentium*, 58: AAS 57 (1965), p. 61.

109. *Roman Missal*, IV Sunday of Advent, Collect. Similarly the Collect of 25 March, which may be used in place of the previous one in the recitation of the Angelus.

110. Pope Pius XII, Letter to the Archbishop of Manila, "*Philippinas Insulas*": AAS 38 (1946), p. 419.

111. Discourse to the participants in the Third Dominican International Rosary Congress: *Insegnamenti di Paolo VI* , 1, (1963) pp. 463-464.

112. In AAS 58 (1966), pp. 745-749.

113. In AAS 61 (1969), pp. 649-654.

114. Cf. 13: AAS 56 (1964), p. 103.

115. Decree on the Lay Apostolate, *Apostolicam Actuositatem*, 11: AAS 58 (1966), p. 848.

116. Cf. Second Vatican Council, Dogmatic Constitution on the Church, *Lumen Gentium*, 11: AAS 57 (1965), p. 16.

117. Cf. Second Vatican Council, Decree on the Lay Apostolate, *Apostolicam Actuositatem*, 11: AAS 58 (1966), p. 848.

118. Op cit., 27.

119. Second Vatican Council, Dogmatic Constitution on the Church, *Lumen Gentium*, 53: AAS 57 (1965), pp. 58-59.

120. *La Divina Commedia*, Paradiso XXXIII, 4-6.

121. Cf. Second Vatican Council, Dogmatic Constitution on the Church, *Lumen Gentium*, 60-63; AAS 57 (1965), pp. 62-64.

122. Cf. ibid., 65: AAS 57 (1965), pp. 64-65.

123. Ibid., 65: AAS 57 (1965), p. 64.

124. Cf. Second Vatican Council, Pastoral Constitution on the Church in the Modern World, *Gaudium et Spes*, 22: AAS 58 (1966), pp. 1042-1044.

125. Cf. *Roman Missal*, 31 May, Collect.

REDEMPTORIS MATER (THE MOTHER OF THE REDEEMER): ON THE BLESSED VIRGIN MARY IN THE LIFE OF THE PILGRIM CHURCH

An Encyclical Letter of His Holiness Pope John Paul II

MARCH 25, 1987

Venerable Brothers and dear Sons and Daughters,
Health and the Apostolic Blessing.

INTRODUCTION

1.   The Mother of the Redeemer has a precise place in the plan of salvation, for "when the time had fully come, God sent forth his Son, born of woman, born under the law, to redeem those who were under the law, so that we might receive adoption as sons. And because you are sons, God has sent the Spirit of his Son into our hearts, crying, 'Abba! Father!'" (Gal 4:4-6)

With these words of the Apostle Paul, which the Second Vatican Council takes up at the beginning of its treatment of the Blessed Virgin Mary,[1] I too wish to begin my reflection on the role of Mary in the mystery of Christ and on her active and exemplary presence in the life of the Church. For they are words which celebrate together the love of the Father, the mission of the Son, the gift of the Spirit, the role of the woman from whom the Redeemer was born, and our own divine filiation, in the mystery of the "fullness of time."[2]

This "fullness" indicates the moment fixed from all eternity when the Father sent his Son "that whoever believes in him should not perish but have eternal life" (Jn 3:16). It denotes the blessed moment when the Word that "was with God . . . became flesh and dwelt among us" (Jn 1:1, 14), and made himself our brother. It marks the moment when the Holy Spirit, who had already infused the fullness of grace into Mary of Nazareth, formed in her virginal womb the human nature of Christ. This "fullness" marks the moment when, with the entrance of the eternal into time, time itself is redeemed, and being filled with the mystery of Christ becomes definitively "salvation time." Finally, this "fullness" designates the hidden beginning of the Church's journey. In the liturgy the Church salutes Mary of Nazareth as the Church's own beginning,[3] for in the event of the Immaculate Conception the Church sees projected, and anticipated in her most noble member, the saving grace of Easter. And above all, in the Incarnation she encounters Christ and Mary indissolubly joined: he who is the Church's Lord and Head and she who, uttering the first fiat of the New Covenant, prefigures the Church's condition as spouse and mother.

2.   Strengthened by the presence of Christ (cf. Mt 28:20), the Church journeys through time towards the consummation of the ages and goes to meet the Lord who comes. But on this journey—and I wish to make this point straightaway—she proceeds along the path already trodden by the Virgin Mary, who "*advanced in her pilgrimage of faith, and loyally persevered in her union with her Son unto the cross.*"[4]

I take these very rich and evocative words from the Constitution *Lumen Gentium*, which in its concluding part offers a clear summary of the Church's doctrine on the Mother of Christ, whom she venerates as her beloved Mother and as her model in faith hope and charity.

Shortly after the Council, my great predecessor Paul VI decided to speak further of the Blessed Virgin. In the Encyclical *Epistle Christi Matri* and subsequently in the Apostolic Exhortations *Signum Magnum* and *Marialis Cultus*[5] he expounded the foundations and criteria of the special veneration which the Mother of Christ receives in the Church, as well as the various forms of Marian devotion—liturgical, popular and private—which respond to the spirit of faith.

3.   The circumstance which now moves me to take up this subject once more is *the prospect of the year 2000*, now drawing near, in which the Bimillennial Jubilee of the birth of Jesus Christ at the same time directs our gaze towards his Mother. In recent years, various opinions have been voiced suggesting that it would be fitting to precede that anniversary by a similar Jubilee in celebration of the birth of Mary.

In fact, even though it is not possible to establish an exact *chronological point* for identifying the date of Mary's birth, the Church has constantly been aware that *Mary appeared* on the horizon *of salvation history before Christ.*[6] It is a fact that when "the fullness of time" was definitively drawing near—the saving advent of Emmanuel—he who was from eternity destined to be his Mother already existed on earth. The fact that she "preceded" the coming of Christ is reflected every year *in the liturgy of Advent.* Therefore, if to that ancient historical expectation of the Savior we compare these years which are bringing us closer to the end of the second Millennium after Christ and to the beginning of the third, it becomes fully comprehensible that in this present period we wish to turn in a special way to her, the one who in the "night" of the Advent expectation began to shine like a true "Morning Star" (*Stella Matutina*). For just as this star, together with the "dawn," precedes the rising of the sun, so Mary from the time of her Immaculate Conception preceded the coming of the Savior, the rising of the "Sun of Justice" in the history of the human race.[7]

Her presence in the midst of Israel—a presence so discreet as to pass almost unnoticed by the eyes of her contemporaries—shone very clearly before the Eternal One, who had associated this hidden "daughter of Sion" (cf. Zep 3:14; Zec 2:10) with the plan of salvation embracing the whole history of humanity. With good reason, then, at the end of this Millennium, we Christians who know that the providential plan of the Most Holy Trinity is *the central reality of Revelation and of faith* feel the need to emphasize the unique presence of the Mother of Christ in history, especially during these last years leading up to the year 2000.

4.   The Second Vatican Council prepares us for this by presenting in its teaching *the Mother of God in the mystery of Christ and of the Church.* If it is true, as the Council itself proclaims,[8] that "only in the mystery of the Incarnate Word does the mystery of man take on light," then this principle must be applied in a very particular way to that exceptional "daughter of the human race," that extraordinary "woman" who became the Mother of Christ. Only *in the mystery of Christ is her mystery fully made clear.* Thus has the Church sought to interpret it from the very beginning: the mystery of the Incarnation has enabled her to penetrate and to make ever clearer the mystery of the Mother of the Incarnate Word. The Council of Ephesus (AD 431) was of decisive importance in clarifying this, for during that Council, to the great joy of Christians, the truth of the divine motherhood of Mary was solemnly confirmed as a truth of the Church's faith. Mary *is the Mother of God* (*Theotókos*), since by the power of the Holy Spirit she conceived in her virginal womb and brought into the world Jesus Christ, the Son of God, who is of one being

with the Father.[9] "The Son of God . . . born of the Virgin Mary . . . has truly been made one of us,"[10] has been made man. Thus, through the mystery of Christ, on the horizon of the Church's faith there shines in its fullness the mystery of his Mother. In turn, the dogma of the divine motherhood of Mary was for the Council of Ephesus and is for the Church like a seal upon the dogma of the Incarnation, in which the Word truly assumes human nature into the unity of his person, without cancelling out that nature.

5.   The Second Vatican Council, by presenting Mary in the mystery of Christ, also finds the path to a deeper understanding of the mystery of the Church. Mary, as the Mother of Christ, *is in a particular way united with the Church*, "which the Lord established as his own body."[11] It is significant that the conciliar text places this truth about the Church as the Body of Christ (according to the teaching of the Pauline Letters) in close proximity to the truth that the Son of God "through the power of the Holy Spirit was born of the Virgin Mary." The reality of the Incarnation finds a sort of extension *in the mystery of the Church—the Body of Christ*. And one cannot think of the reality of the Incarnation without referring to Mary, the Mother of the Incarnate Word.

In these reflections, however, I wish to consider primarily that "pilgrimage of faith" in which "the Blessed Virgin advanced," faithfully preserving her union with Christ.[12] In this way the *"twofold bond"* which unites the Mother of God *with Christ and with the Church* takes on historical significance. Nor is it just a question of the Virgin Mother's life-story, of her personal journey of faith and "the better part" which is hers in the mystery of salvation; it is also a question of the history of the whole People of God, *of all those who take part* in the same *"pilgrimage of faith."*

The Council expresses this when it states in another passage that Mary "has gone before," becoming "a model of the Church in the matter of faith, charity and perfect union with Christ."[13] This *"going before" as a figure or model* is in reference to the intimate mystery of the Church, as she actuates and accomplishes her own saving mission by uniting in herself—as Mary did—the qualities *of mother and virgin*. She is a virgin who "keeps whole and pure the fidelity she has pledged to her Spouse" and "becomes herself a mother," for "she brings forth to a new and immortal life children who are conceived of the Holy Spirit and born of God."[14]

6.   All this is accomplished in a great historical process, comparable "to a journey." *The pilgrimage of faith indicates the interior history*, that is, the story of souls. But it is also the story of all human beings, subject here on earth to transitoriness, and part

of the historical dimension. In the following reflections we wish to concentrate first of all on the present, which in itself is not yet history, but which nevertheless is constantly forming it, also in the sense of the history of salvation. Here there opens up a broad prospect, within which the *Blessed Virgin Mary continues to "go before" the People of God.* Her exceptional pilgrimage of faith represents a constant point of reference for the Church, for individuals and for communities, for peoples and nations and, in a sense, for all humanity. It is indeed difficult to encompass and measure its range.

The Council emphasizes that *the Mother of God is already the eschatological fulfillment of the Church:* "In the most holy Virgin the Church has already reached that perfection whereby she exists without spot or wrinkle (cf. Eph 5:27)"; and at the same time the Council says that "the followers of Christ still strive to increase in holiness by conquering sin, and *so they raise their eyes to Mary,* who shines forth to the whole community of the elect as a model of the virtues."[15] The pilgrimage of faith no longer belongs to the Mother of the Son of God: glorified at the side of her Son in heaven, Mary has already crossed the threshold between faith and that vision which is "face to face" (1 Cor 13:12). At the same time, however, in this eschatological fulfillment, Mary does not cease to be the "Star of the Sea" (*Maris Stella*)[16] for all those who are still on the journey of faith. If they lift their eyes to her from their earthly existence, they do so because "the Son whom she brought forth is he whom God placed as the first-born among many brethren (Rom 8:29),"[17] and also because "in the birth and development" of these brothers and sisters "she cooperates with a maternal love."[18]

Part I

MARY IN THE MYSTERY OF CHRIST

1. FULL OF GRACE

7.   "Blessed be the God and Father of our Lord Jesus Christ, who has blessed us in Christ with every spiritual blessing in the heavenly places" (Eph 1:3). These words of the *Letter to the Ephesians* reveal the eternal design of God the Father, his plan of man's salvation in Christ. It is a universal plan, which concerns all men and women created in the image and likeness of God (cf. Gn 1:26). Just as all are included in the creative work of God "in the beginning," so all are eternally included in the divine plan of salvation, which is to be completely revealed, in the "fullness of time," with the final coming of Christ. In fact, the God who is the "Father of our

Lord Jesus Christ"—these are the next words of the same *Letter*—"*chose us* in him *before the foundation of the world*, that we should be holy and blameless before him. He destined us in love to be his sons through Jesus Christ, according to the purpose of his will, to the praise of his glorious grace, which he freely bestowed on us in *the Beloved*. In him we have redemption through his blood, the forgiveness of our trespasses, according to the riches of his grace" (Eph 1:4-7).

The divine plan of salvation—which was fully revealed to us with the coming of Christ—is eternal. And according to the teaching contained in the Letter just quoted and in other Pauline Letters (cf. Col 1:12-14; Rom 3:24; Gal 3:13; 2 Cor 5:18-29), it is also *eternally linked to Christ*. It includes everyone, but it reserves a special place for the "*woman*" who is the Mother of him to whom the Father has entrusted the work of salvation.[19] As the Second Vatican Council says, "she is already prophetically foreshadowed in that promise made to our first parents after their fall into sin"—according to the Book of *Genesis* (cf. 3:15). "Likewise she is the Virgin who is to conceive and bear a son, whose name will be called Emmanuel"— according to the words of Isaiah (cf. 7:14).[20] In this way the Old Testament prepares that "fullness of time" when God "sent forth his Son, born of woman . . . so that we might receive adoption as sons." The coming into the world of the Son of God is an event recorded in the first chapters of the Gospels according to Luke and Matthew.

8.   Mary is definitively *introduced into the mystery of Christ* through this event: *the Annunciation* by the angel. This takes place at Nazareth, within the concrete circumstances of the history of Israel, the people which first received God's promises. The divine messenger says to the Virgin: "Hail, full of grace, the Lord is with you" (Lk 1:28). Mary "was greatly troubled at the saying, and considered in her mind what sort of greeting this might be" (Lk 1:29): what could those extraordinary words mean, and in particular the expression "full of grace" (*kecharitoméne*).[21]

If we wish to meditate together with Mary on these words, and especially on the expression "full of grace," we can find a significant echo in the very passage from the *Letter to the Ephesians* quoted above. And if after the announcement of the heavenly messenger the Virgin of Nazareth is also called "blessed among women" (cf. Lk 1:42), it is because of that blessing with which "God the Father" has filled us "in the heavenly places, in Christ." It is a *spiritual blessing* which is meant for all people and which bears in itself fullness and universality ("every blessing"). It flows from that love which, in the Holy Spirit, unites the consubstantial Son to the Father. At the same time, it is a blessing poured out through Jesus Christ upon human history until the end: upon all people. This blessing, however, refers *to Mary in a special and exceptional degree*: for she was greeted by Elizabeth as "blessed among women."

The double greeting is due to the fact that in the soul of this "daughter of Sion" there is manifested, in a sense, all the "glory of grace," that grace which "the Father . . . has given us in his beloved Son." For the messenger greets Mary as "full of grace"; he calls her thus as if it were her real name. He does not call her by her proper earthly name: Miryam (Mary), but *by this new name: "full of grace."* What does this name mean? Why does the archangel address the Virgin of Nazareth in this way?

In the language of the Bible "grace" means a special gift, which according to the New Testament has its source precisely in the Trinitarian life of God himself, God who is love (cf. 1 Jn 4:8). The fruit of this love is *"the election"* of which the *Letter to the Ephesians* speaks. On the part of God, this election is the eternal desire to save man through a sharing in his own life (cf. 2 Pt 1:4) in Christ: it is salvation through a sharing in supernatural life. The effect of this eternal gift, of this grace of man's election by God, is like a *seed of holiness*, or a spring which rises in the soul as a gift from God himself, who through grace gives life and holiness to those who are chosen. In this way there is fulfilled, that is to say there comes about, that "blessing" of man "with every spiritual blessing," that "being his adopted sons and daughters . . . in Christ," in him who is eternally the "beloved Son" of the Father.

When we read that the messenger addresses Mary as "full of grace," the Gospel context, which mingles revelations and ancient promises, enables us to understand that among all the "spiritual blessings in Christ" this is a special "blessing." In the mystery of Christ she is *present* even "before the creation of the world," as the one whom the Father "has chosen" *as Mother* of his Son in the Incarnation. And, what is more, together with the Father, the Son has chosen her, entrusting her eternally to the Spirit of holiness. In an entirely special and exceptional way Mary is united to Christ, and similarly she *is eternally loved in this "beloved Son,"* this Son who is of one being with the Father, in whom is concentrated all the "glory of grace." At the same time, she is and remains perfectly open to this "gift from above" (cf. Jas 1:17). As the Council teaches, Mary "stands out among the poor and humble of the Lord, who confidently await and receive salvation from him."[22]

9.   If the greeting and the name "full of grace" say all this, in the context of the angel's announcement they refer first of all *to the election of Mary as Mother of the Son of God*. But at the same time the "fullness of grace" indicates all the supernatural

munificence from which Mary benefits by being chosen and destined to be the Mother of Christ. If this election is fundamental for the accomplishment of God's salvific designs for humanity, and if the eternal choice in Christ and the vocation to the dignity of adopted children is the destiny of everyone, then the election of Mary is wholly exceptional and unique. Hence also the singularity and uniqueness of her place in the mystery of Christ.

The divine messenger says to her: "Do not be afraid, Mary, for you have found favor with God. And behold, you will conceive in your womb and bear a son, and you shall call his name Jesus. He will be great, and will be called the Son of the Most High" (Lk 1:30-32). And when the Virgin, disturbed by that extraordinary greeting, asks: "How shall this be, since I have no husband?" she receives from the angel the confirmation and explanation of the preceding words. Gabriel says to her: "*The Holy Spirit will come upon you*, and the power of the Most High will overshadow you; therefore the child to be born will be called holy, the Son of God" (Lk 1:35).

The Annunciation, therefore, is the revelation of the mystery of the Incarnation at the very beginning of its fulfillment on earth. God's salvific giving of himself and his life, in some way to all creation but directly to man, reaches *one of its high points in the mystery of the Incarnation.* This is indeed a high point among all the gifts of grace conferred in the history of man and of the universe: Mary is "full of grace," because it is precisely in her that the Incarnation of the Word, the hypostatic union of the Son of God with human nature, is accomplished and fulfilled. As the Council says, Mary is "the Mother of the Son of God. As a result she is also the favorite daughter of the Father and the temple of the Holy Spirit. Because of this gift of sublime grace, she far surpasses all other creatures, both in heaven and on earth."[23]

10.   The *Letter to the Ephesians*, speaking of the "glory of grace" that "God, the Father . . . has bestowed on us in his beloved Son," adds: "In him we have redemption through his blood" (Eph 1:7). According to the belief formulated in solemn documents of the Church, this "glory of grace" is manifested in the Mother of God through the fact that she has been "redeemed in a more sublime manner."[24] By virtue of the richness of the grace of the beloved Son, by reason of the redemptive merits of him who willed to become her Son, Mary was *preserved from the inheritance of original sin.*[25] In this way, from the first moment of her conception—which is to say of her existence-she belonged to Christ, sharing in the salvific and sanctifying grace and in that love which has its beginning in the "Beloved," the Son of the Eternal Father, who through the Incarnation became her own Son. Consequently, through the power of the Holy Spirit, in the order of grace, which is a participation

in the divine nature, *Mary receives life from him to whom* she herself, in the order of earthly generation, *gave life* as a mother. The liturgy does not hesitate to call her "mother of her Creator"[26] and to hail her with the words which Dante Alighieri places on the lips of St. Bernard: "daughter of your Son."[27] And since Mary receives this "new life" with a fullness corresponding to the Son's love for the Mother, and thus corresponding to the dignity of the divine motherhood, the angel at the Annunciation calls her "full of grace."

11.   In the salvific design of the Most Holy Trinity, the mystery of the Incarnation constitutes the superabundant *fulfillment of the promise* made by God to man *after original sin*, after that first sin whose effects oppress the whole earthly history of man (cf. Gn 3:15). And so, there comes into the world a Son, "the seed of the woman" who will crush the evil of sin in its very origins: "he will crush the head of the serpent." As we see from the words of the Proto-gospel, the victory of the woman's Son will not take place without a hard struggle, a struggle that is to extend through the whole of human history. The "enmity," foretold at the beginning, is confirmed in the Apocalypse (the book of the final events of the Church and the world), in which there recurs the sign of the "woman," this time "clothed with the sun" (Rev 12:1).

Mary, Mother of the Incarnate Word, is placed *at the very center of that enmity*, that struggle which accompanies the history of humanity on earth and the history of salvation itself. In this central place, she who belongs to the "weak and poor of the Lord" bears in herself, like no other member of the human race, that "glory of grace" which the Father "has bestowed on us in his beloved Son," and this *grace determines the extraordinary greatness and beauty* of her whole being. Mary thus remains before God, and also before the whole of humanity, as the unchangeable and inviolable sign of God's election, spoken of in Paul's Letter: "in Christ . . . he chose us . . . before the foundation of the world, . . . he destined us . . . to be his sons" (Eph 1:4, 5). This election is more powerful than any experience of evil and sin, than all that "enmity" which marks the history of man. In this history Mary remains a sign of sure hope.

2. BLESSED IS SHE WHO BELIEVED

12.   Immediately after the narration of the Annunciation, the Evangelist Luke guides us in the footsteps of the Virgin of Nazareth towards "a city of Judah" (Lk 1:39). According to scholars this city would be the modern Ain Karim, situated

in the mountains, not far from Jerusalem. Mary arrived there "in haste," *to visit Elizabeth* her kinswoman. The reason for her visit is also to be found in the fact that at the Annunciation Gabriel had made special mention of Elizabeth, who in her old age had conceived a son by her husband Zechariah, through the power of God: "your kinswoman Elizabeth in her old age has also conceived a Son; and this is the sixth month with her who was called barren. *For with God nothing will be impossible*" (Lk 1:36-37). The divine messenger had spoken of what had been accomplished in Elizabeth in order to answer Mary's question. "How shall this be, since I have no husband?" (Lk 1:34) It is to come to pass precisely through the "power of the Most High," just as it happened in the case of Elizabeth, and even more so.

Moved by charity, therefore, Mary goes to the house of her kinswoman. When Mary enters, Elizabeth replies to her greeting and feels the child leap in her womb, and being "filled with the Holy Spirit" she *greets Mary* with a loud cry: "Blessed are you among women, and blessed is the fruit of your womb!" (cf. Lk 1:40-42) Elizabeth's exclamation or acclamation was subsequently to become part of the Hail Mary, as a continuation of the angel's greeting, thus becoming one of the Church's most frequently used prayers. But still more significant are the words of Elizabeth in the question which follows: "And why is this granted me, that the mother of my Lord should come to me?" (Lk 1:43) Elizabeth bears witness to Mary: she recognizes and proclaims that before her stands the Mother of the Lord, the Mother of the Messiah. The son whom Elizabeth is carrying in her womb also shares in this witness: "The babe in my womb leaped for joy" (Lk 1:44). This child is the future John the Baptist, who at the Jordan will point out Jesus as the Messiah.

While every word of Elizabeth's greeting is filled with meaning, her final words would seem to have *fundamental importance*: "And blessed is she who believed that there would be a fulfillment of what was spoken to her from the Lord" (Lk 1:45).[28] These words can be linked with the little "full of grace" of the angel's greeting. Both of these texts reveal an essential Mariological content, namely the truth about Mary, who has become really present in the mystery of Christ precisely because she "has believed." The *fullness of grace* announced by the angel means the gift of God himself. *Mary's faith*, proclaimed by Elizabeth at the Visitation, indicates *how* the Virgin of Nazareth *responded to this gift*.

13.   As the Council teaches, "'The obedience of faith' (Rom 16:26; cf. Rom 1:5; 2 Cor 10:5-6) must be given to God who reveals, an obedience by which man entrusts his whole self freely to God."[29] This description of faith found perfect realization in Mary. The "decisive" moment was the Annunciation, and the very words of Elizabeth: "And blessed is she who believed" refer primarily to that very moment.[30]

Indeed, at the Annunciation Mary entrusted herself to God completely, with the "full submission of intellect and will," manifesting "the obedience of faith" to him who spoke to her through his messenger.[31] She responded, therefore, *with all her human and feminine "I,"* and this response of faith included both perfect cooperation with "the grace of God that precedes and assists" and perfect openness to the action of the Holy Spirit, who "constantly brings faith to completion by his gifts."[32]

The word of the living God, announced to Mary by the angel, referred to her: "And behold, you will conceive in your womb and bear a son" (Lk 1:31). By accepting this announcement, Mary was to become the "Mother of the Lord," and the divine mystery of the Incarnation was to be accomplished in her: "The Father of mercies willed that the consent of the predestined Mother should precede the Incarnation."[33] And Mary gives this consent, after she has heard everything the messenger has to say. She says: "Behold, I am the handmaid of the Lord; let it be to me according to your word" (Lk 1:38). This fiat of Mary—"let it be to me"—was decisive, on the human level, for the accomplishment of the divine mystery. There is a complete harmony with the words of the Son, who, according to the *Letter to the Hebrews*, says to the Father as he comes into the world: "Sacrifices and offering you have not desired, but *a body you have prepared for me.* . . . Lo, I have come to do your will, O God" (Heb 10:5-7). The mystery of the Incarnation was accomplished when Mary uttered her fiat: "Let it be to me according to your word," which made possible, as far as it depended upon her in the divine plan, the granting of her Son's desire.

Mary uttered this *fiat in faith.* In faith she entrusted herself to God without reserve and "devoted herself totally as the handmaid of the Lord to the person and work of her Son."[34] And as the Fathers of the Church teach—she conceived this Son in her mind before she conceived him in her womb: precisely in faith![35] Rightly therefore does Elizabeth praise Mary: "And blessed is she who believed *that there would be a fulfillment* of what was spoken to her from the Lord." These words have already been fulfilled: Mary of Nazareth presents herself at the threshold of Elizabeth and Zechariah's house as the Mother of the Son of God. This is Elizabeth's joyful discovery: "The mother of my Lord comes to me"!

14. Mary's faith can also be *compared to that of Abraham,* whom St. Paul calls "our father in faith" (cf. Rom 4:12). In the salvific economy of God's revelation, Abraham's faith constitutes the beginning of the Old Covenant; Mary's faith at the Annunciation inaugurates the New Covenant. Just as Abraham "*in hope believed against hope,* that he should become the father of many nations" (cf. Rom 4:18), so Mary, at the Annunciation, having professed her virginity ("How shall this be, since

I have no husband?") *believed* that through the power of the Most High, by the power of the Holy Spirit, she would become the Mother of God's Son in accordance with the angel's revelation: "The child to be born will be called holy, the Son of God" (Lk 1:35).

However, Elizabeth's words "And blessed is she who believed" do not apply only to that particular moment of the Annunciation. Certainly the Annunciation is the culminating moment of Mary's faith in her awaiting of Christ, but it is also the point of departure from which her whole "journey towards God" begins, her whole pilgrimage of faith. And on this road, in an eminent and truly heroic manner—indeed with an ever greater heroism of faith—the "obedience" which she professes to the word of divine revelation will be fulfilled. Mary's "obedience of faith" during the whole of her pilgrimage will show surprising similarities to the faith of Abraham. Just like the Patriarch of the People of God, so too Mary, during the pilgrimage of her filial and maternal *fiat*, "in hope believed against hope." Especially during certain stages of this journey the blessing granted to her "who believed" will be revealed with particular vividness. To believe means "to abandon oneself" to the truth of the word of the living God, knowing and humbly recognizing "how unsearchable are his judgments and how *inscrutable his ways*" (Rom 11:33). Mary, who by the eternal will of the Most High stands, one may say, at the very center of those "inscrutable ways" and "unsearchable judgments" of God, conforms herself to them in the dim light of faith, accepting fully and with a ready heart everything that is decreed in the divine plan.

15.   When at the Annunciation Mary hears of the Son whose Mother she is to become and to whom "she will give the name Jesus" (Savior), she also learns that "the Lord God will give to him the throne of his father David," and that "he will reign over the house of Jacob for ever and of his kingdom there will be no end" (Lk 1:32-33). The hope of the whole of Israel was directed towards this. The promised Messiah is to be "great," and the heavenly messenger also announces that "*he will be great*"—great both by bearing the name of Son of the Most High and by the fact that he is to assume the inheritance of David. He is therefore to be a king, he is to reign "over the house of Jacob." Mary had grown up in the midst of these expectations of her people: could she guess, at the moment of the Annunciation, the vital significance of the angel's words? And how is one to understand that "kingdom" which "will have no end"?

Although through faith she may have perceived in that instant the was the mother of the "Messiah King," nevertheless she replied: "*Behold, I am the handmaid of the Lord*; let it be to me according to your word" (Lk 1:38). From the first moment

Mary professed above all the "obedience of faith," abandoning herself to the meaning which was given to the words of the Annunciation by him from whom they proceeded: God himself.

16.   Later, a little further along this way of the "obedience of faith," Mary hears *other words*: those uttered by *Simeon* in the Temple of Jerusalem. It was now forty days after the birth of Jesus when, in accordance with the precepts of the Law of Moses, Mary and Joseph "brought him up to Jerusalem to present him to the Lord" (Lk 2:22). The birth had taken place in conditions of extreme poverty. We know from Luke that when, on the occasion of the census ordered by the Roman authorities, Mary went with Joseph to Bethlehem, having found "no place in the inn," *she gave birth to her Son in a stable* and "laid him in a manger" (cf. Lk 2:7).

A just and God-fearing man, called Simeon, appears at this beginning of Mary's "journey" of faith. His words, suggested by the Holy Spirit (cf. Lk 2:25-27), confirm the truth of the Annunciation. For we read that he took up in his arms the child to whom—in accordance with the angel's command—the name Jesus was given (cf. Lk 2:21). Simeon's words match the meaning of this name, which is Savior: "God is salvation." Turning to the Lord, he says: "For my eyes have seen your salvation which you have prepared *in the presence of all peoples*, a light for revelation to the Gentiles, and for glory to your people Israel" (Lk 2:30-32). At the same time, however, Simeon addresses Mary with the following words: "Behold, this child is set for the fall and rising of many in Israel, and for a *sign that is spoken against*, that thoughts out of many hearts may be revealed"; and he adds with direct reference to her: "and a sword will pierce through your own soul also" (cf. Lk 2:34-35). Simeon's words cast new light on the announcement which Mary had heard from the angel: Jesus is the Savior, he is "a *light* for revelation" to mankind. Is not this what was manifested in a way on Christmas night, when the shepherds come to the stable (cf. Lk 2:8-20)? Is not this what was to be manifested even more clearly in the coming of the *Magi from the East* (cf. Mt 2:1-12)? But at the same time, at the very beginning of his life, the Son of Mary, and his Mother with him, will experience in themselves the truth of those other words of Simeon: "a sign that is spoken against" (Lk 2:34). Simeon's words seem like a *second Annunciation to Mary*, for they tell her of the actual historical situation in which the Son is to accomplish his mission, namely, in misunderstanding and sorrow. While this announcement on the one hand confirms her faith in the accomplishment of the divine promises of salvation, on the other hand it also reveals to her that she will have to live her obedience of faith in suffering, at the side of the suffering Savior, and that her motherhood will be mysterious and sorrowful. Thus, after the visit of the Magi who came from the East, after their homage ("they fell down and worshipped him") and after they had offered gifts (cf. Mt 2:11), Mary together with the child *has to flee into Egypt* in the protective care of Joseph, for "Herod is about to search for the child, to destroy him" (cf. Mt 2:13). And until the death of Herod they will have to remain in Egypt (cf. Mt 2:15).

17.   When the Holy Family returns to Nazareth after Herod's death, there begins the long *period of the hidden life.* She "who believed that there would be a fulfillment of what was spoken to her from the Lord" (Lk 1:45) lives the reality of these words day by day. And daily at her side is the Son to whom "*she gave the name Jesus*"; therefore in contact with him she certainly uses this name, a fact which would have surprised no one, since the name had long been in use in Israel. Nevertheless, Mary knows that he who bears the name *Jesus has been called by the angel "the Son of the Most High"* (cf. Lk 1:32). Mary knows she has conceived and given birth to him "without having a husband," by the power of the Holy Spirit, by the power of the Most High who overshadowed her (cf. Lk 1:35), just as at the time of Moses and the Patriarchs the cloud covered the presence of God (cf. Ex 24:16; 40:34-35; 1 Kgs 8:10-12). Therefore Mary knows that the Son to whom she gave birth in a virginal manner is precisely that "Holy One," the Son of God, of whom the angel spoke to her.

During the years of Jesus' hidden life in the house at Nazareth, *Mary's life* too is "*hid with Christ in God*" (cf. Col 3:3) *through faith.* For faith is contact with the mystery of God. Every day Mary is in constant contact with the ineffable mystery of God made man, a mystery that surpasses everything revealed in the Old Covenant. From the moment of the Annunciation, the mind of the Virgin-Mother has been initiated into the radical "newness" of God's self-revelation and has been made aware of the mystery. She is the first of those "little ones" of whom Jesus will say one day: "Father, . . . you have hidden these things from the wise and understanding and revealed them to babes" (Mt 11:25). For "no one knows the Son except the Father" (Mt 11:27). If this is the case, how can Mary "know the Son"? Of course she does not know him as the Father does; and yet she is *the first of those to whom the Father "has chosen to reveal him"* (cf. Mt 11:26-27; 1 Cor 2:11). If though, from the moment of the Annunciation, the Son—whom only the Father knows completely, as the one who begets him in the eternal "today" (cf. Ps 2:7) was revealed to Mary, she, his Mother, is in contact with the truth about her Son only in faith and through faith! She is therefore blessed, because "she has believed," and continues to *believe day after day* amidst all the trials and the adversities of Jesus' infancy and then during the years of the hidden life at Nazareth, where he "was obedient to them" (Lk 2:51). He was obedient both to Mary and also to Joseph, since Joseph took the place of his father in people's eyes; for this reason, the Son of Mary was regarded by the people as "the carpenter's son" (Mt 13:55).

The Mother of *that Son*, therefore, mindful of what has been told her at the Annunciation and in subsequent events, bears within herself the radical "newness" of faith: *the beginning of the New Covenant*. This is the beginning of the Gospel, the joyful Good News. However, it is not difficult to see in that beginning a particular heaviness of heart, linked with a sort of night of faith"—to use the words of St. John of the Cross—a kind of "veil" through which one has to draw near to the Invisible One and to live in intimacy with the mystery.[36] And this is the way that Mary, for many years, *lived in intimacy with the mystery of her Son*, and went forward in her "pilgrimage of faith," while Jesus "increased in wisdom . . . and in favor with God and man" (Lk 2:52). God's predilection for him was manifested ever more clearly to people's eyes. The first human creature thus permitted to discover Christ was Mary, who lived with Joseph in the same house at Nazareth.

However, when he had been found in the Temple, and his Mother asked him, "Son, why have you treated us so?" *the twelve-year-old Jesus* answered: "Did you not know that I must be in my Father's house?" And the Evangelist adds: "*And they* (Joseph and Mary) *did not understand* the saying which he spoke to them" (Lk 2:48-50). Jesus was aware that "no one knows the Son except the Father" (cf. Mt 11:27); thus even his Mother, to whom had been revealed most completely the mystery of his divine sonship, lived in intimacy with this mystery only through faith! Living side by side with her Son under the same roof, and faithfully persevering "in her union with her Son," she "*advanced in her pilgrimage of faith*," as the Council emphasizes.[37] And so it was during Christ's public life too (cf. Mk 3:21-35) that day by day there was fulfilled in her the blessing uttered by Elizabeth at the Visitation: "Blessed is she who believed."

18.   This blessing reaches its full meaning *when Mary stands beneath the Cross* of her Son (cf. Jn 19:25). The Council says that this happened "not without a divine plan": by "suffering deeply with her only-begotten Son and joining herself with her maternal spirit to his sacrifice, lovingly consenting to the immolation of the victim to whom she had given birth," in this way Mary "faithfully preserved her union with her Son even to the Cross."[38] It is a union through faith—the same faith with which she had received the angel's revelation at the Annunciation. At that moment she had also heard the words: "He will be great . . . and *the Lord God* will give to him the throne of his father David, and he will reign over the house of Jacob for ever; and of his kingdom there will be no end" (Lk 1:32-33).

And now, standing at the foot of the Cross, Mary is the witness, humanly speaking, of the complete *negation of these words*. On that wood of the Cross her Son hangs in agony as one condemned. "He was despised and rejected by men; a man of sorrows . . . he was despised, and we esteemed him not": as one destroyed (cf. Is 53:3-5). How great, how heroic then is the *obedience of faith* shown by Mary in the face of God's "unsearchable judgments"! How completely she "abandons herself to God" without reserve, offering the full assent of the intellect and the will[39] to him whose "ways are inscrutable" (cf. Rom 11:33)! And how powerful too is the action of grace in her soul, how all-pervading is the influence of the Holy Spirit and of his light and power!

Through this faith Mary is perfectly united with Christ in his self-emptying. For "Christ Jesus, who, though he was in the form of God, did not count equality with God a thing to be grasped, but emptied himself, taking the form of a servant, being born in the likeness of men": precisely on Golgotha "humbled himself and became obedient unto death, even death on a cross" (cf. Phil 2:5-8). At the foot of the Cross Mary shares through faith in the shocking mystery of this self-emptying. This is perhaps the deepest *"kenosis" of faith* in human history. Through faith the Mother shares in the death of her Son, in his redeeming death; but in contrast with the faith of the disciples who fled, hers was far more enlightened. On Golgotha, Jesus through the Cross definitively confirmed that he was the "sign of contradiction" foretold by Simeon. At the same time, there were also fulfilled on Golgotha the words which Simeon had addressed to Mary: "and a sword will pierce through your own soul also."[40]

19.   Yes, truly "blessed is she who believed"! These words, spoken by Elizabeth after the Annunciation, here at the foot of the Cross seem to re-echo with supreme eloquence, and the power contained within them becomes something penetrating. From the Cross, that is to say from the very heart of the mystery of Redemption, there radiates and spreads out the prospect of that blessing of faith. It goes right back to "the beginning," and as a sharing in the sacrifice of Christ—the new Adam—it becomes in a certain sense *the counterpoise to the disobedience and disbelief* embodied in the sin of our first parents. Thus teach the Fathers of the Church and especially St. Irenaeus, quoted by the Constitution *Lumen Gentium*: "The knot of Eve's disobedience was untied by Mary's obedience; what the virgin Eve bound through her unbelief, the Virgin Mary *loosened by her faith*."[41] In the light of this comparison with Eve, the Fathers of the Church—as the Council also says— call Mary the "mother of the living" and often speak of "death through Eve, life through Mary."[42]

In the expression "Blessed is she who believed," we can therefore rightly find *a kind of "key"* which unlocks for us the innermost reality of Mary, whom the angel hailed as "full of grace." If as "full of grace" she has been eternally present in the mystery of Christ, through faith she became a sharer in that mystery in every extension of her earthly journey. She "advanced in her pilgrimage of faith" and at the same time, in a discreet yet direct and effective way, she made present to humanity *the mystery of Christ.* And she still continues to do so. Through the mystery of Christ, she too is present within mankind. Thus through the mystery of the Son the mystery of the Mother is also made clear.

3. BEHOLD YOUR MOTHER

20.   The Gospel of Luke records the moment when "a woman in the crowd raised her voice" and said to Jesus: *"Blessed is the womb that bore you, and the breasts that you sucked!"* (Lk 11:27) These words were an expression of praise of Mary as Jesus' mother according to the flesh. Probably the Mother of Jesus was not personally known to this woman; in fact, when Jesus began his messianic activity Mary did not accompany him but continued to remain at Nazareth. One could say that the words of that unknown woman in a way brought Mary out of her hiddenness.

Through these words, there flashed out in the midst of the crowd, at least for an instant, the Gospel of Jesus' infancy. This is the Gospel in which Mary is present as the mother who conceives Jesus in her womb, gives him birth and nurses him: the nursing mother referred to by the woman in the crowd. *Thanks to this motherhood, Jesus,* the Son of the Most High (cf. Lk 1:32), is a true *son of man.* He is "flesh," like every other man: he is "the Word (who) became flesh" (cf. Jn 1:14). He is of the flesh and blood of Mary![43]

But to the blessing uttered by that woman upon her who was his mother according to the flesh, Jesus replies in a significant way: "Blessed rather are *those who hear the word of God and keep it*" (Lk 11:28). He wishes to divert attention from motherhood understood only as a fleshly bond, in order to direct it towards those mysterious bonds of the spirit which develop from hearing and keeping God's word.

This same shift into the sphere of spiritual values is seen even more clearly in another response of Jesus reported by all the Synoptics. When Jesus is told that "his mother and brothers are standing outside and wish to see him," he replies: "*My mother and my brothers are those who hear the word of God and do it*" (cf. Lk

8:20-21). This he said "looking around on those who sat about him," as we read in Mark (3:34) or, according to Matthew (12:49), "stretching out his hand towards his disciples."

These statements seem to *fit in with the reply which the twelve-year-old Jesus* gave to Mary and Joseph when he was found after three days in the Temple at Jerusalem.

Now, when Jesus left Nazareth and began his public life throughout Palestine, *he was completely and exclusively "concerned with his Father's business"* (cf. Lk 2:49). He announced the Kingdom: the "Kingdom of God" and "his Father's business," which add a new dimension and meaning to everything human, and therefore to every human bond, insofar as these things relate to the goals and tasks assigned to every human being. Within this new dimension, also a bond such as that of "brotherhood" means something different from "brotherhood according to the flesh" deriving from a common origin from the same set of parents. "*Motherhood,*" too, *in the dimension of the Kingdom of God and in the radius of the fatherhood of God himself, takes on another meaning.* In the words reported by Luke, Jesus teaches precisely this new meaning of motherhood.

Is Jesus thereby distancing himself from his mother according to the flesh? Does he perhaps wish to leave her in the hidden obscurity which she herself has chosen? If this seems to be the case from the tone of those words, one must nevertheless note that the new and different motherhood which Jesus speaks of to his disciples refers precisely to Mary in a very special way. Is not Mary *the first of "those who hear the word of God and do it"*? And therefore does not the blessing uttered by Jesus in response to the woman in the crowd refer primarily to her? Without any doubt, Mary is worthy of blessing by the very fact that she became the mother of Jesus according to the flesh ("Blessed is the womb that bore you, and the breasts that you sucked"), but also and especially because already at the Annunciation she accepted the word of God, because she believed it, *because she was obedient to God,* and because she "kept" the word and "pondered it in her heart" (cf. Lk 1:38, 45; 2:19, 51) and by means of her whole life accomplished it. Thus we can say that the blessing proclaimed by Jesus is not in opposition, despite appearances, to the blessing uttered by the unknown woman, but rather coincides with that blessing in the person of this Virgin Mother, who called herself only "the handmaid of the Lord" (Lk 1:38). If it is true that "all generations will call her blessed" (cf. Lk 1:48), then it can be said that the unnamed woman was the first to confirm unwittingly that prophetic phrase of Mary's *Magnificat* and to begin the *Magnificat* of the ages.

If *through faith* Mary became the bearer of the Son given to her by the Father through the power of the Holy Spirit, while preserving her virginity intact, in that same faith she *discovered and accepted the other dimension of motherhood* revealed by Jesus during his messianic mission. One can say that this dimension of motherhood belonged to Mary from the beginning, that is to say from the moment of the conception and birth of her Son. From that time she was "the one who believed." But as the messianic mission of her Son grew clearer to her eyes and spirit, she herself as a mother became ever more open to *that new dimension of motherhood* which was to constitute her "part" beside her Son. Had she not said from the very beginning: "Behold, I am the handmaid of the Lord; let it be to me according to your word" (Lk 1:38)? Through faith Mary continued to hear and to ponder that word, in which there became ever clearer, in a way "which surpasses knowledge" (Eph 3:19), the self-revelation of the living God. Thus *in a sense* Mary as Mother became *the first "disciple" of her Son*, the first to whom he seemed to say: "Follow me," even before he addressed this call to the Apostles or to anyone else (cf. Jn 1:43).

21.   From this point of view, particularly eloquent is the passage in the *Gospel of John* which presents Mary at the wedding feast of Cana. She appears there as the Mother of Jesus at the beginning of his public life: "There was a *marriage at Cana in Galilee*, and the mother of Jesus was there; Jesus also was invited to the marriage, with his disciples" (Jn 2:1-2). From the text it appears that Jesus and his disciples were invited together with Mary, as if by reason of her presence at the celebration: the Son seems to have been invited because of his mother. We are familiar with the sequence of events which resulted from that invitation, that "beginning of the signs" wrought by Jesus—the water changed into wine—which prompts the Evangelist to say that Jesus "manifested his glory; and his disciples believed in him" (Jn 2:11).

Mary is present at Cana in Galilee as the *Mother of Jesus*, and in a significant way she *contributes* to that "beginning of the signs" which reveal the messianic power of her Son. We read: "When the wine gave out, the mother of Jesus said to him, 'They have no wine.' And Jesus said to her, 'O woman, what have you to do with me? My hour has not yet come'" (Jn 2:3-4). In John's Gospel that "hour" means the time appointed by the Father when the Son accomplishes his task and is to be glorified (cf. Jn 7:30; 8:20; 12:23, 27; 13:1; 17:1; 19:27). Even though Jesus' reply to his mother sounds like a refusal (especially if we consider the blunt statement "My hour has not yet come" rather than the question), Mary nevertheless turns to the servants and says to them: "Do whatever he tells you" (Jn 2:5). Then Jesus orders the servants to fill the stone jars with water, and the water becomes wine, better than the wine which has previously been served to the wedding guests.

What deep understanding existed between Jesus and his mother? How can we probe the mystery of their intimate spiritual union? But the fact speaks for itself. It is certain that that event already quite clearly outlines *the new dimension*, the new meaning *of Mary's motherhood*. Her motherhood has a significance which is not exclusively contained in the words of Jesus and in the various episodes reported by the Synoptics (Lk 11:27-28 and Lk 8:19-21; Mt 12:46-50; Mk 3:31-35). In these texts Jesus means above all to contrast the motherhood resulting from the fact of birth with what this "motherhood" (and also "brotherhood") is to be in the dimension of the Kingdom of God, in the salvific radius of God's fatherhood. In John's text on the other hand, the description of the Cana event outlines what is actually manifested as a new kind of motherhood according to the spirit and not just according to the flesh, that is to say *Mary's solicitude for human beings*, her coming to them in the wide variety of their wants and needs. At Cana in Galilee there is shown only one concrete aspect of human need, apparently a small one of little importance ("They have no wine"). But it has a symbolic value: this coming to the aid of human needs means, at the same time, bringing those needs within the radius of Christ's messianic mission and salvific power. Thus there is a mediation: Mary places herself between her Son and mankind in the reality of their wants, needs and sufferings. *She puts herself "in the middle," that is to say she acts as a mediatrix not as an outsider, but in her position as mother.* She knows that as such she can point out to her Son the needs of mankind, and in fact, she "has the right" to do so. Her mediation is thus in the nature of intercession: Mary "intercedes" for mankind. And that is not all. As a mother she also *wishes the messianic power of her Son to be manifested*, that salvific power of his which is meant to help man in his misfortunes, to free him from the evil which in various forms and degrees weighs heavily upon his life. Precisely as the Prophet Isaiah had foretold about the Messiah in the famous passage which Jesus quoted before his fellow townsfolk in Nazareth: "To preach good news to the poor . . . to proclaim release to the captives and recovering of sight to the blind . . ." (cf. Lk 4:18).

Another essential element of Mary's maternal task is found in her words to the servants: "Do whatever he tells you." *The Mother of Christ presents herself as the spokeswoman of her Son's will*, pointing out those things which must be done so that the salvific power of the Messiah may be manifested. At Cana, thanks to the intercession of Mary and the obedience of the servants, Jesus begins "his hour." At Cana Mary appears as *believing in Jesus*. Her faith evokes his first "sign" and helps to kindle the faith of the disciples.

22.   We can therefore say that in this passage of John's Gospel we find as it were a first manifestation of the truth concerning Mary's maternal care. This truth has

also found expression *in the teaching of the Second Vatican Council.* It is important to note how the Council illustrates Mary's maternal role as it relates to the mediation of Christ. Thus we read: "Mary's maternal function towards mankind in no way obscures or diminishes the unique mediation of Christ, but rather shows its efficacy," because "there is one mediator between God and men, the man Christ Jesus" (1 Tm 2:5). This maternal role of Mary flows, according to God's good pleasure, "from the superabundance of the merits of Christ; it is founded on his mediation, absolutely depends on it, and draws all its efficacy from it."[44] It is precisely in this sense that the episode at Cana in Galilee offers us *a sort of first announcement of Mary's mediation,* wholly oriented towards Christ and tending to the revelation of his salvific power.

From the *text of John* it is evident that it is a mediation which is maternal. As the Council proclaims: Mary became "a mother to us in the order of grace." This motherhood in the order of grace flows from her divine motherhood. Because she was, by the design of divine Providence, the mother who nourished the divine Redeemer, Mary became "an associate of unique nobility, and the Lord's humble handmaid," who "cooperated by her obedience, faith, hope and burning charity in the Savior's work of restoring supernatural life to souls."[45] And "this *maternity of Mary in the order of grace* . . . will last without interruption until the eternal fulfillment of all the elect."[46]

23.   If John's description of the event at Cana presents Mary's caring motherhood at the beginning of Christ's messianic activity, another passage from the same Gospel confirms this motherhood in the salvific economy of grace at its crowning moment, namely when Christ's sacrifice on the Cross, his Paschal Mystery, is accomplished. John's description is concise: "*Standing by the cross of Jesus* were his mother, and his mother's sister, Mary the wife of Clopas, and Mary Magdalene. When Jesus saw his mother, and the disciple whom he loved standing near, he said to his mother: 'Woman, behold your son!' Then he said to the disciple, 'Behold, your mother!' And from that hour the disciple took her to his own home" (Jn 19:25-27).

Undoubtedly, we find here an expression of the Son's particular solicitude for his Mother, whom he is leaving in such great sorrow. And yet the "testament of Christ's Cross" says more. Jesus highlights a new relationship between Mother and Son, the whole truth and reality of which he solemnly confirms. One can say that if Mary's motherhood of the human race had already been outlined, now it is clearly stated and established. It *emerges* from the definitive accomplishment of *the Redeemer's Paschal Mystery.* The Mother of Christ, who stands at the very center of this mystery—a mystery which embraces each individual and all humanity—is given as mother to every single individual and all mankind. The man at the foot of the Cross is John, "the disciple whom he loved."[47] But it is not he alone. Following tradition, the Council does not hesitate to call Mary *"the Mother of Christ and mother of mankind"*: since she "belongs to the offspring of Adam she is one with all human beings. . . . Indeed she is 'clearly the mother of the members of Christ . . . since she cooperated out of love so that there might be born in the Church the faithful.'"[48]

And so this "new motherhood of Mary," generated by faith, is *the fruit of the "new" love* which came to definitive maturity in her at the foot of the Cross, through her sharing in the redemptive love of her Son.

24.   Thus we find ourselves at the very center of the fulfillment of the promise contained in the Proto-gospel: the "seed of the woman . . . will crush the head of the serpent" (cf. Gn 3:15). By his redemptive death Jesus Christ conquers the evil of sin and death at its very roots. It is significant that, as he speaks to his mother from the Cross, he calls her "woman" and says to her: "Woman, behold your son!" Moreover, he had addressed her by the same term at Cana too (cf. Jn 2:4). How can one doubt that especially now, on Golgotha, this expression goes to the very heart of the mystery of Mary, and indicates the unique *place* which she occupies *in the whole economy of salvation?* As the Council teaches, in Mary "the exalted Daughter of Sion, and after a long expectation of the promise, the times were at length ful-filled and the new dispensation established. All this occurred when the Son of God took a human nature from her, that he might in the mysteries of his flesh free man from sin."[49]

The words uttered by Jesus from the Cross signify that *the motherhood* of her who bore Christ finds a "new" continuation *in the Church and through the Church,* sym-bolized and represented by John. In this way, she who as the one "full of grace" was brought into the mystery of Christ in order to be his Mother and thus the Holy Mother of God, through the Church remains in that mystery as *"the woman"* spo-ken of by the Book of *Genesis* (3:15) at the beginning and by the *Apocalypse* (12:1) at the end of the history of salvation. In accordance with the eternal plan of Providence, Mary's divine motherhood is to be poured out upon the Church, as indicated by statements of Tradition, according to which Mary's "motherhood" of the Church is the reflection and extension of her motherhood of the Son of God.[50]

According to the Council the very moment of the Church's birth and full manifes-tation to the world enables us to glimpse this continuity of Mary's motherhood:

"Since it pleased God not to manifest solemnly the mystery of the salvation of the human race until he poured forth the Spirit promised by Christ, we see the Apostles before the day of Pentecost 'continuing with one mind *in prayer* with the women and *Mary the mother of Jesus*, and with his brethren' (Acts 1:14). We see Mary prayerfully imploring the gift of the Spirit, who had already overshadowed her in the Annunciation."[51]

And so, in the redemptive economy of grace, brought about through the action of the Holy Spirit, there is a unique correspondence between the moment of the Incarnation of the Word and the moment of the birth of the Church. The person who links these two moments is Mary: *Mary at Nazareth* and *Mary in the Upper Room at Jerusalem*. In both cases her discreet yet essential presence indicates the path of "birth from the Holy Spirit." Thus she who is present in the mystery of Christ as Mother becomes—by the will of the Son and the power of the Holy Spirit—present in the mystery of the Church. In the Church too she continues to be *a maternal presence*, as is shown by the words spoken from the Cross: "Woman, behold your son!"; "Behold, your mother."

Part II
THE MOTHER OF GOD
AT THE CENTER OF THE PILGRIM CHURCH

1. THE CHURCH, THE PEOPLE OF GOD PRESENT IN ALL THE NATIONS OF THE EARTH

25. "The Church 'like a pilgrim in a foreign land, presses forward amid the persecutions of the world and the consolations of God,[52] announcing the Cross and Death of the Lord until he comes (cf. 1 Cor 11:26)."[53] "Israel according to the flesh, which wandered as an exile in the desert, was already called the Church of God (cf. 2 Esd. 13:1; Nm 20:4; Dt 23:1ff.). Likewise the new Israel . . . is also called the Church of Christ (cf. Mt 16:18). For he has bought it for himself with his blood (Acts 20:28), has filled it with his Spirit, and provided it with those means which befit it as a visible and social unity. *God has gathered together as one all those who in faith look upon Jesus* as the author of salvation and the source of unity and peace, and has established them as Church, that for each and all she may be the visible sacrament of this saving unity."[54]

The Second Vatican Council speaks of the pilgrim Church, establishing an analogy with the Israel of the Old Covenant journeying through the desert. The journey also has an *external character*, visible in the time and space in which it historically takes place. For the Church "is destined to extend to all regions of the earth and so to enter into the history of mankind," but at the same time "she transcends all limits of time and of space."[55] And yet the essential *character* of her pilgrimage is *interior*: it is a question of a *pilgrimage through faith*, by "the power of the Risen Lord,"[56] a pilgrimage in the Holy Spirit, given to the Church as the invisible Comforter (*parákletos*) (cf. Jn 14:26; 15:26; 16:7): "Moving forward through trial and tribulation, the Church is strengthened by the power of God's grace promised to her by the Lord, so that . . . moved by the Holy Spirit, she may never cease to renew herself, until through the Cross she arrives at the light which knows no setting."[57]

It is precisely *in this ecclesial journey or pilgrimage* through space and time, and even more through the history of souls, that *Mary is present*, as the one who is "blessed because she believed," as the one who advanced on the pilgrimage of faith, sharing unlike any other creature in the mystery of Christ. The Council further says that "Mary figured profoundly in the history of salvation and in a certain way unites and mirrors within herself the central truths of the faith."[58] Among all believers she is *like a "mirror"* in which are reflected in the most profound and limpid way "the mighty works of God" (Acts 2:11).

26.   Built by Christ upon the Apostles, the Church became fully aware of these mighty works of God *on the day of Pentecost*, when those gathered together in the Upper Room "were all filled with the Holy Spirit and began to speak in other tongues, as the Spirit gave them utterance" (Acts 2:4). From that moment there also *begins* that journey of faith, *the Church's pilgrimage* through the history of individuals and peoples. We know that at the beginning of this journey Mary is present. We see her in the midst of the Apostles in the Upper Room, "prayerfully imploring the gift of the Spirit."[59]

In a sense her journey of faith is longer. The Holy Spirit had already come down upon her, and she became his faithful spouse *at the Annunciation*, welcoming the Word of the true God, offering "the full submission of intellect and will . . . and freely assenting to the truth revealed by him," indeed abandoning herself totally to God through "the obedience of faith,"[60] whereby she replied to the angel: "Behold, I am the handmaid of the Lord; let it be to me according to your word." The journey of faith made by Mary, whom we see praying in the Upper Room, is thus longer than that of the others gathered there: Mary "goes before them," "leads the way" for them.[61] *The moment of Pentecost* in Jerusalem had been prepared for by the *moment of the Annunciation* in Nazareth, as well as by the Cross. In the Upper Room Mary's journey meets the Church's journey of faith. In what way?

Among those who devoted themselves to prayer in the Upper Room, preparing to go "into the whole world" after receiving the Spirit, some *had been called by Jesus* gradually from the beginning of his mission in Israel. Eleven of them *had been made Apostles*, and to them Jesus had passed on the mission which he himself had received from the Father. "As the Father has sent me, even so I send you" (Jn 20:21), he had said to the Apostles after the Resurrection. And forty days later, before returning to the Father, he had added: "when the Holy Spirit has come upon you . . . *you shall be my witnesses* . . . to the end of the earth" (cf. Acts 1:8). This mission of the Apostles began the moment they left the Upper Room in Jerusalem. The Church is born and then grows through the testimony that Peter and the Apostles bear to the Crucified and Risen Christ (cf. Acts 2:31-34; 3:15-18; 4:10-12; 5:30-32).

Mary did not directly receive this apostolic mission. She was not among those whom Jesus sent "to the whole world to teach all nations" (cf. Mt 28:19) when he conferred this mission on them. But she was in the Upper Room, where the Apostles were preparing to take up this mission with the coming of the Spirit of Truth: she was present with them. In their midst Mary was "devoted to prayer" as the "mother of Jesus" (cf. Acts 1:13-14), of the Crucified and Risen Christ. And that first group of those who in faith looked "upon Jesus as the author of salvation,"[62] knew that Jesus was the Son of Mary, and that she was his Mother, and that as such she was from the moment of his conception and birth a unique witness to *the mystery of Jesus*, that mystery which before their eyes had been disclosed and confirmed in the Cross and Resurrection. Thus, from the very first moment, the Church "looked at" Mary through Jesus, just as she "looked at" Jesus through Mary. For the Church of that time and of every time Mary is a singular witness to the years of Jesus' infancy and hidden life at Nazareth, when she "kept all these things, pondering them in her heart" (Lk 2:19; cf. Lk 2:51).

But above all, in the Church of that time and of every time Mary was and is the one who is "blessed because she believed"; *she was the first to believe.* From the moment of the Annunciation and conception, from the moment of his birth in the stable at Bethlehem, Mary followed Jesus step by step in her maternal pilgrimage of faith. She followed him during the years of his hidden life at Nazareth; she followed him also during the time after he left home, when he began "to do and to teach" (cf. Acts 1:1) in the midst of Israel. Above all she followed him in the tragic experience of Golgotha. Now, while Mary was with the Apostles in the Upper Room in Jerusalem at the dawn of the Church, *her faith, born from the words of the Annunciation, found confirmation.* The angel had said to her then: "You will conceive in your womb and bear a son, and you shall call his name Jesus. He will be great . . . and he will reign over the house of Jacob for ever; and of his kingdom there will be no end." The recent events on Calvary had shrouded that promise in darkness, yet not even beneath the Cross did Mary's faith fail. She had still remained the one who, like Abraham, "in hope believed against hope" (Rom 4:18). But it is only after the Resurrection that hope had shown its true face and *the promise had begun to be transformed into reality.* For Jesus, before returning to the Father, had said to the Apostles: "Go therefore and make disciples of all nations . . . lo, I am with you always, to the close of the age" (cf. Mt 28:19-20). Thus had spoken the one who by his Resurrection had revealed himself as the conqueror of death, as the one who possessed the kingdom of which, as the angel said, "there will be no end."

27.   Now, at the first dawn of the Church, at the beginning of the long journey through faith which began at Pentecost in Jerusalem, Mary was with all those who were the seed of the "new Israel." She was present among them as an exceptional witness to the mystery of Christ. And the Church was assiduous in prayer together with her, and at the same time *"contemplated her in the light of the Word made man."* It was always to be so. For when the Church "enters more intimately into the supreme mystery of the Incarnation," she thinks of the Mother of Christ with profound reverence and devotion.[63] Mary belongs indissolubly to the mystery of Christ, and she belongs also to the mystery of the Church from the beginning, from the day of the Church's birth. At the basis of what the Church has been from the beginning, and of what she must continually become from generation to generation, in the midst of all the nations of the earth, we find the one "who believed that there would be a fulfillment of what was spoken to her from the Lord" (Lk 1:45). It is precisely Mary's faith which marks the beginning of the new and eternal Covenant of God with man in Jesus Christ; this heroic *faith* of hers *"precedes"* the apostolic *witness* of the Church, and ever remains in the Church's heart hidden like a special heritage of God's revelation. All those who from generation to generation accept the apostolic witness of the Church share in that mysterious inheritance, and *in a sense share in Mary's faith.*

Elizabeth's words "Blessed is she who believed" continue to accompany the Virgin also at Pentecost; they accompany her from age to age, wherever knowledge of Christ's salvific mystery spreads, through the Church's apostolic witness and service. Thus is fulfilled the prophecy of the *Magnificat*: "All generations will call me *blessed*; for he who is mighty has done great things for me, and holy is his name" (Lk 1:48-49). For knowledge of the mystery of Christ leads us to bless his Mother, in the form of special veneration for the *Theotókos*. But this veneration always includes a blessing of her faith, for the Virgin of Nazareth became blessed above all through this faith, in accordance with Elizabeth's words. Those who from generation to generation among the different peoples and nations of the earth accept with faith the mystery of Christ, the Incarnate Word and Redeemer of the world, not only turn with veneration to Mary and confidently have recourse to her as his Mother, but also *seek in her faith support for their own*. And it is precisely this lively sharing in Mary's faith that determines her special place in the Church's pilgrimage as the new People of God throughout the earth.

28.   As the Council says, "Mary figured profoundly in the history of salvation. . . . Hence when she is being preached and venerated, she summons the faithful to her Son and his sacrifice, and to love for the Father."[64] For this reason, Mary's faith, according to the Church's apostolic witness, in some way continues to become the faith of the pilgrim People of God: the faith of individuals and communities, of places and gatherings, and of the various groups existing in the Church. It is a faith that is passed on simultaneously through both the mind and the heart. It is gained or regained continually through prayer. Therefore, "*the Church* in her apostolic work also *rightly looks to her who brought forth Christ*, conceived by the Holy Spirit and born of the Virgin, so that through the Church Christ *may be born and increase in the hearts of the faithful also*."[65]

Today, as on this pilgrimage of faith we draw near to the end of the second Christian Millennium, the Church, through the teaching of the Second Vatican Council, calls our attention to her vision of herself, as the "one People of God . . . among all the nations of the earth." And she reminds us of that truth according to which all the faithful, though "scattered throughout the world, are in communion with each other in the Holy Spirit."[66] We can therefore say that in this union the mystery of Pentecost is continually being accomplished. At the same time, the Lord's apostles and disciples, in all the nations of the earth, "devote themselves to prayer *together with Mary, the mother of Jesus*" (Acts 1:14). As they constitute from generation to generation the "sign of the Kingdom" which is not of his world,[67] they are also aware that in the midst of this world they must *gather around that King* to whom the nations have been given in heritage (cf. Ps 2:8), to whom the Father has given "the throne of David his father," so that he "will reign over the house of Jacob for ever, and of his kingdom there will be no end."

During this time of vigil, Mary, through the same faith which made her blessed, especially from the moment of the Annunciation, is *present* in the Church's mission, *present* in the Church's work of introducing into the world *the Kingdom of her Son*.[68]

This presence of Mary finds many different expressions in our day, just as it did throughout the Church's history. It also has a wide field of action. Through the faith and piety of individual believers; through the traditions of Christian families or "domestic churches," of parish and missionary communities, religious institutes and dioceses; through the radiance and attraction of the great shrines where not only individuals or local groups, but sometimes whole nations and societies, even whole continents, seek to meet the Mother of the Lord, the one who is blessed because she believed is the first among believers and therefore became the Mother of Emmanuel. This is the message of the Land of Palestine, the spiritual homeland of all Christians because it was the homeland of the Savior of the world and of his Mother. This is the message of the many churches in Rome and throughout the world which have been raised up in the course of the centuries by the faith of Christians. This is the message of centers like Guadalupe, Lourdes, Fatima and the others situated in the various countries. Among them how could I fail to mention the one in my own native land, Jasna Góra? One could perhaps speak of a specific "geography" of faith and Marian devotion, which includes all these special places of pilgrimage where the People of God seek to meet the Mother of God in order to find, within the radius of the maternal presence of her "who believed," a strengthening of their own faith. For *in Mary's faith*, first at the Annunciation and then fully at the foot of the Cross, an *interior space* was reopened within humanity which the eternal Father can fill "with every spiritual blessing." It is the space "of the new and eternal Covenant,"[69] and it continues to exist in the Church, which in Christ is "a kind of sacrament or sign of intimate union with God, and of the unity of all mankind."[70]

In the faith which Mary professed at the Annunciation as the "handmaid of the Lord" and in which she constantly "precedes" the pilgrim People of God throughout the earth, the *Church* "strives energetically and constantly to bring all humanity . . . back to Christ its Head* in the unity of his Spirit."[71]

2. THE CHURCH'S JOURNEY AND THE UNITY OF ALL CHRISTIANS

29.   "In all of Christ's disciples the Spirit arouses the desire to be peacefully *united*, in the manner determined by Christ, as one flock *under one shepherd*."[72] The journey of the Church, especially in our own time, is marked by the sign of ecumenism: Christians are seeking ways to restore that unity which Christ implored from the Father for his disciples on the day before his Passion: "*That they may all be*

one; even as you, Father, are in me, and I in you that they also may be in us, so that the world *may believe* that you have sent me" (Jn 17:21). The unity of Christ's disciples, therefore, is a great sign given in order to kindle faith in the world while their division constitutes a scandal.[73]

The ecumenical movement, on the basis of a clearer and more widespread awareness of the urgent need to achieve the unity of all Christians, has found on the part of the Catholic Church its culminating expression in the work of the Second Vatican Council: Christians must deepen in themselves and each of their communities that "obedience of faith" of which Mary is the first and brightest example. And since she "shines forth on earth, . . . as a sign of sure hope and solace for the pilgrim People of God," "it gives great joy and comfort to this most holy Synod that *among the divided brethren*, too, there are those who live due honor to the Mother of our Lord and Savior. This is especially so among the Easterners."[74]

30.   Christians know that their unity will be truly rediscovered only if it is based on the unity of their faith. They must resolve considerable discrepancies of doctrine concerning the mystery and ministry of the Church, and sometimes also concerning the role of Mary in the work of salvation.[75] The dialogues begun by the Catholic Church with the Churches and Ecclesial Communities of the West[76] are steadily converging upon these *two inseparable aspects* of the same mystery of salvation. If the mystery of the Word made flesh enables us to glimpse the mystery of the divine motherhood and is, in turn, contemplation of the Mother of God brings us to a more profound understanding of the mystery of the Incarnation, then the same must be said for the mystery of the Church and Mary's role in the work of salvation. By a more profound study of both Mary and the Church, clarifying each by the light of the other, Christians who are eager to do what Jesus tells them—as their Mother recommends (cf. Jn 2:5)—will be able to go forward together on this "pilgrimage of faith." Mary, who is still the model of this pilgrimage, is to lead them to the unity which is willed by their one Lord and so much desired by those who are attentively listening to what "the Spirit is saying to the Churches" today (Rev 2:7, 11, 17).

Meanwhile, it is a hopeful sign that these Churches and Ecclesial Communities are finding agreement with the Catholic Church on fundamental points of Christian belief, including matters relating to the Virgin Mary. For they recognize her as the Mother of the Lord and hold that this forms part of our faith in Christ, true God and true man. They look to her who at the foot of the Cross accepts as her son the beloved disciple, the one who in his turn accepts her as his mother.

Therefore, why should we not all together look to her as *our common Mother*, who prays for the unity of God's family and who "precedes" us all at the head of the long line of witnesses of faith in the one Lord, the Son of God, who was conceived in her virginal womb by the power of the Holy Spirit?

31.   On the other hand, I wish to emphasize how profoundly the Catholic Church, the Orthodox Church and the ancient Churches of the East feel united by love and praise of the *Theotókos*. Not only "basic dogmas of the Christian faith concerning the Trinity and God's Word made flesh of the Virgin Mary were defined in Ecumenical Councils held in the East,"[77] but also in their liturgical worship "the Orientals pay high tribute, in very beautiful hymns, to Mary ever Virgin . . . God's Most Holy Mother."[78]

The brethren of these Churches have experienced a complex history, but it is one that has always been marked by an intense desire for Christian commitment and apostolic activity, despite frequent persecution, even to the point of bloodshed. It is a history of fidelity to the Lord, an authentic "pilgrimage of faith" in space and time, during which Eastern Christians have always looked with boundless trust to the Mother of the Lord, celebrated her with praise and invoked her with unceasing prayer. In the difficult moments of their troubled Christian existence, "they have taken refuge under her protection,"[79] conscious of having in her a powerful aid. The Churches which profess the doctrine of Ephesus proclaim the Virgin as "true Mother of God," since "our Lord Jesus Christ, born of the Father before time began according to his divinity, in the last days, for our sake and for our salvation, was himself begotten of Mary, the Virgin Mother of God according to his humanity."[80] The Greek Fathers and the Byzantine tradition contemplating the Virgin in the light of the Word made flesh, have sought to penetrate the depth of that bond which unites Mary, as the Mother of God, to Christ and the Church: the Virgin is a permanent presence in the whole reality of the salvific mystery.

The Coptic and Ethiopian traditions were introduced to this contemplation of the mystery of Mary by St. Cyril of Alexandria, and in their turn they have celebrated it with a profuse poetic blossoming.[81] The poetic genius of St. Ephrem the Syrian, called "the lyre of the Holy Spirit," tirelessly sang of Mary, leaving a still living mark on the whole tradition of the Syriac Church.[82]

In his panegyric of the *Theotókos*, St. Gregory of Narek, one of the outstanding glories of Armenia, with powerful poetic inspiration ponders the different aspects of the mystery of the Incarnation, and each of them is for him an occasion to sing and extol the extraordinary dignity and magnificent beauty of the Virgin Mary, Mother of the Word made flesh.[83]

It does not surprise us therefore that Mary occupies a privileged place in the worship or the ancient Oriental Churches with an incomparable abundance of feasts and hymns.

32.   In the Byzantine liturgy, in all the hours of the Divine Office, praise of the Mother is linked with praise of her Son and with the praise which, through the Son, is offered up to the Father in the Holy Spirit. In the Anaphora or Eucharistic Prayer of St. John Chrysostom, immediately after the epiclesis the assembled community sings in honor of the Mother of God: "It is truly just to proclaim you blessed, O Mother of God, who are most blessed, all pure and Mother of our God. We magnify you who are more honorable than the Cherubim and incomparably more glorious than the Seraphim. You who, without losing your virginity, gave birth to the Word of God. You who are truly the Mother of God."

These praises, which in every celebration of the Eucharistic Liturgy are offered to Mary, have molded the faith, piety and prayer of the faithful. In the course of the centuries they have permeated their whole spiritual outlook, fostering in them a profound devotion to the "All Holy Mother of God."

33.   This year there occurs the twelfth centenary of the Second Ecumenical Council of Nicaea (AD 787). Putting an end to the well-known controversy about the cult of sacred images, this Council defined that, according to the teaching of the holy Fathers and the universal tradition of the Church, there could be exposed for the veneration of the faithful, together with the Cross, also images of the Mother of God, of the angels and of the saints, in churches and houses and at the roadside.[84] This custom has been maintained in the whole of the East and also in the West. Images of the Virgin have a place of honor in churches and houses. In them Mary is represented in a number of ways: as the throne of God carrying the Lord and giving him to humanity (*Theotókos*); as the way that leads to Christ and manifests him (*Hodegetria*); as a praying figure in an attitude of intercession and as a sign of the divine presence on the journey of the faithful until the day of the Lord (*Deësis*); as the protectress who stretches out her mantle over the peoples (*Pokrov*), or as the merciful Virgin of tenderness (*Eleousa*). She is usually represented with her Son, the child Jesus, in her arms: it is the relationship with the Son which glorifies the Mother. Sometimes she embraces him with tenderness (*Glykophilousa*); at other times she is a hieratic figure, apparently rapt in contemplation of him who is the Lord of history (cf. Rev 5:9-14).[85]

It is also appropriate to mention the icon of Our Lady of Vladimir, which continually accompanied the pilgrimage of faith of the peoples of ancient Rus'. The first Millennium of the conversion of those noble lands to Christianity is approaching: lands of humble folk, of thinkers and of saints. The Icons are still venerated in the Ukraine, in Byelorussia and in Russia under various titles. They are images which witness to the faith and spirit of prayer of that people, who sense the presence and protection of the Mother of God. In these Icons the Virgin shines as the image of divine beauty, the abode of Eternal Wisdom, the figure of the one who prays, the prototype of contemplation, the image of glory: she who even in her earthly life possessed the spiritual knowledge inaccessible to human reasoning and who attained through faith the most sublime knowledge. I also recall the Icon of the Virgin of the Cenacle, praying with the Apostles as they awaited the Holy Spirit: could she not become the sign of hope for all those who, in fraternal dialogue, wish to deepen their obedience of faith?

34.   Such a wealth of praise, built up by the different forms of the Church's great tradition, could help us to hasten the day when the Church can begin once more to breathe fully with her "two lungs," the East and the West. As I have often said, this is more than ever necessary today. It would be an effective aid in furthering the progress of the dialogue already taking place between the Catholic Church and the Churches and Ecclesial Communities of the West.[86] It would also be the way for the pilgrim Church to sing and to live more perfectly her "*Magnificat.*"

3. THE "MAGNIFICAT" OF THE PILGRIM CHURCH

35.   At the present stage of her journey, therefore, the Church seeks to rediscover the unity of all who profess their faith in Christ, in order to show obedience to her Lord, who prayed for this unity before his Passion. "Like a pilgrim in a foreign land, the Church presses forward amid the persecutions of the world and the consolations of God, announcing the Cross and Death of the Lord until he comes."[87] "Moving forward through trial and tribulation, *the Church is strengthened by the power of God's grace promised to her by the Lord,* so that in the weakness of the flesh she may not waver from perfect fidelity, but remain a bride worthy of her Lord; that moved by the Holy Spirit she may never cease to renew herself, until through the Cross she arrives at the light which knows no setting."[88]

The Virgin Mother is constantly present on this journey of faith of the People of God towards the light. This is shown in a special way by *the canticle of the*

"Magnificat," *which, having welled up from the depths of Mary's faith* at the Visitation, ceaselessly re-echoes in the heart of the Church down the centuries. This is proved by its daily recitation in the liturgy of Vespers and at many other moments of both personal and communal devotion.

> "My soul magnifies the Lord,
> and my spirit rejoices in God my Savior,
> for he has looked on his servant in her lowliness.
> For behold, henceforth all generations
> will call me blessed;
> *for he who is mighty has done great things for me,*
> and holy is his name:
> and his mercy is from age to age
> on those who fear him.
> He has shown strength with his arm,
> he has scattered the proud-hearted,
> he has cast down the mighty from their thrones,
> and lifted up the lowly;
> he has filled the hungry with good things,
> sent the rich away empty.
> He has helped his servant Israel,
> remembering his mercy,
> as he spoke to our fathers,
> to Abraham and to his posterity for ever." (Lk 1:46-55)

36.   When Elizabeth greeted her young kinswoman coming from Nazareth, *Mary replied with the Magnificat.* In her greeting, Elizabeth first called Mary "blessed" because of "the fruit of her womb," and then she called her "blessed" because of her faith (cf. Lk 1:42, 45). These two blessings referred directly to the Annunciation. Now, at the Visitation, when Elizabeth's greeting bears witness to that culminating moment, Mary's faith acquires a new consciousness and a new expression. That which remained hidden in the depths of the "obedience of faith" at the Annunciation can now be said to spring forth like a clear and life-giving flame of the spirit. The words used by Mary on the threshold of Elizabeth's house are *an inspired profession of her faith,* in which *her response to the revealed word* is expressed with the religious and poetical exultation of her whole being towards God. In these sublime words, which are simultaneously very simple and wholly inspired by the sacred texts of the people of Israel,[89] Mary's personal experience, the ecstasy of her heart, shines forth. In them shines a ray of the mystery of God, the glory of his ineffable holiness, the *eternal love which, as an irrevocable gift, enters into human history.*

Mary is the first to share in this new revelation of God and, within the same, in this new "self-giving" of God. Therefore she proclaims: "For he who is mighty has done great things for me, and holy is his name." Her words reflect a joy of spirit which is difficult to express: "My spirit rejoices in God my Savior." Indeed, "the deepest truth about God and the salvation of man is made clear to us in Christ, who is at the same time the mediator and the fullness of all revelation."[90] In her exultation Mary confesses that she finds herself *in the very heart of this fullness* of Christ. She is conscious that the promise made to the fathers, first of all "to Abraham and to his posterity for ever," is being fulfilled in herself. She is thus aware that concentrated within herself as the mother of Christ is the *whole salvific economy*, in which "from age to age" is manifested he who as the God of the Covenant, "remembers his mercy."

37.   The Church, which from the beginning has modelled her earthly journey on that of the Mother of God, constantly repeats after her the words of the *Magnificat*. From the depths of the Virgin's faith at the Annunciation and the Visitation, the Church derives the truth about the God of the Covenant: the God who is Almighty and does "great things" for man: "holy is his name." In the *Magnificat* the Church sees uprooted that sin which is found at the outset of the earthly history of man and woman, the sin of disbelief and of "little faith" in God. In contrast with the "suspicion" which the "father of lies" sowed in the heart of Eve the first woman, Mary, whom tradition is wont to call the "new Eve"[91] and the true "Mother of the living,"[92] boldly proclaims the *undimmed* truth about God: the holy and almighty God, who from the beginning is *the source of all gifts*, he who "has done great things" in her, as well as in the whole universe. In the act of creation God gives existence to all that is. In creating man, God gives him the dignity of the image and likeness of himself in a special way as compared with all earthly creatures. Moreover, in his desire to give *God gives himself in the Son*, notwithstanding man's sin: "He so loved the world that he gave his only Son" (Jn 3:16). Mary is the first witness of this marvelous truth, which will be fully accomplished through "the works and words" (cf. Acts 1:1) of her Son and definitively through his Cross and Resurrection.

The Church, which even "amid trials and tribulations" does not cease repeating with Mary the words of the *Magnificat*, is sustained by the power of God's truth, proclaimed on that occasion with such extraordinary simplicity. At the same time, *by means of this truth about God*, the Church *desires to shed light upon* the difficult and sometimes tangled paths of man's earthly existence. The Church's journey, therefore, near the end of the second Christian Millennium, involves a renewed commitment to her mission. Following him who said of himself: "(God) has anointed me *to preach good news to the poor*" (cf. Lk 4:18), the Church has sought from generation to generation and still seeks today to accomplish that same mission.

The Church's *love of preference for the poor* is wonderfully inscribed in Mary's *Magnificat*. The God of the Covenant, celebrated in the exultation of her spirit by the Virgin of Nazareth, is also he who "has cast down the mighty from their thrones, and lifted up the lowly, . . . filled the hungry with good things, sent the rich away empty, . . . scattered the proud-hearted . . . and his mercy is from age to age on those who fear him." Mary is deeply imbued with the spirit of the "poor of Yahweh," who in the prayer of the Psalms awaited from God their salvation, placing all their trust in him (cf. Ps 25; 31; 35; 55). Mary truly proclaims the coming of the "Messiah of the poor" (cf. Is 11:4; 61:1). Drawing from Mary's heart, from the depth of her faith expressed in the words of the *Magnificat*, the Church renews ever more effectively in herself the awareness that *the truth about God who saves*, the truth about God who is the source of every gift, *cannot be separated from the manifestation of his love of preference for the poor and humble*, that love which, celebrated in the *Magnificat*, is later expressed in the words and works of Jesus.

The Church is thus aware—and at the present time this awareness is particularly vivid—not only that these two elements of the message contained in the *Magnificat* cannot be separated, but also that there is a duty to safeguard carefully the importance of "the poor" and of "the option in favor of the poor" in the word of the living God. These are matters and questions intimately connected with the *Christian meaning of freedom and liberation*. "Mary is totally dependent upon God and completely directed towards him, and at the side of her Son, she is the *most perfect image of freedom and of the liberation* of humanity and of the universe. It is to her as Mother and Model that the Church must look in order to understand in its completeness the meaning of her own mission."[93]

Part III
MATERNAL MEDIATION

1. MARY, THE HANDMAID OF THE LORD

38.   The Church knows and teaches with St. Paul that there is only one mediator: "For there is one God, and *there is one mediator* between God and men, the man Christ Jesus, who gave himself as a ransom for all" (1 Tm 2:5-6). "The maternal role of Mary towards people in no way obscures or diminishes the unique mediation of Christ, but rather shows its power":[94] it is mediation in Christ.

The Church knows and teaches that "all *the saving influences of the Blessed Virgin* on mankind originate . . . from the divine pleasure. They flow forth *from the super-*

abundance of the merits of Christ, rest on his mediation, depend entirely on it, and draw all their power from it. In no way do they impede the immediate union of the faithful with Christ. Rather, they foster this union."[95] This saving influence is sustained by the Holy Spirit, who, just as he overshadowed the Virgin Mary when he began in her the divine motherhood, in a similar way constantly sustains her solicitude for the brothers and sisters of her Son.

In effect, Mary's mediation is *intimately linked with her motherhood*. It possesses a specifically maternal character, which distinguishes it from the mediation of the other creatures who in various and always subordinate ways share in the one mediation of Christ, although her own mediation is also a shared mediation.[96] In fact, while it is true that "no creature could ever be classed with the Incarnate Word and Redeemer," at the same time "the unique mediation of the Redeemer does not exclude but rather gives rise among creatures to *a manifold cooperation* which is but a sharing in this unique source." And thus "the one goodness of God is in reality communicated diversely to his creatures."[97]

The teaching of the Second Vatican Council presents the truth of Mary's mediation as "*a sharing in the one unique source that is the mediation of Christ himself.*" Thus we read: "The Church does not hesitate to profess this subordinate role of Mary. She experiences it continuously and commends it to the hearts of the faithful, so that, encouraged by this maternal help, they may more closely adhere to the Mediator and Redeemer."[98] This role is at the same time *special and extraordinary*. It flows from her divine motherhood and can be understood and lived in faith only on the basis of the full truth of this motherhood. Since by virtue of divine election Mary is the earthly Mother of the Father's consubstantial Son and his "generous companion" in the work of redemption "she is a mother to us in the order of grace."[99] This role constitutes a real dimension of her presence in the saving mystery of Christ and the Church.

39.   From this point of view we must consider once more the fundamental event in the economy of salvation, namely the Incarnation of the Word at the moment of the Annunciation. It is significant that Mary, recognizing in the words of the divine messenger the will of the Most High and submitting to his power, says: "*Behold, I am the handmaid* of the Lord; let it be to me according to your word" (Lk 1:38). The first moment of submission to the one mediation "between God and men"—the mediation of Jesus Christ—is the Virgin of Nazareth's acceptance of motherhood. Mary consents to God's choice, in order to become through the power of the Holy Spirit the Mother of the Son of God. It can be said that a *consent to motherhood* is

above all *a result of her total self-giving to God in virginity*. Mary accepted her election as Mother of the Son of God, guided by spousal love, the love which totally "consecrates" a human being to God. By virtue of this love, Mary wished to be always and in all things "given to God," living in virginity. The words "Behold, I am the handmaid of the Lord" express the fact that from the outset she accepted and understood her own motherhood as a total *gift of self*, a gift of her person to the service of the saving plans of the Most High. And to the very end she lived her entire maternal sharing in the life of Jesus Christ, her Son, in a way that matched her vocation to virginity.

Mary's motherhood, completely pervaded by her spousal attitude as the "handmaid of the Lord," constitutes the first and fundamental dimension of that mediation which the Church confesses and proclaims in her regard[100] and continually "commends to the hearts of the faithful," since the Church has great trust in her. For it must be recognized that before anyone else it was God himself, the Eternal Father, *who entrusted himself to the Virgin of Nazareth*, giving her his own Son in the mystery of the Incarnation. Her election to the supreme office and dignity of Mother of the Son of God refers, on the ontological level, to the very reality of the union of the two natures in the person of the Word (*hypostatic union*). This basic fact of being the Mother of the Son of God is from the very beginning a complete openness to the person of Christ, to his whole work, to his whole mission. The words "Behold, I am the handmaid of the Lord" testify to Mary's openness of spirit: she perfectly unites in herself the love proper to virginity and the love characteristic of motherhood, which are joined and, as it were, fused together.

For this reason Mary became not only the "nursing mother" of the Son of Man but also the "associate of unique nobility"[101] of the Messiah and Redeemer. As I have already said, she advanced in her pilgrimage of faith, and in this *pilgrimage* to the foot of the Cross there was simultaneously accomplished her maternal *cooperation* with the Savior's whole mission through her actions and sufferings. Along the path of this collaboration with the work of her Son, the Redeemer, Mary's motherhood itself underwent a singular transformation, becoming ever more imbued with "burning charity" towards all those to whom Christ's mission was directed. Through this "burning charity," which sought to achieve, in union with Christ, the restoration of "supernatural life to souls,"[102] Mary *entered, in a way all her own, into the one mediation* "between God and men" *which is the mediation of the man Christ Jesus*. If she was the first to experience within herself the supernatural consequences of this one mediation—in the Annunciation she had been greeted as "full of grace"—then we must say that through this fullness of grace and supernatural life she was especially predisposed to cooperation with Christ, the one Mediator of human salvation. *And such cooperation is precisely this mediation subordinated* to the mediation of Christ.

In Mary's case we have a special and exceptional mediation, based upon her "fullness of grace," which was expressed in the complete willingness of the "handmaid of the Lord." In response to this interior willingness of his Mother, *Jesus Christ prepared her* ever more completely to become for all people their "mother in the order of grace." This is indicated, at least indirectly, by certain details noted by the Synoptics (cf. Lk 11:28; 8:20-21; Mk 3:32-35; Mt 12:47-50) and still more so by the Gospel of John (cf. 2:1-12; 19:25-27), which I have already mentioned. Particularly eloquent in this regard are the words spoken by Jesus on the Cross to Mary and John.

40.   After the events of the Resurrection and Ascension Mary entered the Upper Room together with the Apostles to await Pentecost, and was present there as the Mother of the glorified Lord. She was not only the one who "advanced in her pilgrimage of faith" and loyally persevered in her union with her Son "unto the Cross," *but she was also the "handmaid of the Lord," left by her Son as Mother in the midst of the infant Church*: "Behold your mother." Thus there began to develop a special bond between this Mother and the Church. For the infant Church was the fruit of the Cross and Resurrection of her Son. Mary, who from the beginning had given herself without reserve to the person and work of her Son, could not but pour out upon the Church, from the very beginning, her maternal self-giving. After her Son's departure, her motherhood remains in the Church as maternal mediation: interceding for all her children, the Mother cooperates in the saving work of her Son, the Redeemer of the world. In fact the Council teaches that the "motherhood of Mary in the order of grace . . . *will last without interruption* until the eternal fulfillment of all the elect."[103] With the redeeming death of her Son, the maternal mediation of the handmaid of the Lord took on a universal dimension, for the work of redemption embraces the whole of humanity. Thus there is manifested in a singular way the efficacy of the one and universal mediation of Christ "between God and men" Mary's cooperation shares, in its subordinate character, *in the universality of the mediation of the Redeemer*, the one Mediator. This is clearly indicated by the Council in the words quoted above.

"For," the text goes on, "taken up to heaven, she did not lay aside this saving role, but by her manifold acts of intercession continues to win for us gifts of eternal salvation."[104] With this character of "intercession," first manifested at Cana in Galilee,

Mary's mediation continues in the history of the Church and the world. We read that Mary "by her maternal charity, cares for the brethren of her Son who still journey on earth surrounded by dangers and difficulties, until they are led to their happy homeland."[105] In this way Mary's motherhood continues unceasingly in the Church as the mediation which intercedes, and the Church expresses her faith in this truth by invoking Mary "under the titles of Advocate, Auxiliatrix, Adjutrix and Mediatrix."[106]

41.   Through her mediation, subordinate to that of the Redeemer, Mary contributes *in a special way to the union of the pilgrim Church* on earth with the eschatological and heavenly *reality* of the Communion of Saints, since she has already been "assumed into heaven."[107] The truth of the Assumption, defined by Pius XII, is reaffirmed by the Second Vatican Council, which thus expresses the Church's faith: "Preserved free from all guilt of original sin, the Immaculate Virgin *was taken up body and soul into heavenly glory* upon the completion of her earthly sojourn. She was *exalted* by the Lord *as Queen of the Universe*, in order that she might be the more thoroughly conformed to her Son, the Lord of lords (cf. Rev 19:16) and the conqueror of sin and death."[108] In this teaching Pius XII was in continuity with Tradition, which has found many different expressions in the history of the Church, both in the East and in the West.

By the mystery of the Assumption into heaven there were definitively accomplished in Mary all the effects of the one mediation of *Christ the Redeemer of the world* and *Risen Lord*: "In Christ shall all be made alive. But each in his own order: Christ the first fruits, then at his coming those who belong to Christ" (1 Cor 15:22-23). In the mystery of the Assumption is expressed the faith of the Church, according to which Mary is "united by a close and indissoluble bond" to Christ, for, if as Virgin and Mother she was singularly united with him *in his first coming*, so through her continued collaboration with him she will also be united with him in expectation of the second; "redeemed in an especially sublime manner by reason of the merits of her Son,"[109] she also has that specifically maternal role of mediatrix of mercy *at his final coming*, when all those who belong to Christ "shall be made alive," when "the last enemy to be destroyed is death" (1 Cor 15:26).[110]

Connected with this exaltation of the noble "Daughter of Sion"[111] through her Assumption into heaven is the mystery of her eternal glory. For the Mother of Christ is glorified as "Queen of the Universe."[112] She who at the Annunciation called herself the "handmaid of the Lord" remained throughout her earthly life faithful to what this name expresses. In this she confirmed that she was a true "disciple" of Christ, who strongly emphasized that his mission was one of service: the Son of Man came not to be served but to serve, and to give his life as a ransom for many" (Mt 20:28). In this way Mary became the first of those who, "serving Christ also in others, with humility and patience lead their brothers and sisters to that King whom to serve is to reign,"[113] and she fully obtained that "state of royal freedom" proper to Christ's disciples: to serve means to reign!

"Christ obeyed even at the cost of death, and was therefore raised up by the Father (cf. Phil 2:8-9). Thus he entered into the glory of his kingdom. To him all things are made subject until he subjects himself and all created things to the Father, that God may be all in all (cf. 1 Cor 15:27-28)."[114] Mary, the handmaid of the Lord, has a share in this Kingdom of the Son.[115] The *glory of serving* does not cease to be her royal exaltation: assumed into heaven, she does not cease her saving service, which expresses her maternal mediation "until the eternal fulfillment of all the elect."[116] Thus, she who here on earth "loyally preserved in her union with her Son unto the Cross," continues to remain united with him, while now "*all things are subjected to him, until he subjects to the Father himself and all things.*" Thus in her Assumption into heaven, Mary is as it were clothed by the whole reality of the Communion of Saints, and her very union with the Son in glory is wholly oriented towards the definitive fullness of the Kingdom, *when "God will be all in all."*

In this phase too Mary's maternal mediation does not cease to be subordinate to him who is the one Mediator, *until the final realization of "the fullness of time,"* that is to say until "all things are united in Christ" (cf. Eph 1:10).

2. MARY IN THE LIFE OF THE CHURCH AND OF EVERY CHRISTIAN

42.   Linking itself with Tradition, the Second Vatican Council brought new light to bear on the role of the Mother of Christ in the life of the Church. "Through the gift . . . of divine motherhood, Mary is united with her Son, the Redeemer, and with his singular graces and offices. By these, the Blessed Virgin is also intimately united with the Church: *the Mother of God is a figure of the Church* in the matter of faith, charity and perfect union with Christ."[117] We have already noted how, from the beginning, Mary remains with the Apostles in expectation of Pentecost and how, as "the blessed one who believed," she is present in the midst of the pilgrim Church from generation to generation through faith and as the model of the hope which does not disappoint (cf. Rom 5:5).

Mary believed in the fulfillment of what had been said to her by the Lord. As Virgin, she believed that she would conceive and bear a son: the "Holy One," who bears the name of "Son of God," the name "Jesus" (God who saves). As handmaid of the Lord, she remained in perfect fidelity to the person and mission of this Son. As Mother, "*believing and obeying* . . . she brought forth on earth the *Father's Son*. This she did, knowing not man but overshadowed by the Holy Spirit."[118]

For these reasons Mary is honored in the Church "with special reverence. Indeed, from most ancient times the Blessed Virgin Mary has been venerated under the title of 'God-bearer.' In all perils and needs, the faithful have fled prayerfully to her protection."[119] This cult is altogether special: it bears in itself and *expresses* the profound *link* which exists *between the Mother of Christ and the Church*.[120] As Virgin and Mother, Mary remains for the Church a "permanent model." It can therefore be said that especially under this aspect, namely as a model, or rather as a "figure," Mary, present in the mystery of Christ, remains constantly present also in the mystery of the Church. For the Church too is "called mother and virgin," and these names have a profound biblical and theological justification.[121]

43. The *Church* "*becomes* herself *a mother* by accepting God's word with fidelity."[122] Like Mary, who first believed by accepting the word of God revealed to her at the Annunciation and by remaining faithful to that word in all her trials even unto the Cross, so too the Church becomes a mother when, *accepting with fidelity the word of God*, "by her preaching and by baptism *she brings forth to a new and immortal life children* who are conceived *of the Holy Spirit* and born of God."[123] This "maternal" characteristic of the Church was expressed in a particularly vivid way by the Apostle to the Gentiles when he wrote: "My little children, with whom I am again in travail until Christ be formed in you!" (Gal 4:19) These words of St. Paul contain an interesting sign of the early Church's awareness of her own motherhood, linked to her apostolic service to mankind. This awareness enabled and still enables the Church to see the mystery of her life and mission modelled *upon the example of the Mother of the Son*, who is "the first-born among many brethren" (Rom 8:29).

It can be said that from Mary the Church also learns her own motherhood: she recognizes the maternal dimension of her vocation, which is essentially bound to her sacramental nature, in "contemplating Mary's mysterious sanctity, imitating her charity and faithfully fulfilling the Father's will."[124] If the Church is the sign and instrument of intimate union with God, she is so by reason of her motherhood, because, receiving life from the Spirit, she "generates" sons and daughters of the human race to a new life in Christ. For, just as *Mary is at the service of the mystery of* the Incarnation, so the Church is always *at the service of the mystery of adoption to sonship* through grace.

Likewise, following the example of Mary, the Church remains the virgin faithful to her spouse: The Church herself is a virgin who keeps whole and pure the fidelity she has pledged to her Spouse."[125] For the Church is the spouse of Christ, as is clear from the Pauline Letters (cf. Eph 5:21-33; 2 Cor 11:2), and from the title found in John: "bride of the Lamb" (Rev 21:9). If *the Church* as spouse "keeps the fidelity she *has pledged* to Christ," this fidelity, even though in the Apostle's teaching it has become an image of marriage (cf. Eph 5:23-33), also has value as a model of total self-giving to God in celibacy "for the kingdom of heaven," *in virginity consecrated to God* (cf. Mt 19:11-12; 2 Cor 11:2). Precisely such virginity, after the example of the Virgin of Nazareth, is the source of a special spiritual fruitfulness: *it is the source of motherhood in the Holy Spirit.*

But *the Church* also preserves the faith *received from Christ.* Following the example of Mary, who kept and pondered in her heart everything relating to her divine Son (cf. Lk 2:19, 51), the Church is committed to preserving the word of God and investigating its riches with discernment and prudence, in order to bear faithful witness to it before all mankind in every age.[126]

44.   Given Mary's relationship to the Church as an exemplar, the Church is close to her and seeks to become like her: "Imitating the Mother of her Lord, and by the power of the Holy Spirit, she preserves with virginal purity an integral faith, a firm hope, and a sincere charity."[127] Mary is thus present in the mystery of the Church as a *model.* But the Church's mystery also consists in generating people to a new and immortal life: this is her motherhood in the Holy Spirit. And here Mary is not only the model and figure of the Church; she is much more. For, *"with maternal love she cooperates in the birth and development"* of the sons and daughters of Mother Church. The Church's motherhood is accomplished not only according to the model and figure of the Mother of God but also with her "cooperation." The Church draws abundantly from this cooperation, that is to say from the maternal mediation which is characteristic of Mary, insofar as already on earth she cooperated in the rebirth and development of the Church's sons and daughters, as the Mother of that Son whom the Father "placed as the first-born among many brethren."[128]

She cooperated, as the Second Vatican Council teaches, with a maternal love.[129] Here we perceive the real value of the words spoken by Jesus to his Mother at the hour of the Cross: "Woman, behold your son" and to the disciple: "Behold your mother" (Jn 19:26-27). They are words which determine *Mary's place in the life of Christ's disciples* and they express—as I have already said—the new motherhood of the Mother of the Redeemer: a spiritual motherhood, born from the heart of the Paschal Mystery of the Redeemer of the world. It is a motherhood in the order of grace, for it implores the gift of the Spirit, who raises up the new children of God, redeems through the sacrifice of Christ that Spirit whom Mary too, together with the Church, received on the day of Pentecost.

Her motherhood is particularly noted and experienced by the Christian people at the *Sacred Banquet*—the liturgical celebration of the mystery of the Redemption—at which Christ, his *true body born of the Virgin Mary*, becomes present.

The piety of the Christian people has always very rightly sensed a *profound link* between devotion to the Blessed Virgin and worship of the Eucharist: this is a fact that can be seen in the liturgy of both the West and the East, in the traditions of the Religious Families, in the modern movements of spirituality, including those for youth, and in the pastoral practice of the Marian Shrines. *Mary guides the faithful to the Eucharist.*

45.   Of the essence of motherhood is the fact that it concerns the person. Motherhood always establishes *a unique and unrepeatable relationship* between two people: *between mother and child* and *between child and mother*. Even when the same woman is the mother of many children, her personal relationship with each one of them is of the very essence of motherhood. For each child is generated in a unique and unrepeatable way, and this is true both for the mother and for the child. Each child is surrounded in the same way by that maternal love on which are based the child's development and coming to maturity as a human being.
It can be said that motherhood "in the order of grace" preserves the analogy with what "in the order of nature" characterizes the union between mother and child. In the light of this fact it becomes easier to understand why in Christ's testament on Golgotha his Mother's new motherhood is expressed in the singular, in reference to one man: "Behold your son."

It can also be said that these same words fully show the reason *for the Marian dimension of the life of Christ's disciples.* This is true not only of John, who at that hour stood at the foot of the Cross together with his Master's Mother, but it is also true of every disciple of Christ, of every Christian. The Redeemer entrusts his mother to the disciple, and at the same time he gives her to him as his mother. Mary's motherhood, which becomes man's inheritance, is a gift: *a gift which Christ himself makes* personally to every individual. The Redeemer entrusts Mary to John because he entrusts John to Mary. At the foot of the Cross there begins that special *entrusting of humanity to the Mother of Christ*, which in the history of the Church has been practiced and expressed in different ways. The same Apostle and Evangelist, after reporting the words addressed by Jesus on the Cross to his Mother and to himself, adds: "And from that hour the disciple took her to his own home" (Jn 19:27). This statement certainly means that the role of son was attributed to the disciple and that he assumed responsibility for the Mother of his beloved Master. And since Mary was given as a mother to him personally, the statement indicates, even though indirectly, everything expressed by the intimate relationship of a child with its mother. And all of this can be included in the word "entrusting." Such entrusting is *the response* to a person's love, and in particular *to the love of a mother*.

The Marian dimension of the life of a disciple of Christ is expressed in a special way precisely through this filial entrusting to the Mother of Christ, which began with the testament of the Redeemer on Golgotha. Entrusting himself to Mary in a filial manner, the Christian, like the Apostle John, "welcomes" the Mother of Christ "into his own home"[130] and brings her into everything that makes up his inner life, that is to say into his human and Christian "I": he "*took her to his own home*." Thus the Christian seeks to be taken into that "maternal charity" with which the Redeemer's Mother "cares for the brethren of her Son,"[131] "in whose birth and development she cooperates"[132] in the measure of the gift proper to each one through the power of Christ's Spirit. Thus also is exercised that motherhood in the Spirit which became Mary's role at the foot of the Cross and in the Upper Room.

46.   This filial relationship, this self-entrusting of a child to its mother, not only has its *beginning in Christ* but can also be said to be *definitively directed towards him*. Mary can be said to continue to say to each individual the words which she spoke at Cana in Galilee: "Do whatever he tells you." For he, Christ, is the one Mediator between God and mankind; he is "the way, and the truth, and the life" (Jn 14:6); it is he whom the Father has given to the world, so that man "should not perish but have eternal life" (Jn 3:16). The Virgin of Nazareth became the first "witness" of this saving love of the Father, and she also wishes *to remain* its *humble handmaid always and everywhere*. For every Christian, for every human being, Mary is the one who first "believed," and precisely with her faith as Spouse and Mother she wishes to act upon all those who entrust themselves to her as her children. And it is well known that the more her children persevere and progress in this attitude, the nearer Mary leads them to the "unsearchable riches of Christ" (Eph 3:8). And to the same degree they recognize more and more clearly the dignity of man in all its

fullness and the definitive meaning of his vocation, for "Christ . . . fully reveals man to man himself."[133]

This Marian dimension of Christian life takes on special importance in relation to women and their status. In fact, femininity has a *unique relationship* with the Mother of the Redeemer, a subject which can be studied in greater depth elsewhere. Here I simply wish to note that the figure of Mary of Nazareth sheds light on *womanhood as such* by the very fact that God, in the sublime event of the Incarnation of his Son, entrusted himself to the ministry, the free and active ministry of a woman. It can thus be said that women, by looking to Mary, find in her the secret of living their femininity with dignity and of achieving their own true advancement. In the light of Mary, the Church sees in the face of women the reflection of a beauty which mirrors the loftiest sentiments of which the human heart is capable: the self-offering totality of love; the strength that is capable of bearing the greatest sorrows; limitless fidelity and tireless devotion to work; the ability to combine penetrating intuition with words of support and encouragement.

47.   At the Council Paul VI solemnly proclaimed that *Mary is the Mother of the Church*, "that is, Mother of the entire Christian people, both faithful and pastors."[134] Later, in 1968, in the Profession of faith known as the "Credo of the People of God." he restated this truth in an even more forceful way in these words: "We believe that the Most Holy Mother of God, the new Eve, the Mother of the Church, carries on in heaven her maternal role with regard to the members of Christ, cooperating in the birth and development of divine life in the souls of the redeemed."[135]

The Council's teaching emphasized that the truth concerning the Blessed Virgin, Mother of Christ, is an effective aid in exploring more deeply the truth concerning the Church. When speaking of the Constitution *Lumen Gentium*, which had just been approved by the Council, Paul VI said: "Knowledge of the true Catholic doctrine regarding the Blessed Virgin Mary will always be a key to the *exact understanding of the mystery of Christ and of the Church*."[136] Mary is present in the Church as the Mother of Christ, and at the same time as that Mother whom Christ, in the mystery of the Redemption, gave to humanity in the person of the Apostle John. Thus, in her new motherhood in the Spirit, Mary embraces each and every one *in* the Church, and embraces each and every one *through* the Church. In this sense Mary, Mother of the Church, is also the Church's model. Indeed, as Paul VI hopes and asks, the Church must draw "from the Virgin Mother of God the most authentic form of perfect imitation of Christ."[137]

Thanks to this special bond linking the Mother of Christ with the Church, there is further *clarified the mystery of that "woman"* who, from the first chapters of the Book of *Genesis* until the Book of *Revelation*, accompanies the revelation of God's salvific plan for humanity. For Mary, present in the Church as the Mother of the Redeemer, takes part, as a mother, in that monumental struggle; against the powers of darkness"[138] which continues throughout human history. And by her ecclesial identification as the "woman clothed with the sun" (Rev 12:1),[139] it can be said that "in the Most Holy Virgin the Church has already reached that perfection whereby she exists without spot or wrinkle." Hence, as Christians raise their eyes with faith to Mary in the course of their earthly pilgrimage, they "strive to increase in holiness."[140] Mary, the exalted Daughter of Sion, helps all her children, wherever they may be and whatever their condition, *to find in Christ the path to the Father's house.*

Thus, throughout her life, the Church maintains with the Mother of God a link which embraces, in the saving mystery, the past, the present and the future, and venerates her as the spiritual mother of humanity and the advocate of grace.

3. THE MEANING OF THE MARIAN YEAR

48.   It is precisely the special bond between humanity and this Mother which has led me to proclaim a Marian Year in the Church, in this period before the end of the Second Millennium since Christ's birth, a similar initiative was taken in the past. when Pius XII proclaimed 1954 as a Marian Year, in order to highlight the exceptional holiness of the Mother of Christ as expressed in the mysteries of her Immaculate Conception (defined exactly a century before) and of her Assumption into heaven.[141]

Now, following the line of the Second Vatican Council, I wish to emphasize the *special presence* of the Mother of God in the mystery of Christ and his Church. For this is a fundamental dimension emerging from the Mariology of the Council, the end of which is now more than twenty years behind us. The Extraordinary Synod of Bishops held in 1985 exhorted everyone to follow faithfully the teaching and guidelines of the Council We can say that these two events—the Council and the synod—embody what the Holy Spirit himself wishes "to say to the Church" in the present phase of history.

In this context, the Marian Year is meant to promote a new and more careful reading of what the Council said about the Blessed Virgin Mary, Mother of God, in the mystery of Christ and of the Church, the topic to which the contents of this

Encyclical are devoted. Here we speak not only of *the doctrine of faith* but also of *the life of faith*, and thus of authentic "Marian spirituality," seen in the light of Tradition, and especially the spirituality to which the Council exhorts us.[142] Furthermore, Marian *spirituality*, like its corresponding *devotion*, finds a very rich source in the historical experience of individuals and of the various Christian communities present among the different peoples and nations of the world. In this regard, I would like to recall, among the many witnesses and teachers of this spirituality, the figure of St. Louis Marie Grignion de Montfort,[143] who proposes consecration to Christ through the hands of Mary, as an effective means for Christians to live faithfully their baptismal commitments. I am pleased to note that in our own time too new manifestations of this spirituality and devotion are not lacking.

There thus exist solid points of reference to look to and follow in the context of this Marian Year.

49.   This Marian Year *will begin on the Solemnity of Pentecost, on June 7 next.* For it is a question not only of recalling that Mary "preceded" the entry of Christ the Lord into the history of the human family, but also of emphasizing, in the light of Mary, that from the moment when the mystery of the Incarnation was accomplished, human history entered "the fullness of time," and that the Church is the sign of this fullness. As the People of God, the Church makes her pilgrim way towards eternity through faith, in the midst of all the peoples and nations, beginning from the day of Pentecost. *Christ's Mother*, who was present at the beginning of "the time of the Church," when in expectation of the coming of the Holy Spirit she devoted herself to prayer in the midst of the Apostles and her Son's disciples—constantly "precedes" *the Church* in her *journey* through human history. She is also the one who, precisely as the "handmaid of the Lord," cooperates unceasingly with the work of salvation accomplished by Christ, her Son.

Thus by means of this Marian Year *the Church is called* not only to remember everything in her past that testifies to the special maternal cooperation of the Mother of God in the work of salvation in Christ the lord, but also, on her own part, *to prepare* for the future the paths of this cooperation. For the end of the second Christian Millennium opens up as a new prospect.

50.   As has already been mentioned, also among our divided brethren many honor and celebrate the Mother of the Lord, especially among the Orientals. It is a Marian light cast upon ecumenism. In particular, I wish to mention once more that during the Marian Year there will occur the *Millennium of the Baptism* of St. Vladimir, Grand Duke of Kiev (AD 988). This marked the beginning of Christianity in the territories of what was then called Rus', and subsequently in other territories of Eastern Europe.

In this way, through the work of evangelization, Christianity spread beyond Europe, as far as the northern territories of the Asian continent. We would therefore like, especially during this Year, to join in prayer with all those who are celebrating the Millennium of this Baptism, both Orthodox and Catholics, repeating and confirming with the Council those sentiments of joy and comfort that "the Easterners . . . with ardent emotion and devout mind concur in reverencing the Mother of God, ever Virgin."[144] Even though we are still experiencing the painful effects of the separation which took place some decades later (AD 1054), we can say that *in the presence of the Mother of Christ we feel that we are true brothers and sisters* within that messianic People, which is called to be the one family of God on earth. As I announced at the beginning of the New Year "We desire to reconfirm this universal inheritance of all the Sons and daughters of this earth."[145]

In announcing the Year of Mary, I also indicated that it will end next year on *the Solemnity of the Assumption of the Blessed Virgin into Heaven*, in order to emphasize the "great sign in heaven" spoken of by the *Apocalypse*. In this way we also wish to respond to the exhortation of the Council, which looks to Mary as "a sign of sure hope and solace for the pilgrim People of God." And the Council expresses this exhortation in the following words: "Let the entire body of the faithful pour forth persevering prayer to the Mother of God and Mother of mankind. Let them implore that she who aided the beginning of the Church by her prayers may now, exalted as she is in heaven above all the saints and angels, intercede with her Son in the fellowship of all the saints. May she do so until all the peoples of the human family, whether they are honored with the name of Christian or whether they still do not know their Savior, are happily gathered together in peace and harmony into the one People of God, for the glory of the Most Holy and Undivided Trinity."[146]

CONCLUSION

51.   At the end of the daily Liturgy of the Hours, among the invocations addressed to Mary by the Church is the following:

> Loving Mother of the Redeemer, gate of heaven, star of the sea,
> assist your people who have fallen yet strive to rise again.
> To the wonderment of nature you bore your Creator!

"To the wonderment of nature"! These words of the antiphon express that *wonderment of faith* which accompanies the mystery of Mary's divine motherhood. In a sense, it does so in the heart of the whole of creation, and, directly, in the heart of the whole People of God, in the heart of the Church. How wonderfully far God has gone, the Creator and Lord of all things, in the "revelation of himself" to man![147] How clearly he has bridged all the spaces of that infinite "distance" which separates the Creator from the creature! If in himself he remains *ineffable and unsearchable*, still more *ineffable and unsearchable is he in the reality of the Incarnation* of the Word, who became man through the Virgin of Nazareth.

If he has eternally willed to call man to share in the divine nature (cf. 2 Pt 1:4), it can be said that he has matched the "divinization" of man to humanity's historical conditions, so that even after sin he is ready to restore at a great price the eternal plan of his love through the "humanization" of his Son, who is of the same being as himself. The whole of creation, and more directly man himself, cannot fail to be amazed at this gift in which he has become a sharer, in the Holy Spirit: "God so loved the world that he gave his only Son" (Jn 3:16).

At the center of this mystery, in the midst of this wonderment of faith, stands Mary. As the loving Mother of the Redeemer, she was the first to experience it: "To the wonderment of nature you bore your Creator"!

52.   The words of this liturgical antiphon also express *the truth of the "great transformation"* which the mystery of the Incarnation establishes for man. It is a transformation which belongs to his entire history, from that beginning which is revealed to us in the first chapters of *Genesis* until the final end, in the perspective of the end of the world, of which Jesus has revealed to us "neither the day nor the hour" (Mt 25:13). It is an unending and continuous transformation between falling and rising again, between the man of sin and the man of grace and justice. The Advent liturgy in particular is at the very heart of this transformation and captures its unceasing "here and now" when it exclaims: "Assist your people who have fallen yet strive to rise again"!

These words apply to every individual, every community, to nations and peoples, and to the generations and epochs of human history, to our own epoch, to these years of the Millennium which is drawing to a close: "Assist, yes assist, your people who have fallen"!

This is the invocation addressed to Mary, the "loving Mother of the Redeemer," the invocation addressed to Christ, who through Mary entered human history. Year after year the antiphon rises to Mary, evoking that moment which saw the accomplishment of this essential historical transformation, which irreversibly continues: the transformation from "falling" to "rising."

Mankind has made wonderful discoveries and achieved extraordinary results in the fields of science and technology. It has made great advances along the path of progress and civilization, and in recent times one could say that it has succeeded in speeding up the pace of history. But the fundamental transformation, the one which can be called "original," constantly accompanies man's journey, and through all the events of history accompanies each and every individual. It is the transformation from "falling" to "rising," from death to life. It is also *a constant challenge* to people's consciences, a challenge to man's whole historical awareness: the challenge to follow the path of "not falling" in ways that are ever old and ever new, and of "rising again" if a fall has occurred.

As she goes forward with the whole of humanity towards the frontier between the two Millennia, the Church, for her part, with the whole community of believers and in union with all men and women of good will, takes up the great challenge contained in these words of the Marian antiphon: "the people who have fallen yet strive to rise again," and she addresses both the Redeemer and his Mother with the plea: "Assist us." For, as this prayer attests, the Church sees the Blessed Mother of God in the saving mystery of Christ and in her own mystery. She sees Mary deeply rooted in humanity's history, in man's eternal vocation according to the providential plan which God has made for him from eternity She sees Mary maternally present and sharing in the many complicated problems which *today* beset the lives of individuals, families and nations; she sees her helping the Christian people in the constant struggle between good and evil, to ensure that it "does not fall," or, if it has fallen, that it "rises again."

I hope with all my heart that the reflections contained in the present Encyclical will also serve to renew this vision in the hearts of all believers.

As Bishop of Rome, I send to all those to whom these thoughts are addressed the kiss of peace, my greeting and my blessing in our Lord Jesus Christ. Amen.

Given in Rome, at St. Peter's, on March 25, the Solemnity of the Annunciation of the Lord, in the year 1987, the ninth of my Pontificate.

NOTES

1.   Cf. Second Vatican Ecumenical Council, Dogmatic Constitution on the Church *Lumen Gentium*, 52 and the whole of Chapter VIII, entitled "The Role of the Blessed Virgin Mary, Mother of God, in the Mystery of Christ and the Church."

2. The expression "fullness of time" (*pleroma tou chronou*) is parallel with similar expressions of Judaism, both Biblical (cf. Gn 29:21; 1 Sm 7:12; Tb 14:5) and extra-Biblical, and especially of the New Testament (cf. Mk 1:15; Lk 21:24; Jn 7:8; Eph 1:10). From the point of view of form, it means not only the conclusion of a chronological process but also and especially the coming to maturity or completion of a particularly important period, one directed towards the fulfillment of an expectation, a coming to completion which thus takes on an eschatological dimension. According to Galatians 4:4 and its context, it is the coming of the Son of God that reveals that time has, so to speak, reached its limit. That is to say, the period marked by the promise made to Abraham and by the Law mediated by Moses has now reached its climax, in the sense that Christ fulfills the divine promise and supersedes the old law.

3. Cf. *Roman Missal*, Preface of December 8, Immaculate Conception of the Blessed Virgin Mary; St. Ambrose, *De Institutione Virginis*, XV, 93-94: *PL* 16, 342; Second Vatican Ecumenical Council, Dogmatic Constitution on the Church *Lumen Gentium*, 68.

4. Second Vatican Ecumenical Council, Dogmatic Constitution on the Church *Lumen Gentium*, 58.

5. Pope Paul VI, Encyclical Epistle *Christi Matri* (September 15, 1966): *AAS* 58 (1966) 745-749, Apostolic Exhortation *Signum Magnum* (May 13, 1967): *AAS* 59 (1967) 465:475; Apostolic Exhortation *Marialis Cultus* (February 2, 1974): *AAS* 66 (1974) 113-168.

6. The Old Testament foretold in many different ways the mystery of Mary: cf. St. John Damascene, *Hom. in Dormitionem* 1, 8-9: *S. Ch.* 80, 103-107.

7. Cf. *Insegnamenti di Giovanni Paolo II*, VI/2 (1983) 225f.; Pope Pius IX, Apostolic Letter *Ineffabilis Deus* (December 8, 1854): *Pii IX P. M. Acta*, pars I, 597-599.

8. Cf. Pastoral Constitution on the Church in the Modern World *Gaudium et Spes*, 22.

9. Ecumenical Council of Ephesus, in *Conciliorum Oecumenicorum Decreta*, Bologna 1973, 41-44; 59-61: *DS* 250-264; cf. Ecumenical Council of Chalcedon, o. c. 84-87: *DS* 300-303.

10. Second Vatican Ecumenical Council, Pastoral Constitution on the Church in the Modern World *Gaudium et Spes*, 22.

11. Dogmatic Constitution on the Church *Lumen Gentium*, 52.

12. Cf. ibid., 58.

13. Ibid., 63, cf. St. Ambrose, *Expos. Evang. sec. Lucam*, II, 7: *CSEL* 32/4, 45; *De Institutione Virginis*, XIV, 88-89: *PL* 16, 341.

14. Cf. Dogmatic Constitution on the Church *Lumen Gentium*, 64.

15. Ibid., 65.

16. "Take away this star of the sun which illuminates the world: where does the day go? Take away Mary, this star of the sea, of the great and boundless sea: what is left but a vast obscurity and the shadow of death and deepest darkness?": St. Bernard, *In Navitate B. Mariae Sermo—De aquaeductu*, 6: *S. Bernardi Opera*, V, 1968, 279; cf. *In Laudibus Virginis Matris Homilia II*, 17: ed. cit., IV, 1966, 34f.

17. Dogmatic Constitution on the Church *Lumen Gentium*, 63.

18. Ibid., 63.

19. Concerning the predestination of Mary, cf. St. John Damascene, *Hom. in Nativitatem*, 7, 10: *S. Ch.* 80, 65; 73; *Hom. in Dormitionem* 1, 3: *S. Ch.* 80, 85: "For it is she, who, chosen from the ancient generations, by virtue of the predestination and benevolence of the God and Father who generated you (the Word of God) outside time without coming out of himself or suffering change, it is she who gave you birth, nourished of her flesh, in the last time. . . ."

20. Dogmatic Constitution on the Church *Lumen Gentium*, 55.

21. In Patristic tradition there is a wide and varied interpretation of this expression: cf. Origen, *In Lucam Homiliae*, VI, 7: *S. Ch.* 87, 148; Severianus of Gabala, *In Mundi Creationem, Oratio VI*, 10: *PG* 56, 497f.; St. John Chrysostom (Pseudo), *In Annunhationem Deiparae et contra Arium Impium*, *PG* 62, 765f.; Basil of Seleucia, *Oratio 39, In Sanctissimae Deiparae Annuntiationem*, 5: *PG* 85, 441-46; Antipater of Bosra, *Hom. II, In Sanctissimae Deiparae Annuntiationem*, 3-11: *PG* 85, 1777-1783; St. Sophronius of Jerusalem, *Oratio 11, In Sanctissimae Deiparae Annuntiationem*, 17-19: *PG* 87/3, 3235-3240; St. John Damascene, *Hom. in Dormitionem*, 1, 70: *S. Ch.* 80, 96-101; St. Jerome, *Epistola 65*, 9: *PL* 22, 628, St. Ambrose, *Expos. Evang. sec. Lucam*, II, 9: *CSEL* 32/4, 45f.; St. Augustine, *Sermo 291*, 4-6: *PL* 38, 131 8f.; *Enchiridion*, 36, 11: *PL* 40, 250; St. Peter Chrysologus, *Sermo 142*: *PL* 52, 579f.; *Sermo 143*: *PL* 52, 583; St. Fulgentius of Ruspe, *Epistola 17*, VI 12: *PL* 65 458; St. Bernard, *In Laudibus Virginis Matris, Homilia III*, 2-3: *S. Bernardi Opera*, IV, 1966, 36-38.

22. Dogmatic Constitution on the Church *Lumen Gentium*, 55.
23. Ibid., 53.
24. Cf. Pope Pius XI, Apostolic Letter *Ineffabilis Deus* (December 8, 1854): *Pii IX P.M. Acta*, pars I, 616; Second Vatican Ecumenical Council, Dogmatic Constitution on the Church *Lumen Gentium*, 53.
25. Cf. St. Germanus of Constantinople, *In Annuntiationem SS. Deiparae Hom.*: PG 98, 327f.; St. Andrew of Crete, *Canon in B. Mariae Natalem*, 4. PG 97, 1321f., *In Nativitatem B. Mariae*, I: PG 97, 81 1f. *Hom. in Dormitionem S. Mariae* 1: PG 97, 1067f.
26. *Liturgy of the Hours* of August 15, Assumption of the Blessed Virgin Mary, Hymn at First and Second Vespers; St. Peter Damian, *Carmina et Preces*, XLVII: PL 145, 934.
27. *Divina Commedia, Paradiso*, XXXIII, 1; cf. *Liturgy of the Hours*, Memorial of the Blessed Virgin Mary on Saturday, Hymn II in the Office of Readings.
28. Cf. St. Augustine, *De Sancta Virginitate*, III, 3: PL 40, 398; *Sermo* 25, 7: PL 46,
29. Dogmatic Constitution on Divine Revelation *Dei Verbum*, 5
30. This is a classic theme, already expounded by St. Irenaeus: "And, as by the action of the disobedient virgin, man was afflicted and, being cast down, died, so also by the action of the Virgin who obeyed the word of God, man being regenerated received, through life, life. . . . For it was meet and Just . . . that Eve should be "recapitulated" in Mary, so that the Virgin, becoming the advocate of the virgin, should dissolve and destroy the virginal disobedience by means of virginal obedience": *Expositio Doctrinae Apostolicae*, 33: S. Ch. 62, 83-86; cf. also *Adversus Haereses*, V, 19, 1: S. Ch. 153, 248-250.
31. Second Vatican Ecumenical Council, Dogmatic Constitution on Divine Revelation *Dei Verbum*, 5.
32. Ibid., 5, cf. Dogmatic Constitution on the Church *Lumen Gentium*, 56.
33. Second Vatican Ecumenical Council, Dogmatic Constitution on the Church *Lumen Gentium*, 56.
34. Ibid., 56.
35. Cf. ibid., 53; St. Augustine, *De Sancta Virginitate*, III, 3: PL 40, 398; *Sermo* 215, 4; PL 38, 1074; *Sermo* 196, I: PL 38, 1019; *De Peccatorum Meritis et Remissione*, I, 29, 57: PL 44, 142; *Sermo* 25, 7: PL 46, 937-938; St. Leo the Great, *Tractatus* 21, *De Natale Domini*, I: CCL 138, 86.
36. *Ascent of Mount Carmel*, 1. II, Ch. 3, 4-6.
37. Cf. Dogmatic Constitution on the Church *Lumen Gentium*, 58.
38. Ibid., 58.
39. Cf. Second Vatican Ecumenical Council, Dogmatic Constitution on Divine Revelation *Dei Verbum*, 5.
40. Concerning Mary's participation or "compassion" in the death of Christ, cf. St. Bernard, *In Dominica Infra Octavam Assumptionis Sermo*, 14: *S. Bernardi Opera*, V, 1968, 273.
41. St. Irenaeus, *Adversus Haereses* III, 22, 4: S. Ch. 211, 438-444; cf. Dogmatic Constitution on the Church *Lumen Gentium*, 56, Note 6.
42. Cf. Dogmatic Constitution on the Church *Lumen Gentium*, 56, and the Fathers quoted there in Notes 8 and 9.
43. "Christ is truth, Christ is flesh: Christ truth in the mind of Mary, Christ flesh in the womb of Mary": St. Augustine, *Sermo* 25 (*Sermones inediti*), 7: PL 46, 938.
44. Dogmatic Constitution on the Church *Lumen Gentium*, 60.
45. Ibid., 61.
46. Ibid., 62.
47. There is a well-known passage of Origen on the presence of Mary and John on Calvary: "The Gospels are the first fruits of all Scripture and the Gospel of John is the first of the Gospels: no one can grasp its meaning without having leaned his head on Jesus' breast and having received from Jesus Mary as Mother": *Comm. in Ioan.*, I, 6: PG 14, 31; cf. St. Ambrose, *Expos. Evang. sec. Lucam*, X, 129-131: CSEL 32/4, 504f.
48. Dogmatic Constitution on the Church *Lumen Gentium*, 54 and 53; the latter text quotes St. Augustine, *De Sancta Virginitate*, VI, 6: PL 40, 399.
49. Dogmatic Constitution on the Church *Lumen Gentium*, 55.
50. Cf. St. Leo the Great, *Tractatus* 26, *De Natale Domini*, 2: CCL 138, 126.
51. Dogmatic Constitution on the Church *Lumen Gentium*, 59.

52. St. Augustine, *De Civitate Dei*, XVIII, 51: CCL 48, 650.
53. Second Vatican Ecumenical Council, Dogmatic Constitution on the Church *Lumen Gentium*, 8.
54. Ibid., 9.
55. Ibid., 9.
56. Ibid., 8.
57. Ibid., 9.
58. Ibid., 65.
59. Ibid., 59.
60. Cf. Second Vatican Ecumenical Council, Dogmatic Constitution on Divine Revelation *Dei Verbum*, 5.
61. Cf. Second Vatican Ecumenical Council, Dogmatic Constitution on the Church *Lumen Gentium*, 63.
62. Cf. ibid., 9.
63. Cf. ibid., 65.
64. Ibid., 65.
65. Ibid., 65.
66. Cf. ibid., 13.
67. Cf. ibid., 13.
68. Cf. ibid., 13.
69. Cf. *Roman Missal*, formula of the Consecration of the Chalice in the Eucharistic Prayers.
70. Second Vatican Ecumenical Council, Dogmatic Constitution on the Church *Lumen Gentium*, 1.
71. Ibid., 13.
72. Ibid., 15.
73. Cf. Second Vatican Ecumenical Council, Decree on Ecumenism *Unitatis Redintegratio*, 1.
74. Dogmatic Constitution on the Church *Lumen Gentium*, 68, 69. On Mary Most Holy, promoter of Christian unity, and on the cult of Mary in the East, cf. Leo XIII, Encyclical Epistle *Adiutricem Populi* (September 5, 1985): *Acta Leonis* XV, 300-312.
75. Cf. Second Vatican Ecumenical Council, Decree on Ecumenism *Unitatis Redintegratio*, 20.
76. Cf. ibid., 19.
77. Ibid., 14.
78. Ibid., 15.
79. Second Vatican Ecumenical Council, Dogmatic Constitution on the Church *Lumen Gentium*, 66.
80. Ecumenical Council of Chalcedon, *Definitio Fidei: Conciliorum Oecumenicorum Decreta*, Bologna 1973, 86 (DS 301).
81. Cf. the *Weddâsê Mâryâm* (*Praises of Mary*), which follows the Ethiopian Psalter and contains hymns and prayers to Mary for each day of the week. Cf. also the *Matshafa Kidâna Mehrat* (*Book of the Pact of Mercy*); the importance given to Mary in the Ethiopian hymnology and liturgy deserves to be emphasized.
82. Cf. St. Ephrem, *Hymn. de Nativitate: Scriptores Syri*, 82, CSCO, 186.
83. Cf. St. Gregory of Narek, *Le Livre de Prières: S. Ch.* 78, 160-163; 428-432.
84. Second Ecumenical Council of Nicaea: *Conciliorum Oecumenicorum Decreta*, Bologna 1973, 135-138 (DS 600-609).
85. Cf. Second Vatican Ecumenical Council, Dogmatic Constitution on the Church *Lumen Gentium*, 59.
86. Cf. Second Vatican Ecumenical Council, Decree on Ecumenism *Unitatis Redintegratio*, 19.
87. Second Vatican Ecumenical Council, Dogmatic Constitution on the Church *Lumen Gentium*, 8.
88. Ibid., 9.
89. As is well known, the words of the *Magnificat* contain or echo numerous passages of the Old Testament.
90. Second Vatican Ecumenical Council, Dogmatic Constitution on Divine Revelation *Dei Verbum*, 2.
91. Cf. for example St. Justin, *Dialogus cum Tryphone Iudaeo*, 100: Otto II, 358; St. Irenaeus, *Adversus Haereses* III, 22, 4: S. Ch. 211, 439-445; Tertullian, *De Carne Christi*, 17, 4-6: CCL 2, 904f.
92. Cf. St. Epiphanius, *Panarion*, III, 2; *Haer.* 78, 18: PG 42, 727-730.
93. Congregation for the Doctrine of the Faith, *Instruction on Christian Freedom and Liberation* (March 22, 1986), 97.
94. Second Vatican Ecumenical Council, Dogmatic Constitution on the Church *Lumen Gentium*, 60.

95. Ibid., 60.
96. Cf. the formula of mediatrix *"ad Mediatorem"* of St. Bernard, *In Dominica infra oct. Assumptionis Sermo*, 2: *S. Bernardi Opera*, V, 1968, 263. Mary as a pure mirror sends back to her Son all the glory and honor which she receives: Id., *In Nativitate B. Mariae Sermo—De Aquaeductu*, 12: ed. cit., 283.
97. Second Vatican Ecumenical Council, Dogmatic Constitution on the Church *Lumen Gentium*, 62.
98. Ibid., 62.
99. Ibid., 61.
100. Ibid., 62.
101. Ibid., 61.
102. Ibid., 61.
103. Ibid., 62.
104. Ibid., 62.
105. Ibid., 62; in her prayer too the Church recognizes and celebrates Mary's "maternal role": it is a role "of intercession and forgiveness, petition and grace, reconciliation and peace" (cf. Preface of the Mass of the Blessed Virgin Mary, Mother and Mediatrix of Grace, in *Collectio Missarum de Beata Maria Virgine*, ed. typ. 1987, I, 120).
106. Ibid., 62.
107. Ibid., 62; cf. St. John Damascene, *Hom. in Dormitionem*, I, 11; II, 2, 14; III, 2: *S. Ch.* 80, 111f.; 127-131; 157-161; 181-185; St. Bernard, *In Assumptione Beatae Mariae Sermo*, 1-2: *S. Bernardi Opera*, V, 1968, 228-238.
108. Dogmatic Constitution on the Church *Lumen Gentium*, 59; cf. Pope Pius XII, Apostolic Constitution *Munificentissimus Deus* (November 1, 1950): AAS 42 (1950) 769-771; St. Bernard presents Mary immersed in the splendor of the Son's glory: *In Dominica infra oct. Assumptionis Sermo*, 3; *S. Bernardi Opera*, V, 1968, 263f.
109. Dogmatic Constitution on the Church *Lumen Gentium*, 53.
110. On this particular aspect of Mary's mediation *as implorer of clemency* from the "Son as Judge," cf. St. Bernard, *In Dominica infra oct. Assumptionis Sermo*, 1-2: *S. Bernardi Opera*, V, 1968, 262f; Pope Leo XIII, Encyclical Epistle *Octobri Mense* (September 22, 1891): *Acta Leonis*, XI, 299-315.
111. Second Vatican Ecumenical Council, Dogmatic Constitution on the Church *Lumen Gentium*, 55.
112. Ibid., 59.
113. Ibid., 36.
114. Ibid., 36.
115. With regard to Mary as Queen, cf. St. John Damascene, *Hom. in Nativitatem*, 6; 12; *Hom. in Dormitionem*, 1, 2, 12, 14; II, 11;III, 4: *S. Ch.* 80, 59f.; 77f.; 83f.; 113f.; 117; 151f.; 189-193.
116. Second Vatican Ecumenical Council. Dogmatic Constitution on the Church *Lumen Gentium*, 62.
117. Ibid., 63.
118. Ibid., 63.
119. Ibid., 66.
120. Cf. St. Ambrose, *De Institutione Virginis*, XIV, 88-89: *PL* 16, 341, St. Augustine, *Sermo* 215, 4: *PL* 38, 1074; *De Sancta Virginitate*, II, 2; V, 5; VI, 6: *PL* 40, 397-398f.; 399; *Sermo* 191, II, 3: *PL* 38, 1010f.
121. Cf. Second Vatican Ecumenical Council, Dogmatic Constitution on the Church *Lumen Gentium*, 63.
122. Ibid., 64.
123. Ibid., 64.
124. Ibid., 64.
125. Ibid., 64.
126. Cf. Second Vatican Ecumenical Council, Dogmatic Constitution on Divine Revelation *Dei Verbum*, 8; St. Bonaventure, *Comment. in Evang. Lucae*, Ad Claras Aquas, VII, 53, No. 40, 68, No. 109.
127. Second Vatican Ecumenical Council, Dogmatic Constitution on the Church *Lumen Gentium*, 64.
128. Ibid., 63.
129. Cf. ibid., 63.

130. Clearly, in the Greek text the expression "eis ta idia" goes beyond the mere acceptance of Mary by the disciple in the sense of material lodging and hospitality in his house; it indicates rather a *communion of life* established between the two as a result of the words of the dying Christ: cf. St. Augustine, *In Ioan. Evang. tract.* 119, 3: CCL 36, 659: "He took her to himself, not into his own property, for he possessed nothing of his own, but among his own duties, which he attended to with dedication."

131. Second Vatican Ecumenical Council, Dogmatic Constitution on the Church *Lumen Gentium,* 62.

132. Ibid., 63.

133. Second Vatican Ecumenical Council, Pastoral Constitution on the Church in the Modern World *Gaudium et Spes,* 22.

134. Cf. Pope Paul VI, *Discourse of November 21, 1964:* AAS 56 (1964) 1015.

135. Pope Paul VI, *Solemn Profession of Faith* (June 30, 1968), 15: AAS 60 (1968) 438f.

136. Pope Paul VI, *Discourse of November 21, 1964:* AAS 56 (1964) 1015.

137. Ibid., 1016.

138. Cf. Second Vatican Ecumenical Council, Pastoral Constitution on the Church in the Modern World *Gaudium et Spes,* 37.

139. Cf. St. Bernard, *In Dominica infra oct. Assumptionis Sermo: S. Bernardi Opera,* V, 1968, 262-274.

140. Second Vatican Ecumenical Council, Dogmatic Constitution on the Church *Lumen Gentium,* 65.

141. Cf. Encyclical Letter *Fulgens Corona* (September 8, 1953): AAS 45 (1953) 577-592. Pius X with his Encyclical Letter *Ad Diem Illum* (February 2, 1904), on the occasion of the 50th anniversary of the dogmatic definition of the Immaculate Conception of the Blessed Virgin Mary, had proclaimed an Extraordinary jubilee of a few months; *Pii X P. M. Acta,* I, 147-166.

142. Cf. Dogmatic Constitution on the Church *Lumen Gentium,* 66-67.

143. St. Louis Marie Grignion de Montfort, *Traite de la Varie Devotion a la Sainte Vierge.* This saint can rightly be linked with the figure of St. Alfonso Maria de' Liguori, the second centenary of whose death occurs this year; cf. among his works *Le Glorie di Maria.*

144. Dogmatic Constitution on the Church, *Lumen Gentium,* 69.

145. Homily on January 1, 1987.

146. Dogmatic Constitution on the Church, *Lumen Gentium,* 69.

147. Cf. Second Vatican Ecumenical Council, Dogmatic Constitution on Divine Revelation, *Dei Verbum,* 2: "Through this revelation . . . the invisible God . . . out of the abundance of his love speaks to men as friends . . . and lives among them . . . , so that he may invite and take them into fellowship with himself."

ROSARIUM VIRGINIS MARIAE: ON THE MOST HOLY ROSARY

An Apostolic Letter of His Holiness John Paul II

OCTOBER 16, 2002

INTRODUCTION

1.   The Rosary of the Virgin Mary, which gradually took form in the second millennium under the guidance of the Spirit of God, is a prayer loved by countless Saints and encouraged by the Magisterium. Simple yet profound, it still remains, at the dawn of this third millennium, a prayer of great significance, destined to bring forth a harvest of holiness. It blends easily into the spiritual journey of the Christian life, which, after two thousand years, has lost none of the freshness of its beginnings and feels drawn by the Spirit of God to "set out into the deep" (*duc in altum!*) in order once more to proclaim, and even cry out, before the world that Jesus Christ is Lord and Savior, "the way, and the truth and the life" (Jn 14:6), "the goal of human history and the point on which the desires of history and civilization turn."[1] The Rosary, though clearly Marian in character, is at heart a Christocentric prayer.

In the sobriety of its elements, it has all the *depth of the Gospel message in its entirety*, of which it can be said to be a compendium.[2] It is an echo of the prayer of Mary, her perennial *Magnificat* for the work of the redemptive Incarnation which began in her virginal womb. With the Rosary, the Christian people *sits at the school of Mary* and is led to contemplate the beauty on the face of Christ and to experience the depths of his love. Through the Rosary the faithful receive abundant grace, as though from the very hands of the Mother of the Redeemer.

2.   Numerous predecessors of mine attributed great importance to this prayer. Worthy of special note in this regard is Pope Leo XIII who on September 1, 1883 promulgated the Encyclical *Supremi Apostolatus Officio*,[3] a document of great worth, the first of his many statements about this prayer, in which he proposed the Rosary as an effective spiritual weapon against the evils afflicting society. Among the more recent Popes who, from the time of the Second Vatican Council, have distinguished themselves in promoting the Rosary I would mention Blessed John XXIII[4] and above all Pope Paul VI, who in his Apostolic Exhortation *Marialis Cultus* emphasized, in the spirit of the Second Vatican Council, the Rosary's evangelical character and its Christocentric inspiration. I myself have often encouraged the frequent recitation of the Rosary. From my youthful years this prayer has held an important place in my spiritual life. I was powerfully reminded of this during my recent visit to Poland, and in particular at the Shrine of Kalwaria. The Rosary has accompanied me in moments of joy and in moments of difficulty. To it I have entrusted any number of concerns; in it I have always found comfort. Twenty-four years ago, on October 29, 1978, scarcely two weeks after my election to the See of Peter, I frankly admitted: "The Rosary is my favorite prayer. A marvelous prayer! Marvelous in its simplicity and its depth. [. . .]. It can be said that the Rosary is, in some sense, a prayer-commentary on the final chapter of the Vatican II Constitution *Lumen Gentium*, a chapter which discusses the wondrous presence of the Mother of God in the mystery of Christ and the Church. Against the background of the words *Ave Maria* the principal events of the life of Jesus Christ pass before the eyes of the soul. They take shape in the complete series of the joyful, sorrowful and glorious mysteries, and they put us in living communion with Jesus through—we might say—the heart of his Mother. At the same time our heart can embrace in the decades of the Rosary all the events that make up the lives of individuals, families, nations, the Church, and all mankind. Our personal concerns and those of our neighbor, especially those who are closest to us, who are dearest to us. Thus the simple prayer of the Rosary marks the rhythm of human life."[5]

With these words, dear brothers and sisters, I set *the first year of my Pontificate* within the daily rhythm of the Rosary. Today, *as I begin the twenty-fifth year of my service as the Successor of Peter*, I wish to do the same. How many graces have I received in these years from the Blessed Virgin through the Rosary: *Magnificat anima mea Dominum!* I wish to lift up my thanks to the Lord in the words of his Most Holy Mother, under whose protection I have placed my Petrine ministry: *Totus Tuus!*

3.   Therefore, in continuity with my reflection in the Apostolic Letter *Novo Millennio Ineunte*, in which, after the experience of the Jubilee, I invited the people of God to "start afresh from Christ,"[6] I have felt drawn to offer a reflection on the Rosary, as a kind of Marian complement to that Letter and an exhortation to contemplate the face of Christ in union with, and at the school of, his Most Holy Mother. To recite the Rosary is nothing other than to *contemplate with Mary the face of Christ*. As a way of highlighting this invitation, prompted by the forthcoming 120th anniversary of the aforementioned Encyclical of Leo XIII, I desire that during the course of this year the Rosary should be especially emphasized and promoted in the various Christian communities. I therefore proclaim the year from October 2002 to October 2003 *the Year of the Rosary*.

I leave this pastoral proposal to the initiative of each ecclesial community. It is not my intention to encumber but rather to complete and consolidate pastoral programs of the Particular Churches. I am confident that the proposal will find a ready and generous reception. The Rosary, reclaimed in its full meaning, goes to the very heart of Christian life; it offers a familiar yet fruitful spiritual and educational opportunity for personal contemplation, the formation of the People of God, and the new evangelization. I am pleased to reaffirm this also in the joyful remembrance of another anniversary: the fortieth anniversary of the opening of the Second Vatican Ecumenical Council on October 11, 1962, the "great grace" disposed by the Spirit of God for the Church in our time.[7]

OBJECTIONS TO THE ROSARY

4.   The timeliness of this proposal is evident from a number of considerations. First, the urgent need to counter a certain crisis of the Rosary, which in the present historical and theological context can risk being wrongly devalued, and therefore no longer taught to the younger generation. There are some who think that the centrality of the Liturgy, rightly stressed by the Second Vatican Ecumenical Council, necessarily entails giving lesser importance to the Rosary. Yet, as Pope Paul VI made clear, not only does this prayer not conflict with the Liturgy, *it sustains it*, since it serves as an excellent introduction and a faithful echo of the Liturgy, enabling people to participate fully and interiorly in it and to reap its fruits in their daily lives.

Perhaps too, there are some who fear that the Rosary is somehow unecumenical because of its distinctly Marian character. Yet the Rosary clearly belongs to the kind of veneration of the Mother of God described by the Council: a devotion directed to the Christological centre of the Christian faith, in such a way that "when the Mother is honored, the Son . . . is duly known, loved and glorified."[8] If properly revitalized, the Rosary is an aid and certainly not a hindrance to ecumenism!

A PATH OF CONTEMPLATION

5.   But the most important reason for strongly encouraging the practice of the Rosary is that it represents a most effective means of fostering among the faithful that *commitment to the contemplation of the Christian mystery* which I have proposed in the Apostolic Letter *Novo Millennio Ineunte* as a genuine "training in holiness": "What is needed is a Christian life distinguished above all in the *art of prayer*."[9] Inasmuch as contemporary culture, even amid so many indications to the contrary, has witnessed the flowering of a new call for spirituality, due also to the influence of other religions, it is more urgent than ever that our Christian communities should become "genuine schools of prayer."[10]

The Rosary belongs among the finest and most praiseworthy traditions of Christian contemplation. Developed in the West, it is a typically meditative prayer, corresponding in some way to the "prayer of the heart" or "Jesus prayer" which took root in the soil of the Christian East.

PRAYER FOR PEACE AND FOR THE FAMILY

6.   A number of historical circumstances also make a revival of the Rosary quite timely. First of all, the need to implore from God *the gift of peace*. The Rosary has many times been proposed by my predecessors and myself as a prayer for peace. At the start of a millennium which began with the terrifying attacks of September 11, 2001, a millennium which witnesses every day innumerous parts of the world fresh scenes of bloodshed and violence, to rediscover the Rosary means to immerse oneself in contemplation of the mystery of Christ who "is our peace," since he made "the two of us one, and broke down the dividing wall of hostility" (Eph 2:14). Consequently, one cannot recite the Rosary without feeling caught up in a clear commitment to advancing peace, especially in the land of Jesus, still so sorely afflicted and so close to the heart of every Christian.

A similar need for commitment and prayer arises in relation to another critical contemporary issue: *the family*, the primary cell of society, increasingly menaced by forces of disintegration on both the ideological and practical planes, so as to make us fear for the future of this fundamental and indispensable institution and, with it, for the future of society as a whole. The revival of the Rosary in Christian families, within the context of a broader pastoral ministry to the family, will be an effective aid to countering the devastating effects of this crisis typical of our age.

"BEHOLD, YOUR MOTHER" (JN 19:27)

7.   Many signs indicate that still today the Blessed Virgin desires to exercise through this same prayer that maternal concern to which the dying Redeemer entrusted, in the person of the beloved disciple, all the sons and daughters of the Church: "Woman, behold your son!" (Jn 19:26). Well-known are the occasions in the nineteenth and the twentieth centuries on which the Mother of Christ made her presence felt and her voice heard, in order to exhort the People of God to this form of contemplative prayer. I would mention in particular, on account of their great influence on the lives of Christians and the authoritative recognition they have received from the Church, the apparitions of Lourdes and of Fatima;[11] these shrines continue to be visited by great numbers of pilgrims seeking comfort and hope.

FOLLOWING THE WITNESSES

8.   It would be impossible to name all the many Saints who discovered in the Rosary a genuine path to growth in holiness. We need but mention St. Louis Marie Grignion de Montfort, the author of an excellent work on the Rosary,[12] and, closer to ourselves, Padre Pio of Pietrelcina, whom I recently had the joy of canonizing. As a true apostle of the Rosary, Blessed Bartolo Longo had a special charism. His path to holiness rested on an inspiration heard in the depths of his heart: "Whoever spreads the Rosary is saved!"[13] As a result, he felt called to build a Church dedicated to Our Lady of the Holy Rosary in Pompei, against the background of the ruins of the ancient city, which scarcely heard the proclamation of Christ before being buried in AD 79 during an eruption of Mount Vesuvius, only to emerge centuries later from its ashes as a witness to the lights and shadows of classical civilization. By his whole life's work and especially by the practice of the "Fifteen Saturdays," Bartolo Longo promoted the Christocentric and contemplative heart of the Rosary, and received great encouragement and support from Leo XIII, the "Pope of the Rosary."

Chapter One
CONTEMPLATING CHRIST WITH MARY

A FACE RADIANT AS THE SUN

9. "And he was transfigured before them, and his face shone like the sun" (Mt 17:2). The Gospel scene of Christ's transfiguration, in which the three Apostles Peter, James and John appear entranced by the beauty of the Redeemer, can be seen as *an icon of Christian contemplation*. To look upon the face of Christ, to recognize its mystery amid the daily events and the sufferings of his human life, and then to grasp the divine splendor definitively revealed in the Risen Lord, seated in glory at the right hand of the Father: this is the task of every follower of Christ and therefore the task of each one of us. In contemplating Christ's face we become open to receiving the mystery of Trinitarian life, experiencing ever anew the love of the Father and delighting in the joy of the Holy Spirit. St. Paul's words can then be applied to us: "Beholding the glory of the Lord, we are being changed into his likeness, from one degree of glory to another; for this comes from the Lord who is the Spirit" (2 Cor 3:18).

MARY, MODEL OF CONTEMPLATION

10. The contemplation of Christ has an *incomparable model* in Mary. In a unique way the face of the Son belongs to Mary. It was in her womb that Christ was formed, receiving from her a human resemblance which points to an even greater spiritual closeness. No one has ever devoted himself to the contemplation of the face of Christ as faithfully as Mary. The eyes of her heart already turned to him at the Annunciation, when she conceived him by the power of the Holy Spirit. In the months that followed she began to sense his presence and to picture his features. When at last she gave birth to him in Bethlehem, her eyes were able to gaze tenderly on the face of her Son, as she "wrapped him in swaddling cloths, and laid him in a manger" (Lk 2:7).

Thereafter Mary's gaze, ever filled with adoration and wonder, would never leave him. At times it would be *a questioning look*, as in the episode of the finding in the Temple: "Son, why have you treated us so?" (Lk 2:48); it would always be *a penetrating gaze*, one capable of deeply understanding Jesus, even to the point of perceiving his hidden feelings and anticipating his decisions, as at Cana (cf. Jn 2:5). At other times it would be *a look of sorrow*, especially beneath the Cross, where her vision would still be that of a mother giving birth, for Mary not only shared the passion and death of her Son, she also received the new son given to her in the beloved disciple (cf. Jn 19:26-27). On the morning of Easter hers would be a *gaze radiant with the joy of the Resurrection*, and finally, on the day of Pentecost, *a gaze afire* with the outpouring of the Spirit (cf. Acts 1:14).

MARY'S MEMORIES

11.   Mary lived with her eyes fixed on Christ, treasuring his every word: "She kept all these things, pondering them in her heart" (Lk 2:19; cf. 2:51). The memories of Jesus, impressed upon her heart, were always with her, leading her to reflect on the various moments of her life at her Son's side. In a way those memories were to be the "rosary" which she recited uninterruptedly throughout her earthly life.

Even now, amid the joyful songs of the heavenly Jerusalem, the reasons for her thanksgiving and praise remain unchanged. They inspire her maternal concern for the pilgrim Church, in which she continues to relate her personal account of the Gospel. *Mary constantly sets before the faithful the "mysteries" of her Son*, with the desire that the contemplation of those mysteries will release all their saving power. In the recitation of the Rosary, the Christian community enters into contact with the memories and the contemplative gaze of Mary.

THE ROSARY, A CONTEMPLATIVE PRAYER

12.   The Rosary, precisely because it starts with Mary's own experience, is *an exquisitely contemplative prayer*. Without this contemplative dimension, it would lose its meaning, as Pope Paul VI clearly pointed out: "Without contemplation, the Rosary is a body without a soul, and its recitation runs the risk of becoming a mechanical repetition of formulas, in violation of the admonition of Christ: 'In praying do not heap up empty phrases as the Gentiles do; for they think they will be heard for their many words' (Mt 6:7). By its nature the recitation of the Rosary calls for a quiet rhythm and a lingering pace, helping the individual to meditate on the mysteries of the Lord's life as seen through the eyes of her who was closest to the Lord. In this way the unfathomable riches of these mysteries are disclosed."[14]

It is worth pausing to consider this profound insight of Paul VI, in order to bring out certain aspects of the Rosary which show that it is really a form of Christocentric contemplation.

REMEMBERING CHRIST WITH MARY

13.   Mary's contemplation is above all *a remembering*. We need to understand this word in the biblical sense of remembrance (*zakar*) as a making present of the works brought about by God in the history of salvation. The Bible is an account of saving events culminating in Christ himself. These events not only belong to "yesterday"; *they are also part of the "today" of salvation*. This making present comes about above all in the Liturgy: what God accomplished centuries ago did not only affect the direct witnesses of those events; it continues to affect people in every age with its gift of grace. To some extent this is also true of every other devout approach to those events: to "remember" them in a spirit of faith and love is to be open to the grace which Christ won for us by the mysteries of his life, death and resurrection.

Consequently, while it must be reaffirmed with the Second Vatican Council that the Liturgy, as the exercise of the priestly office of Christ and an act of public worship, is "the summit to which the activity of the Church is directed and the font from which all its power flows,"[15] it is also necessary to recall that the spiritual life "is not limited solely to participation in the liturgy. Christians, while they are called to prayer in common, must also go to their own rooms to pray to their Father in secret (cf. Mt 6:6); indeed, according to the teaching of the Apostle, they must pray without ceasing (cf. 1 Thes 5:17)."[16] The Rosary, in its own particular way, is part of this varied panorama of "ceaseless" prayer. If the Liturgy, as the activity of Christ and the Church, is *a saving action par excellence*, the Rosary too, as a "meditation" with Mary on Christ, is *a salutary contemplation*. By immersing us in the mysteries of the Redeemer's life, it ensures that what he has done and what the liturgy makes present is profoundly assimilated and shapes our existence.

LEARNING CHRIST FROM MARY

14.   Christ is the supreme Teacher, the revealer and the one revealed. It is not just a question of learning what he taught but of *"learning him."* In this regard could we have any better teacher than Mary? From the divine standpoint, the Spirit is the interior teacher who leads us to the full truth of Christ (cf. Jn 14:26; 15:26; 16:13).

But among creatures no one knows Christ better than Mary; no one can introduce us to a profound knowledge of his mystery better than his Mother.

The first of the "signs" worked by Jesus—the changing of water into wine at the marriage in Cana—clearly presents Mary in the guise of a teacher, as she urges the servants to do what Jesus commands (cf. Jn 2:5). We can imagine that she would have done likewise for the disciples after Jesus' Ascension, when she joined them in awaiting the Holy Spirit and supported them in their first mission. Contemplating the scenes of the Rosary in union with Mary is a means of learning from her to "read" Christ, to discover his secrets and to understand his message.

This school of Mary is all the more effective if we consider that she teaches by obtaining for us in abundance the gifts of the Holy Spirit, even as she offers us the incomparable example of her own "pilgrimage of faith."[17] As we contemplate each mystery of her Son's life, she invites us to do as she did at the Annunciation: to ask humbly the questions which open us to the light, in order to end with the obedience of faith: "Behold I am the handmaid of the Lord; be it done to me according to your word" (Lk 1:38).

BEING CONFORMED TO CHRIST WITH MARY

15.   Christian spirituality is distinguished by the disciple's commitment to become conformed ever more fully to his Master (cf. Rom 8:29; Phil 3:10,12). The outpouring of the Holy Spirit in Baptism grafts the believer like a branch onto the vine which is Christ (cf. Jn 15:5) and makes him a member of Christ's mystical Body (cf. 1 Cor 12:12; Rom 12:5). This initial unity, however, calls for a growing assimilation which will increasingly shape the conduct of the disciple in accordance with the "mind" of Christ: "Have this mind among yourselves, which was in Christ Jesus" (Phil 2:5). In the words of the Apostle, we are called "to put on the Lord Jesus Christ" (cf. Rom 13:14; Gal 3:27).

In the spiritual journey of the Rosary, based on the constant contemplation—in Mary's company—of the face of Christ, this demanding ideal of being conformed to him is pursued through an association which could be described in terms of friendship. We are thereby enabled to enter naturally into Christ's life and as it were to share his deepest feelings. In this regard Blessed Bartolo Longo has written: "Just as two friends, frequently in each other's company, tend to develop similar habits, so too, by holding familiar converse with Jesus and the Blessed Virgin, by meditating on the mysteries of the Rosary and by living the same life in Holy Communion, we can become, to the extent of our lowliness, similar to them and can learn from these supreme models a life of humility, poverty, hiddenness, patience and perfection."[18]

In this process of being conformed to Christ in the Rosary, we entrust ourselves in a special way to the maternal care of the Blessed Virgin. She who is both the Mother of Christ and a member of the Church, indeed her "pre-eminent and altogether singular member,"[19] is at the same time the "Mother of the Church." As such, she continually brings to birth children for the mystical Body of her Son. She does so through her intercession, imploring upon them the inexhaustible outpouring of the Spirit. Mary is *the perfect icon of the motherhood of the Church.*

The Rosary mystically transports us to Mary's side as she is busy watching over the human growth of Christ in the home of Nazareth. This enables her to train us and to mold us with the same care, until Christ is "fully formed" in us (cf. Gal 4:19). This role of Mary, totally grounded in that of Christ and radically subordinated to it, "in no way obscures or diminishes the unique mediation of Christ, but rather shows its power."[20] This is the luminous principle expressed by the Second Vatican Council which I have so powerfully experienced in my own life and have made the basis of my episcopal motto: *Totus Tuus.*[21] The motto is of course inspired by the teaching of St. Louis Marie Grignion de Montfort, who explained in the following words Mary's role in the process of our configuration to Christ: "*Our entire perfection consists in being conformed, united and consecrated to Jesus Christ.* Hence the most perfect of all devotions is undoubtedly that which conforms, unites and consecrates us most perfectly to Jesus Christ. Now, since Mary is of all creatures the one most conformed to Jesus Christ, it follows that among all devotions that which most consecrates and conforms a soul to our Lord is devotion to Mary, his Holy Mother, and that the more a soul is consecrated to her the more will it be consecrated to Jesus Christ."[22] Never as in the Rosary do the life of Jesus and that of Mary appear so deeply joined. Mary lives only in Christ and for Christ!

PRAYING TO CHRIST WITH MARY

16.   Jesus invited us to turn to God with insistence and the confidence that we will be heard: "Ask, and it will be given to you; seek, and you will find; knock, and it will be opened to you" (Mt 7:7). The basis for this power of prayer is the goodness of the Father, but also the mediation of Christ himself (cf. 1Jn 2:1) and the working of the Holy Spirit who "intercedes for us" according to the will of God (cf. Rom 8:26-27). For "we do not know how to pray as we ought" (Rom 8:26), and at times we are not heard "because we ask wrongly" (cf. Jas 4:2-3).

In support of the prayer which Christ and the Spirit cause to rise in our hearts, Mary intervenes with her maternal intercession. "The prayer of the Church is sustained by the prayer of Mary."[23] If Jesus, the one Mediator, is the Way of our prayer, then Mary, his purest and most transparent reflection, shows us the Way. "Beginning with Mary's unique cooperation with the working of the Holy Spirit, the Churches developed their prayer to the Holy Mother of God, centering it on the person of Christ manifested in his mysteries."[24] At the wedding of Cana the Gospel clearly shows the power of Mary's intercession as she makes known to Jesus the needs of others: "They have no wine" (Jn 2:3).

The Rosary is both meditation and supplication. Insistent prayer to the Mother of God is based on confidence that her maternal intercession can obtain all things from the heart of her Son. She is "all-powerful by grace," to use the bold expression, which needs to be properly understood, of Blessed Bartolo Longo in his *Supplication to Our Lady*.[25] This is a conviction which, beginning with the Gospel, has grown ever more firm in the experience of the Christian people. The supreme poet Dante expresses it marvellously in the lines sung by St. Bernard: "Lady, thou art so great and so powerful, that whoever desires grace yet does not turn to thee, would have his desire fly without wings."[26] When in the Rosary we plead with Mary, the sanctuary of the Holy Spirit (cf. Lk 1:35), she intercedes for us before the Father who filled her with grace and before the Son born of her womb, praying with us and for us.

PROCLAIMING CHRIST WITH MARY

17.   The Rosary is also *a path of proclamation and increasing knowledge*, in which the mystery of Christ is presented again and again at different levels of the Christian experience. Its form is that of a prayerful and contemplative presentation, capable of forming Christians according to the heart of Christ. When the recitation of the Rosary combines all the elements needed for an effective meditation, especially in its communal celebration in parishes and shrines, it can present *a significant cate-chetical opportunity* which pastors should use to advantage. In this way too Our Lady of the Rosary continues her work of proclaiming Christ. The history of the Rosary shows how this prayer was used in particular by the Dominicans at a difficult time for the Church due to the spread of heresy. Today we are facing new challenges. Why should we not once more have recourse to the Rosary, with the same faith as those who have gone before us? The Rosary retains all its power and continues to be a valuable pastoral resource for every good evangelizer.

Chapter Two
MYSTERIES OF CHRIST—
MYSTERIES OF HIS MOTHER

THE ROSARY, "A COMPENDIUM OF THE GOSPEL"

18.   The only way to approach the contemplation of Christ's face is by listening in the Spirit to the Father's voice, since "no one knows the Son except the Father" (Mt 11:27). In the region of Caesarea Philippi, Jesus responded to Peter's confession of faith by indicating the source of that clear intuition of his identity: "Flesh and blood has not revealed this to you, but my Father who is in heaven" (Mt 16:17). What is needed, then, is a revelation from above. In order to receive that revelation, attentive listening is indispensable: "Only *the experience of silence and prayer* offers the proper setting for the growth and development of a true, faithful and consistent knowledge of that mystery."[27]

The Rosary is one of the traditional paths of Christian prayer directed to the contemplation of Christ's face. Pope Paul VI described it in these words: "As a Gospel prayer, centered on the mystery of the redemptive Incarnation, the Rosary is a prayer with a clearly Christological orientation. Its most characteristic element, in fact, the litany-like succession of Hail Marys, becomes in itself an unceasing praise of Christ, who is the ultimate object both of the Angel's announcement and of the greeting of the Mother of John the Baptist: 'Blessed is the fruit of your womb' (Lk 1:42). We would go further and say that the succession of Hail Marys constitutes the warp on which is woven the contemplation of the mysteries. The Jesus that each Hail Mary recalls is the same Jesus whom the succession of mysteries proposes to us now as the Son of God, now as the Son of the Virgin."[28]

A PROPOSED ADDITION TO THE TRADITIONAL PATTERN

19.   Of the many mysteries of Christ's life, only a few are indicated by the Rosary in the form that has become generally established with the seal of the Church's approval. The selection was determined by the origin of the prayer, which was based on the number 150, the number of the Psalms in the Psalter.

I believe, however, that to bring out fully the Christological depth of the Rosary it would be suitable to make an addition to the traditional pattern which, while left to the freedom of individuals and communities, could broaden it to include *the mysteries of Christ's public ministry between his Baptism and his Passion*. In the course of those mysteries we contemplate important aspects of the person of Christ as the definitive revelation of God. Declared the beloved Son of the Father at the Baptism in the Jordan, Christ is the one who announces the coming of the Kingdom, bears witness to it in his works and proclaims its demands. It is during the years of his public ministry that *the mystery of Christ is most evidently a mystery of light*: "While I am in the world, I am the light of the world" (Jn 9:5).

Consequently, for the Rosary to become more fully a "compendium of the Gospel," it is fitting to add, following reflection on the Incarnation and the hidden life of Christ (*the joyful mysteries*) and before focusing on the sufferings of his Passion (*the sorrowful mysteries*) and the triumph of his Resurrection (*the glorious mysteries*), a meditation on certain particularly significant moments in his public ministry (*the mysteries of light*). This addition of these new mysteries, without prejudice to any essential aspect of the prayer's traditional format, is meant to give it fresh life and to enkindle renewed interest in the Rosary's place within Christian spirituality as a true doorway to the depths of the Heart of Christ, ocean of joy and of light, of suffering and of glory.

THE JOYFUL MYSTERIES

20.　The first five decades, the "joyful mysteries," are marked by *the joy radiating from the event of the Incarnation*. This is clear from the very first mystery, the Annunciation, where Gabriel's greeting to the Virgin of Nazareth is linked to an invitation to messianic joy: "Rejoice, Mary." The whole of salvation history, in some sense the entire history of the world, has led up to this greeting. If it is the Father's plan to unite all things in Christ (cf. Eph 1:10), then the whole of the universe is in some way touched by the divine favor with which the Father looks upon Mary and makes her the Mother of his Son. The whole of humanity, in turn, is embraced by the *fiat* with which she readily agrees to the will of God.

Exultation is the keynote of the encounter with Elizabeth, where the sound of Mary's voice and the presence of Christ in her womb cause John to "leap for joy" (cf. Lk 1:44). Gladness also fills the scene in Bethlehem, when the birth of the divine Child, the Savior of the world, is announced by the song of the angels and proclaimed to the shepherds as "news of great joy" (Lk 2:10).

The final two mysteries, while preserving this climate of joy, already point to the drama yet to come. The Presentation in the Temple not only expresses the joy of the Child's consecration and the ecstasy of the aged Simeon; it also records the prophecy that Christ will be a "sign of contradiction" for Israel and that a sword will pierce his mother's heart (cf. Lk 2:34-35). Joy mixed with drama marks the fifth mystery, the finding of the twelve-year-old Jesus in the Temple. Here he appears in his divine wisdom as he listens and raises questions, already in effect one who "teaches." The revelation of his mystery as the Son wholly dedicated to his Father's affairs proclaims the radical nature of the Gospel, in which even the closest of human relationships are challenged by the absolute demands of the Kingdom. Mary and Joseph, fearful and anxious, "did not understand" his words (Lk 2:50).

To meditate upon the "joyful" mysteries, then, is to enter into the ultimate causes and the deepest meaning of Christian joy. It is to focus on the realism of the mystery of the Incarnation and on the obscure foreshadowing of the mystery of the saving Passion. Mary leads us to discover the secret of Christian joy, reminding us that Christianity is, first and foremost, *euangelion*, "good news," which has as its heart and its whole content the person of Jesus Christ, the Word made flesh, the one Savior of the world.

THE MYSTERIES OF LIGHT

21.   Moving on from the infancy and the hidden life in Nazareth to the public life of Jesus, our contemplation brings us to those mysteries which may be called in a special way "mysteries of light." Certainly the whole mystery of Christ is a mystery of light. He is the "light of the world" (Jn 8:12). Yet this truth emerges in a special way during the years of his public life, when he proclaims the Gospel of the Kingdom. In proposing to the Christian community five significant moments—"luminous" mysteries—during this phase of Christ's life, I think that the following can be fittingly singled out: (1) his Baptism in the Jordan, (2) his self-manifestation at the wedding of Cana, (3) his proclamation of the Kingdom of God, with his call to conversion, (4) his Transfiguration, and finally, (5) his institution of the Eucharist, as the sacramental expression of the Paschal Mystery.

Each of these mysteries is *a revelation of the Kingdom now present in the very person of Jesus*. The Baptism in the Jordan is first of all a mystery of light. Here, as Christ descends into the waters, the innocent one who became "sin" for our sake (cf. 2 Cor 5:21), the heavens open wide and the voice of the Father declares him the beloved Son (cf. Mt 3:17 and parallels), while the Spirit descends on him to invest him with the mission which he is to carry out. Another mystery of light is the first of the signs, given at Cana (cf. Jn 2:1-12), when Christ changes water into wine and opens the hearts of the disciples to faith, thanks to the intervention of Mary, the first among believers. Another mystery of light is the preaching by which Jesus proclaims the coming of the Kingdom of God, calls to conversion (cf. Mk 1:15) and forgives the sins of all who draw near to him in humble trust (cf. Mk 2:3-13; Lk 7:47-48): the inauguration of that ministry of mercy which he continues to exercise until the end of the world, particularly through the Sacrament of Reconciliation which he has entrusted to his Church (cf. Jn 20:22-23). The mystery of light *par excellence* is the Transfiguration, traditionally believed to have taken place on Mount Tabor. The glory of the Godhead shines forth from the face of Christ as the Father commands the astonished Apostles to "listen to him" (cf. Lk 9:35 and parallels) and to prepare to experience with him the agony of the Passion, so as to come with him to the joy of the Resurrection and a life transfigured by the Holy Spirit. A final mystery of light is the institution of the Eucharist, in which Christ offers his body and blood as food under the signs of bread and wine, and testifies "to the end" his love for humanity (Jn 13:1), for whose salvation he will offer himself in sacrifice.

In these mysteries, apart from the miracle at Cana, *the presence of Mary remains in the background*. The Gospels make only the briefest reference to her occasional presence at one moment or other during the preaching of Jesus (cf. Mk 3:31-5; Jn 2:12), and they give no indication that she was present at the Last Supper and the institution of the Eucharist. Yet the role she assumed at Cana in some way accompanies Christ throughout his ministry. The revelation made directly by the Father at the Baptism in the Jordan and echoed by John the Baptist is placed upon Mary's lips at Cana, and it becomes the great maternal counsel which Mary addresses to the Church of every age: "Do whatever he tells you" (Jn 2:5). This counsel is a fitting introduction to the words and signs of Christ's public ministry and it forms the Marian foundation of all the "mysteries of light."

THE SORROWFUL MYSTERIES

22.   The Gospels give great prominence to the sorrowful mysteries of Christ. From the beginning Christian piety, especially during the Lenten devotion of the *Way of the Cross*, has focused on the individual moments of the Passion, realizing that here is found *the culmination of the revelation of God's love* and the source of our salvation. The Rosary selects certain moments from the Passion, inviting the faithful to contemplate them in their hearts and to relive them. The sequence of meditations begins with Gethsemane, where Christ experiences a moment of great anguish before the will of the Father, against which the weakness of the flesh would be

tempted to rebel. There Jesus encounters all the temptations and confronts all the sins of humanity, in order to say to the Father: "Not my will but yours be done" (Lk 22:42 and parallels). This "Yes" of Christ reverses the "No" of our first parents in the Garden of Eden. And the cost of this faithfulness to the Father's will is made clear in the following mysteries; by his scourging, his crowning with thorns, his carrying the Cross and his death on the Cross, the Lord is cast into the most abject suffering: *Ecce homo!*

This abject suffering reveals not only the love of God but also the meaning of man himself.

Ecce homo: the meaning, origin and fulfilment of man is to be found in Christ, the God who humbles himself out of love "even unto death, death on a cross" (Phil 2:8). The sorrowful mysteries help the believer to relive the death of Jesus, to stand at the foot of the Cross beside Mary, to enter with her into the depths of God's love for man and to experience all its life-giving power.

THE GLORIOUS MYSTERIES

23.   "The contemplation of Christ's face cannot stop at the image of the Crucified One. He is the Risen One!"[29] The Rosary has always expressed this knowledge born of faith and invited the believer to pass beyond the darkness of the Passion in order to gaze upon Christ's glory in the Resurrection and Ascension. Contemplating the Risen One, Christians *rediscover the reasons for their own faith* (cf. 1 Cor 15:14) and relive the joy not only of those to whom Christ appeared—the Apostles, Mary Magdalene and the disciples on the road to Emmaus—but also *the joy of Mary*, who must have had an equally intense experience of the new life of her glorified Son. In the Ascension, Christ was raised in glory to the right hand of the Father, while Mary herself would be raised to that same glory in the Assumption, enjoying beforehand, by a unique privilege, the destiny reserved for all the just at the resurrection of the dead. Crowned in glory—as she appears in the last glorious mystery—Mary shines forth as Queen of the Angels and Saints, the anticipation and the supreme realization of the eschatological state of the Church.

At the center of this unfolding sequence of the glory of the Son and the Mother, the Rosary sets before us the third glorious mystery, Pentecost, which reveals the face of the Church as a family gathered together with Mary, enlivened by the powerful outpouring of the Spirit and ready for the mission of evangelization. The contemplation of this scene, like that of the other glorious mysteries, ought to lead the faithful to an ever greater appreciation of their new life in Christ, lived in the heart of the Church, a life of which the scene of Pentecost itself is the great "icon." The glorious mysteries thus lead the faithful to *greater hope for the eschatological goal* towards which they journey as members of the pilgrim People of God in history. This can only impel them to bear courageous witness to that "good news" which gives meaning to their entire existence.

FROM "MYSTERIES" TO THE "MYSTERY": MARY'S WAY

24.   The cycles of meditation proposed by the Holy Rosary are by no means exhaustive, but they do bring to mind what is essential and they awaken in the soul a thirst for a knowledge of Christ continually nourished by the pure source of the Gospel. Every individual event in the life of Christ, as narrated by the Evangelists, is resplendent with the Mystery that surpasses all understanding (cf. Eph 3:19): the Mystery of the Word made flesh, in whom "all the fullness of God dwells bodily" (Col 2:9). For this reason the *Catechism of the Catholic Church* places great emphasis on the mysteries of Christ, pointing out that "everything in the life of Jesus is a sign of his Mystery."[30] The "*duc in altum*" of the Church of the third millennium will be determined by the ability of Christians to enter into the "perfect knowledge of God's mystery, of Christ, in whom are hidden all the treasures of wisdom and knowledge" (Col 2:2-3). The Letter to the Ephesians makes this heartfelt prayer for all the baptized: "May Christ dwell in your hearts through faith, so that you, being rooted and grounded in love, may have power . . . to know the love of Christ which surpasses knowledge, that you may be filled with all the fullness of God" (3:17-19).

The Rosary is at the service of this ideal; it offers the "secret" which leads easily to a profound and inward knowledge of Christ. We might call it *Mary's way*. It is the way of the example of the Virgin of Nazareth, a woman of faith, of silence, of attentive listening. It is also the way of a Marian devotion inspired by knowledge of the inseparable bond between Christ and his Blessed Mother: *the mysteries of Christ* are also in some sense *the mysteries of his Mother*, even when they do not involve her directly, for she lives from him and through him. By making our own the words of the Angel Gabriel and St. Elizabeth contained in the Hail Mary, we find ourselves constantly drawn to seek out afresh in Mary, in her arms and in her heart, the "blessed fruit of her womb" (cf. Lk 1:42).

25.   In my testimony of 1978 mentioned above, where I described the Rosary as my favorite prayer, I used an idea to which I would like to return. I said then that "the simple prayer of the Rosary marks the rhythm of human life."[31]

In the light of what has been said so far on the mysteries of Christ, it is not difficult to go deeper into this *anthropological significance* of the Rosary, which is far deeper than may appear at first sight. Anyone who contemplates Christ through the various stages of his life cannot fail to perceive in him *the truth about man*. This is the great affirmation of the Second Vatican Council which I have so often discussed in my own teaching since the Encyclical Letter *Redemptor Hominis*: "it is only in the mystery of the Word made flesh that the mystery of man is seen in its true light."[32] The Rosary helps to open up the way to this light. Following in the path of Christ, in whom man's path is "recapitulated,"[33] revealed and redeemed, believers come face to face with the image of the true man. Contemplating Christ's birth, they learn of the sanctity of life; seeing the household of Nazareth, they learn the original truth of the family according to God's plan; listening to the Master in the mysteries of his public ministry, they find the light which leads them to enter the Kingdom of God; and following him on the way to Calvary, they learn the meaning of salvific suffering. Finally, contemplating Christ and his Blessed Mother in glory, they see the goal towards which each of us is called, if we allow ourselves to be healed and transformed by the Holy Spirit. It could be said that each mystery of the Rosary, carefully meditated, sheds light on the mystery of man.

At the same time, it becomes natural to bring to this encounter with the sacred humanity of the Redeemer all the problems, anxieties, labours and endeavours which go to make up our lives. "Cast your burden on the Lord and he will sustain you" (Ps 55:23). To pray the Rosary is to hand over our burdens to the merciful hearts of Christ and his Mother. Twenty-five years later, thinking back over the difficulties which have also been part of my exercise of the Petrine ministry, I feel the need to say once more, as a warm invitation to everyone to experience it personally: the Rosary does indeed "mark the rhythm of human life," bringing it into harmony with the "rhythm" of God's own life, in the joyful communion of the Holy Trinity, our life's destiny and deepest longing.

Chapter Three
"FOR ME, TO LIVE IS CHRIST"

THE ROSARY, A WAY OF ASSIMILATING THE MYSTERY

26.   Meditation on the mysteries of Christ is proposed in the Rosary by means of a method designed to assist in their assimilation. It is a method *based on repetition*. This applies above all to the Hail Mary, repeated ten times in each mystery. If this repetition is considered superficially, there could be a temptation to see the Rosary as a dry and boring exercise. It is quite another thing, however, when the Rosary is thought of as an outpouring of that love which tirelessly returns to the person loved with expressions similar in their content but ever fresh in terms of the feeling pervading them.

In Christ, God has truly assumed a "heart of flesh." Not only does God have a divine heart, rich in mercy and in forgiveness, but also a human heart, capable of all the stirrings of affection. If we needed evidence for this from the Gospel, we could easily find it in the touching dialogue between Christ and Peter after the Resurrection: "Simon, son of John, do you love me?" Three times this question is put to Peter, and three times he gives the reply: "Lord, you know that I love you" (cf. Jn 21:15-17). Over and above the specific meaning of this passage, so important for Peter's mission, none can fail to recognize the beauty of this triple repetition, in which the insistent request and the corresponding reply are expressed in terms familiar from the universal experience of human love. To understand the Rosary, one has to enter into the psychological dynamic proper to love.

One thing is clear: although the repeated Hail Mary is addressed directly to Mary, it is to Jesus that the act of love is ultimately directed, with her and through her. The repetition is nourished by the desire to be conformed ever more completely to Christ, the true program of the Christian life. St. Paul expressed this project with words of fire: "For me to live is Christ and to die is gain" (Phil 1:21). And again: "It is no longer I that live, but Christ lives in me" (Gal 2:20). The Rosary helps us to be conformed ever more closely to Christ until we attain true holiness.

A VALID METHOD . . .

27.   We should not be surprised that our relationship with Christ makes use of a method. God communicates himself to us respecting our human nature and its vital

rhythms. Hence, while Christian spirituality is familiar with the most sublime forms of mystical silence in which images, words and gestures are all, so to speak, superseded by an intense and ineffable union with God, it normally engages the whole person in all his complex psychological, physical and relational reality.

This becomes apparent *in the Liturgy*. Sacraments and sacramentals are structured as a series of rites which bring into play all the dimensions of the person. The same applies to non-liturgical prayer. This is confirmed by the fact that, in the East, the most characteristic prayer of Christological meditation, centered on the words "Lord Jesus Christ, Son of God, have mercy on me, a sinner"[34] is traditionally linked to the rhythm of breathing; while this practice favors perseverance in the prayer, it also in some way embodies the desire for Christ to become the breath, the soul and the "all" of one's life.

... WHICH CAN NEVERTHELESS BE IMPROVED

28.   I mentioned in my Apostolic Letter *Novo Millennio Ineunte* that the West is now experiencing *a renewed demand for meditation*, which at times leads to a keen interest in aspects of other religions.[35] Some Christians, limited in their knowledge of the Christian contemplative tradition, are attracted by those forms of prayer. While the latter contain many elements which are positive and at times compatible with Christian experience, they are often based on ultimately unacceptable premises. Much in vogue among these approaches are methods aimed at attaining a high level of spiritual concentration by using techniques of a psychophysical, repetitive and symbolic nature. The Rosary is situated within this broad gamut of religious phenomena, but it is distinguished by characteristics of its own which correspond to specifically Christian requirements.

In effect, the Rosary is simply *a method of contemplation*. As a method, it serves as a means to an end and cannot become an end in itself. All the same, as the fruit of centuries of experience, this method should not be undervalued. In its favour one could cite the experience of countless Saints. This is not to say, however, that the method cannot be improved. Such is the intent of the addition of the new series of *mysteria lucis* to the overall cycle of mysteries and of the few suggestions which I am proposing in this Letter regarding its manner of recitation. These suggestions, while respecting the well-established structure of this prayer, are intended to help the faithful to understand it in the richness of its symbolism and in harmony with the demands of daily life. Otherwise there is a risk that the Rosary would not only fail to produce the intended spiritual effects, but even that the beads, with which it is usually said, could come to be regarded as some kind of amulet or magic object, thereby radically distorting their meaning and function.

ANNOUNCING EACH MYSTERY

29.   Announcing each mystery, and perhaps even using a suitable icon to portray it, is as it were *to open up a scenario* on which to focus our attention. The words direct the imagination and the mind towards a particular episode or moment in the life of Christ. In the Church's traditional spirituality, the veneration of icons and the many devotions appealing to the senses, as well as the method of prayer proposed by St. Ignatius of Loyola in the Spiritual Exercises, make use of visual and imaginative elements (the *compositio loci*), judged to be of great help in concentrating the mind on the particular mystery. This is a methodology, moreover, which *corresponds to the inner logic of the Incarnation*: in Jesus, God wanted to take on human features. It is through his bodily reality that we are led into contact with the mystery of his divinity.

This need for concreteness finds further expression in the announcement of the various mysteries of the Rosary. Obviously these mysteries neither replace the Gospel nor exhaust its content. The Rosary, therefore, is no substitute for *lectio divina*; on the contrary, it presupposes and promotes it. Yet, even though the mysteries contemplated in the Rosary, even with the addition of the *mysteria lucis*, do no more than outline the fundamental elements of the life of Christ, they easily draw the mind to a more expansive reflection on the rest of the Gospel, especially when the Rosary is prayed in a setting of prolonged recollection.

LISTENING TO THE WORD OF GOD

30.   In order to supply a Biblical foundation and greater depth to our meditation, it is helpful to follow the announcement of the mystery with *the proclamation of a related Biblical passage*, long or short, depending on the circumstances. No other words can ever match the efficacy of the inspired word. As we listen, we are certain that this is the word of God, spoken for today and spoken "for me."

If received in this way, the word of God can become part of the Rosary's methodology of repetition without giving rise to the ennui derived from the simple recollection of something already well known. It is not a matter of recalling information but of *allowing God to speak*. In certain solemn communal celebrations, this word can be appropriately illustrated by a brief commentary.

SILENCE

31.   *Listening and meditation are nourished by silence.* After the announcement of the mystery and the proclamation of the word, it is fitting to pause and focus one's attention for a suitable period of time on the mystery concerned, before moving into vocal prayer. A discovery of the importance of silence is one of the secrets of practicing contemplation and meditation. One drawback of a society dominated by technology and the mass media is the fact that silence becomes increasingly difficult to achieve. Just as moments of silence are recommended in the Liturgy, so too in the recitation of the Rosary it is fitting to pause briefly after listening to the word of God, while the mind focuses on the content of a particular mystery.

THE "OUR FATHER"

32.   After listening to the word and focusing on the mystery, it is natural for *the mind to be lifted up towards the Father*. In each of his mysteries, Jesus always leads us to the Father, for as he rests in the Father's bosom (cf. Jn 1:18) he is continually turned towards him. He wants us to share in his intimacy with the Father, so that we can say with him: "Abba, Father" (Rom 8:15; Gal 4:6). By virtue of his relationship to the Father he makes us brothers and sisters of himself and of one another, communicating to us the Spirit which is both his and the Father's. Acting as a kind of foundation for the Christological and Marian meditation which unfolds in the repetition of the Hail Mary, the Our Father makes meditation upon the mystery, even when carried out in solitude, an ecclesial experience.

THE TEN HAIL MARYS

33.   This is the most substantial element in the Rosary and also the one which makes it a Marian prayer *par excellence*. Yet when the Hail Mary is properly understood, we come to see clearly that its Marian character is not opposed to its Christological character, but that it actually emphasizes and increases it. The first part of the Hail Mary, drawn from the words spoken to Mary by the Angel Gabriel and by St. Elizabeth, is a contemplation in adoration of the mystery accomplished in

the Virgin of Nazareth. These words express, so to speak, the wonder of heaven and earth; they could be said to give us a glimpse of God's own wonderment as he contemplates his "masterpiece"—the Incarnation of the Son in the womb of the Virgin Mary. If we recall how, in the Book of Genesis, God "saw all that he had made" (Gen 1:31), we can find here an echo of that "pathos with which God, at the dawn of creation, looked upon the work of his hands."[36] The repetition of the Hail Mary in the Rosary gives us a share in God's own wonder and pleasure: in jubilant amazement we acknowledge the greatest miracle of history. Mary's prophecy here finds its fulfilment: "Henceforth all generations will call me blessed" (Lk 1:48).

The center of gravity in the Hail Mary, the hinge as it were which joins its two parts, is *the name of Jesus*. Sometimes, in hurried recitation, this centre of gravity can be overlooked, and with it the connection to the mystery of Christ being contemplated. Yet it is precisely the emphasis given to the name of Jesus and to his mystery that is the sign of a meaningful and fruitful recitation of the Rosary. Pope Paul VI drew attention, in his Apostolic Exhortation *Marialis Cultus*, to the custom in certain regions of highlighting the name of Christ by the addition of a clause referring to the mystery being contemplated.[37] This is a praiseworthy custom, especially during public recitation. It gives forceful expression to our faith in Christ, directed to the different moments of the Redeemer's life. It is at once *a profession of faith* and an aid in concentrating our meditation, since it facilitates the process of assimilation to the mystery of Christ inherent in the repetition of the Hail Mary. When we repeat the name of Jesus—the only name given to us by which we may hope for salvation (cf. Acts 4:12)—in close association with the name of his Blessed Mother, almost as if it were done at her suggestion, we set out on a path of assimilation meant to help us enter more deeply into the life of Christ.

From Mary's uniquely privileged relationship with Christ, which makes her the Mother of God, *Theotókos*, derives the forcefulness of the appeal we make to her in the second half of the prayer, as we entrust to her maternal intercession our lives and the hour of our death.

THE "GLORIA"

34.   Trinitarian doxology is the goal of all Christian contemplation. For Christ is the way that leads us to the Father in the Spirit. If we travel this way to the end, we repeatedly encounter the mystery of the three divine Persons, to whom all praise, worship and thanksgiving are due. It is important that the *Gloria, the high-point of*

contemplation, be given due prominence in the Rosary. In public recitation it could be sung, as a way of giving proper emphasis to the essentially Trinitarian structure of all Christian prayer.

To the extent that meditation on the mystery is attentive and profound, and to the extent that it is enlivened—from one Hail Mary to another—by love for Christ and for Mary, the glorification of the Trinity at the end of each decade, far from being a perfunctory conclusion, takes on its proper contemplative tone, raising the mind as it were to the heights of heaven and enabling us in some way to relive the experience of Tabor, a foretaste of the contemplation yet to come: "It is good for us to be here!" (Lk 9:33).

THE CONCLUDING SHORT PRAYER

35.   In current practice, the Trinitarian doxology is followed by a brief concluding prayer which varies according to local custom. Without in any way diminishing the value of such invocations, it is worthwhile to note that the contemplation of the mysteries could better express their full spiritual fruitfulness if an effort were made to conclude each mystery with *a prayer for the fruits specific to that particular mystery*. In this way the Rosary would better express its connection with the Christian life. One fine liturgical prayer suggests as much, inviting us to pray that, by meditation on the mysteries of the Rosary, we may come to "imitate what they contain and obtain what they promise."[38]

Such a final prayer could take on a legitimate variety of forms, as indeed it already does. In this way the Rosary can be better adapted to different spiritual traditions and different Christian communities. It is to be hoped, then, that appropriate formulas will be widely circulated, after due pastoral discernment and possibly after experimental use in centres and shrines particularly devoted to the Rosary, so that the People of God may benefit from an abundance of authentic spiritual riches and find nourishment for their personal contemplation.

THE ROSARY BEADS

36.   The traditional aid used for the recitation of the Rosary is the set of beads. At the most superficial level, the beads often become a simple counting mechanism to mark the succession of Hail Marys. Yet they can also take on a symbolism which can give added depth to contemplation.

Here the first thing to note is the way *the beads converge upon the Crucifix*, which both opens and closes the unfolding sequence of prayer. The life and prayer of believers is centred upon Christ. Everything begins from him, everything leads towards him, everything, through him, in the Holy Spirit, attains to the Father.

As a counting mechanism, marking the progress of the prayer, the beads evoke the unending path of contemplation and of Christian perfection. Blessed Bartolo Longo saw them also as a "chain" which links us to God. A chain, yes, but a sweet chain; for sweet indeed is the bond to God who is also our Father. A "filial" chain which puts us in tune with Mary, the "handmaid of the Lord" (Lk 1:38) and, most of all, with Christ himself, who, though he was in the form of God, made himself a "servant" out of love for us (Phil 2:7).

A fine way to expand the symbolism of the beads is to let them remind us of our many relationships, of the bond of communion and fraternity which unites us all in Christ.

THE OPENING AND CLOSING

37.   At present, in different parts of the Church, there are many ways to introduce the Rosary. In some places, it is customary to begin with the opening words of Psalm 70: "O God, come to my aid; O Lord, make haste to help me," as if to nourish in those who are praying a humble awareness of their own insufficiency. In other places, the Rosary begins with the recitation of the Creed, as if to make the profession of faith the basis of the contemplative journey about to be undertaken. These and similar customs, to the extent that they prepare the mind for contemplation, are all equally legitimate. The Rosary is then ended with a prayer for the intentions of the Pope, as if to expand the vision of the one praying to embrace all the needs of the Church. It is precisely in order to encourage this ecclesial dimension of the Rosary that the Church has seen fit to grant indulgences to those who recite it with the required dispositions.

If prayed in this way, the Rosary truly becomes a spiritual itinerary in which Mary acts as Mother, Teacher and Guide, sustaining the faithful by her powerful intercession. Is it any wonder, then, that the soul feels the need, after saying this prayer and experiencing so profoundly the motherhood of Mary, to burst forth in praise of the Blessed Virgin, either in that splendid prayer the *Salve Regina* or in the Litany of Loreto? This is the crowning moment of an inner journey which has brought the faithful into living contact with the mystery of Christ and his Blessed Mother.

38.   The Rosary can be recited in full every day, and there are those who most laudably do so. In this way it fills with prayer the days of many a contemplative, or keeps company with the sick and the elderly who have abundant time at their disposal. Yet it is clear—and this applies all the more if the new series of *mysteria lucis* is included—that many people will not be able to recite more than a part of the Rosary, according to a certain weekly pattern. This weekly distribution has the effect of giving the different days of the week a certain spiritual "color," by analogy with the way in which the Liturgy colors the different seasons of the liturgical year.

According to current practice, Monday and Thursday are dedicated to the "joyful mysteries," Tuesday and Thursday to the "sorrowful mysteries," and Wednesday, Saturday and Sunday to the "glorious mysteries." Where might the "mysteries of light" be inserted? If we consider that the "glorious mysteries" are said on both Saturday and Sunday, and that Saturday has always had a special Marian flavour, the second weekly meditation on the "joyful mysteries," mysteries in which Mary's presence is especially pronounced, could be moved to Saturday. Thursday would then be free for meditating on the "mysteries of light."

This indication is not intended to limit a rightful freedom in personal and community prayer, where account needs to be taken of spiritual and pastoral needs and of the occurrence of particular liturgical celebrations which might call for suitable adaptations. What is really important is that the Rosary should always be seen and experienced as a path of contemplation. In the Rosary, in a way similar to what takes place in the Liturgy, the Christian week, centred on Sunday, the day of Resurrection, becomes a journey through the mysteries of the life of Christ, and he is revealed in the lives of his disciples as the Lord of time and of history.

CONCLUSION

"BLESSED ROSARY OF MARY, SWEET CHAIN LINKING US TO GOD"

39.   What has been said so far makes abundantly clear the richness of this traditional prayer, which has the simplicity of a popular devotion but also the theological depth of a prayer suited to those who feel the need for deeper contemplation.

The Church has always attributed particular efficacy to this prayer, entrusting to the Rosary, to its choral recitation and to its constant practice, the most difficult problems. At times when Christianity itself seemed under threat, its deliverance was attributed to the power of this prayer, and Our Lady of the Rosary was acclaimed as the one whose intercession brought salvation.

Today I willingly entrust to the power of this prayer—as I mentioned at the beginning—the cause of peace in the world and the cause of the family.

PEACE

40. The grave challenges confronting the world at the start of this new Millennium lead us to think that only an intervention from on high, capable of guiding the hearts of those living in situations of conflict and those governing the destinies of nations, can give reason to hope for a brighter future.

The Rosary is by its nature a prayer for peace, since it consists in the contemplation of Christ, the Prince of Peace, the one who is "our peace" (Eph 2:14). Anyone who assimilates the mystery of Christ—and this is clearly the goal of the Rosary—learns the secret of peace and makes it his life's project. Moreover, by virtue of its meditative character, with the tranquil succession of Hail Marys, the Rosary has a peaceful effect on those who pray it, disposing them to receive and experience in their innermost depths, and to spread around them, that true peace which is the special gift of the Risen Lord (cf. Jn 14:27; 20:21).

The Rosary is also a prayer for peace because of the fruits of charity which it produces. When prayed well in a truly meditative way, the Rosary leads to an encounter with Christ in his mysteries and so cannot fail to draw attention to the face of Christ in others, especially in the most afflicted. How could one possibly contemplate the mystery of the Child of Bethlehem, in the joyful mysteries, without experiencing the desire to welcome, defend and promote life, and to shoulder the burdens of suffering children all over the world? How could one possibly follow in the footsteps of Christ the Revealer, in the mysteries of light, without resolving to bear witness to his "Beatitudes" in daily life? And how could one contemplate Christ carrying the Cross and Christ Crucified, without feeling the need to act as a "Simon of Cyrene" for our brothers and sisters weighed down by grief or crushed by despair? Finally, how could one possibly gaze upon the glory of the Risen Christ or of Mary Queen of Heaven, without yearning to make this world more beautiful, more just, more closely conformed to God's plan?

In a word, by focusing our eyes on Christ, the Rosary also makes us peacemakers in the world. By its nature as an insistent choral petition in harmony with Christ's invitation to "pray ceaselessly" (Lk 18:1), the Rosary allows us to hope that, even today, the difficult "battle" for peace can be won. Far from offering an escape from the problems of the world, the Rosary obliges us to see them with responsible and generous eyes, and obtains for us the strength to face them with the certainty of God's help and the firm intention of bearing witness in every situation to "love, which binds everything together in perfect harmony" (Col 3:14).

THE FAMILY: PARENTS . . .

41.   As a prayer for peace, the Rosary is also, and always has been, *a prayer of and for the family*. At one time this prayer was particularly dear to Christian families, and it certainly brought them closer together. It is important not to lose this precious inheritance. We need to return to the practice of family prayer and prayer for families, continuing to use the Rosary.

In my Apostolic Letter *Novo Millennio Ineunte* I encouraged the celebration of the Liturgy of the Hours by the lay faithful in the ordinary life of parish communities and Christian groups;[39] I now wish to do the same for the Rosary. These two paths of Christian contemplation are not mutually exclusive; they complement one another. I would therefore ask those who devote themselves to the pastoral care of families to recommend heartily the recitation of the Rosary.

The family that prays together stays together. The Holy Rosary, by age-old tradition, has shown itself particularly effective as a prayer which brings the family together. Individual family members, in turning their eyes towards Jesus, also regain the ability to look one another in the eye, to communicate, to show solidarity, to forgive one another and to see their covenant of love renewed in the Spirit of God.

Many of the problems facing contemporary families, especially in economically developed societies, result from their increasing difficulty in communicating. Families seldom manage to come together, and the rare occasions when they do are often taken up with watching television. To return to the recitation of the family Rosary means filling daily life with very different images, images of the mystery of salvation: the image of the Redeemer, the image of his most Blessed Mother. The family that recites the Rosary together reproduces something of the atmosphere of the household of Nazareth: its members place Jesus at the center, they share his joys and sorrows, they place their needs and their plans in his hands, they draw from him the hope and the strength to go on.

. . . AND CHILDREN

42. It is also beautiful and fruitful to entrust to this prayer *the growth and development of children*. Does the Rosary not follow the life of Christ, from his conception to his death, and then to his Resurrection and his glory? Parents are finding it ever more difficult to follow the lives of their children as they grow to maturity. In a society of advanced technology, of mass communications and globalization, everything has become hurried, and the cultural distance between generations is growing ever greater. The most diverse messages and the most unpredictable experiences rapidly make their way into the lives of children and adolescents, and parents can become quite anxious about the dangers their children face. At times parents suffer acute disappointment at the failure of their children to resist the seductions of the drug culture, the lure of an unbridled hedonism, the temptation to violence, and the manifold expressions of meaninglessness and despair.

To pray the Rosary *for children*, and even more, *with children*, training them from their earliest years to experience this daily "pause for prayer" with the family, is admittedly not the solution to every problem, but it is a spiritual aid which should not be underestimated. It could be objected that the Rosary seems hardly suited to the taste of children and young people of today. But perhaps the objection is directed to an impoverished method of praying it. Furthermore, without prejudice to the Rosary's basic structure, there is nothing to stop children and young people from praying it—either within the family or in groups—with appropriate symbolic and practical aids to understanding and appreciation. Why not try it? With God's help, a pastoral approach to youth which is positive, impassioned and creative—as shown by the World Youth Days!—is capable of achieving quite remarkable results. If the Rosary is well presented, I am sure that young people will once more surprise adults by the way they make this prayer their own and recite it with the enthusiasm typical of their age group.

THE ROSARY, A TREASURE TO BE REDISCOVERED

43.   Dear brothers and sisters! A prayer so easy and yet so rich truly deserves to be rediscovered by the Christian community. Let us do so, especially this year, as a means of confirming the direction outlined in my Apostolic Letter *Novo Millennio Ineunte*, from which the pastoral plans of so many particular Churches have drawn inspiration as they look to the immediate future.

I turn particularly to you, my dear Brother Bishops, priests and deacons, and to you, pastoral agents in your different ministries: through your own personal experience of the beauty of the Rosary, may you come to promote it with conviction.

I also place my trust in you, theologians: by your sage and rigorous reflection, rooted in the word of God and sensitive to the lived experience of the Christian people, may you help them to discover the Biblical foundations, the spiritual riches and the pastoral value of this traditional prayer.

I count on you, consecrated men and women, called in a particular way to contemplate the face of Christ at the school of Mary.

I look to all of you, brothers and sisters of every state of life, to you, Christian families, to you, the sick and elderly, and to you, young people: *confidently take up the Rosary once again*. Rediscover the Rosary in the light of Scripture, in harmony with the Liturgy, and in the context of your daily lives.

May this appeal of mine not go unheard! At the start of the twenty-fifth year of my Pontificate, I entrust this Apostolic Letter to the loving hands of the Virgin Mary, *prostrating myself in spirit before her image in the splendid Shrine built for her by Blessed Bartolo Longo*, the apostle of the Rosary. I willingly make my own the touching words with which he concluded his well-known *Supplication to the Queen of the Holy Rosary*: "O Blessed Rosary of Mary, sweet chain which unites us to God, bond of love which unites us to the angels, tower of salvation against the assaults of Hell, safe port in our universal shipwreck, we will never abandon you. You will be our comfort in the hour of death: yours our final kiss as life ebbs away. And the last word from our lips will be your sweet name, O Queen of the Rosary of Pompei, O dearest Mother, O Refuge of Sinners, O Sovereign Consoler of the Afflicted. May you be everywhere blessed, today and always, on earth and in heaven."

From the Vatican, on the 16th day of October in the year 2002, the beginning of the twenty-fifth year of my Pontificate.

1. Pastoral Constitution on the Church in the Modern World *Gaudium et Spes*, 45.
2. Pope Paul VI, Apostolic Exhortation *Marialis Cultus* (February 2, 1974), 42: *Acta Apostolicae Sedis* (AAS) 66 (1974), 153.
3. Cf. *Acta Leonis XIII*, 3 (1884), 280-289.
4. Particularly worthy of note is his Apostolic Epistle on the Rosary *Il religioso convegno* (September 29, 1961): AAS 53 (1961), 641-647.
5. Angelus: *Insegnamenti di Giovanni Paolo II*, I (1978): 75-76.
6. AAS 93 (2001), 285.
7. During the years of preparation for the Council, Pope John XXIII did not fail to encourage the Christian community to recite the Rosary for the success of this ecclesial event: cf. Letter to the Cardinal Vicar (September 28, 1960): AAS 52 (1960), 814-816.
8. Dogmatic Constitution on the Church *Lumen Gentium*, 66.
9. No. 32: AAS 93 (2001), 288.
10. Ibid., 33: loc. cit., 289.
11. It is well-known and bears repeating that private revelations are not the same as public revelation, which is binding on the whole Church. It is the task of the Magisterium to discern and recognize the authenticity and value of private revelations for the piety of the faithful.
12. *The Secret of the Rosary.*
13. Blessed Bartolo Longo, *Storia del Santuario di Pompei*, Pompei, 1990, 59.
14. Apostolic Exhortation *Marialis Cultus* (February 2, 1974), 47: AAS (1974), 156.
15. Constitution on the Sacred Liturgy *Sacrosanctum Concilium*, 10.
16. Ibid., 12.
17. Second Vatican Ecumenical Council, Dogmatic Constitution on the Church *Lumen Gentium*, 58.
18. *I Quindici Sabati del Santissimo Rosario*, 27th ed., Pompei, 1916, 27.
19. Second Vatican Ecumenical Council, Dogmatic Constitution on the Church *Lumen Gentium*, 53.
20. Ibid., 60.
21. Cf. First Radio Address *Urbi et Orbi* (October 17, 1978): AAS 70 (1978), 927.
22. *Treatise on True Devotion to the Blessed Virgin Mary.*
23. *Catechism of the Catholic Church* (CCC), 2679.
24. Ibid., 2675.
25. The *Supplication to the Queen of the Holy Rosary* was composed by Blessed Bartolo Longo in 1883 in response to the appeal of Pope Leo XIII, made in his first Encyclical on the Rosary, for the spiritual commitment of all Catholics in combating social ills. It is solemnly recited twice yearly, in May and October.
26. *Divina Commedia, Paradiso* XXXIII, 13-15.
27. John Paul II, Apostolic Letter *Novo Millennio Ineunte* (January 6, 2001), 20: AAS 93 (2001), 279.
28. Apostolic Exhortation *Marialis Cultus* (February 2, 1974), 46: AAS 6 (1974), 155.
29. John Paul II, Apostolic Letter *Novo Millennio Ineunte* (January 6, 2001), 28: AAS 93 (2001), 284.
30. No. 515.
31. *Angelus* Message of October 29, 1978 : *Insegnamenti*, I (1978), 76.
32. Second Vatican Ecumenical Council, Pastoral Constitution on the Church in the Modern World *Gaudium et Spes*, 22.
33. Cf. St. Irenaeus of Lyons, *Adversus Haereses*, III, 18, 1: PG 7, 932.
34. CCC, 2616.
35. Cf. No. 33: AAS 93 (2001), 289.
36. John Paul II, *Letter to Artists* (April 4, 1999), 1: AAS 91 (1999), 1155.
37. Cf. No. 46: AAS 66 (1974), 155. This custom has also been recently praised by the Congregation for Divine Worship and for the Discipline of the Sacraments in its *Direttorio Su Pietà Popolare e Liturgia. Principi e Orientamenti* (December 17, 2001), 201, Vatican City, 2002, 165.

38. ". . . concede, quaesumus, ut haec mysteria sacratissimo beatae Mariae Virginis Rosario recolentes, et imitemur quod continent, et quod promittunt assequamur." Missale Romanum 1960, in festo B.M. Virginis a Rosario.
39. Cf. No. 34: AAS 93 (2001), 290.